AFRICANISM

Africanism

Blacks in the Medieval Arab Imaginary

NADER KADHEM

Translated by Amir Al-Azraki

McGill-Queen's University Press
Montreal & Kingston · London · Chicago

© McGill-Queen's University Press 2023

ISBN 978-0-2280-1872-8 (cloth)
ISBN 978-0-2280-1965-7 (ePDF)
ISBN 978-0-2280-1966-4 (ePUB)

Legal deposit third quarter 2023
Bibliothèque nationale du Québec

Printed in Canada on acid-free paper that is 100% ancient forest free (100% post-consumer recycled), processed chlorine free

McGill-Queen's University Press is grateful for the financial support of the Bahrain Authority for Culture and Antiquities, which made possible the translation of this book.

Financé par le gouvernement du Canada | Funded by the Government of Canada

We acknowledge the support of the Canada Council for the Arts.

Nous remercions le Conseil des arts du Canada de son soutien.

Library and Archives Canada Cataloguing in Publication

Title: Africanism: Blacks in the medieval Arab imaginary / Nader Kadhem; translated by Amir Al-Azraki.

Other titles: Tamthīlāt al-akher. English

Names: Kāẓim, Nādir, author.

Description: Translation of: Tamthīlāt al-akher: ṣūrat al-Sūd fī al-mutakhayl al-'Arabī al-wasīṭ. | Includes bibliographical references and index.

Identifiers: Canadiana (print) 2023021004X | Canadiana (ebook) 20230210090 | ISBN 9780228018728 (cloth) | ISBN 9780228019657 (ePDF) | ISBN 9780228019664 (ePUB)

Subjects: LCSH: Arabic literature—History and criticism. | LCSH: Literature, Medieval—History and criticism. | LCSH: Black people in literature. | LCSH: Africanisms in literature. | LCSH: Racism—Arab countries—History. | LCSH: Arab countries—Race relations—History.

Classification: LCC PJ7519.B575 K39 2023 | DDC 892.7/09352996—dc23

This book was typeset by Marquis Interscript in 10.5/13 Sabon.

To Robert Fothergill

Contents

Translator's Preface ix

Introduction 3

PART ONE: CULTURAL REPRESENTATIONS AND THE IMAGINARY UNDERPINNINGS 15

1 Blacks in the Arab Imaginary 25

2 The Absolute Other and the Power of Representation 68

PART TWO: THE IMAGINARY AND THE LITERARY REPRESENTATION 95

3 Blacks in Narrative Representation 97

4 Representation of Blacks in Poetry 116

Notes 157

Bibliography 173

Index 183

Translator's Preface

Working on a translation project of this scale has been an honour and a tremendous amount of work at the same time. It is such a pleasure to acquaint English-speaking readers with valuable work in the emerging field of the so-called *al-Istifraq al-Arabi* (the discourse of perceiving, imagining, and writing about black people as a subject of study in Arab culture). Not only is there very little scholarship on anti-black racism in the Arab world but also there is even less in English. With a desire to increase knowledge and awareness of anti-black racism, I decided to translate this book.

I grew up in Basra (Iraq) where the majority of black Iraqis live. However, I was not aware of the extent of racism and discrimination against black Iraqis until I came to Canada. In Canada, and the West, I am no longer a "white" Arab but a person of colour. The implications of my new racial identity have urged me to rethink and investigate anti-black racism globally, within Canada, and in the Arab world.

My first encounter with Dr Nader Kadhem's book (*Tamtheelat al-Akher: Surat al-Sood fii al-Mutakhail al-Arabi al-Waseet*) occurred when I was preparing a presentation on Afro-Iraqis and their rituals. I was amazed by his bold presentation of the subject matter, and his thorough and systematic critical analysis of a wide range of texts. The book was received with extraordinary interest in scholarly circles and prompted numerous responses in the Arab world. For many Arab readers and scholars, Kadhem's book represents a critical milestone, because it is the first Arabic book that offers a solid investigation in the field of cultural criticism and of *al-Istifraq* in particular. The book won the Ministry of Information and Culture Award in Bahrain for the best book published in 2004. It received hundreds of reviews and studies in Arab newspapers and journals. It became a textbook in cultural studies for graduate students in some Arab universities (e.g., La Faculté des Lettres et des Sciences Humaines Ben M'Sik-Casablanca) and a subject for several doctoral dissertations and masters' theses in Morocco, Algeria, and Syria.

Although I have learned a lot from the book, I cannot deny that I have sometimes felt disgusted by the extremely racist portrayals of black people in the texts studied; I was also disillusioned by how deeply this racism is rooted in my own culture. In this translation, I have tried to avoid certain offensive words, like the notorious N word, and to reduce the virulence of some shockingly cruel and distasteful descriptions of black people.

Since the book was written for Arab readers, I have made modest attempts, with the author's permission, to adapt it to a new audience, so that English-speaking readers may learn something about the original audience for which the book was written. Among the changes I have made are: (1) deleting repetitive and redundant parts, examples, digressions; (2) shortening and summarizing the theoretical foundation of the book, as anglophone readers are more likely to be familiar with the Western theoretical concepts elaborated by the author; (3) adding footnotes to explain complicated words, references, and terms such as *al-Zanj* and *al-Fuhula*; and (4) making the language politically correct and gender-inclusive.

Furthermore, understanding and translating classical Arabic poetry is daunting in many ways, even for Arab readers and translators. Its archaic vocabulary, intricate images and metaphors, complicated rhyme and rhythm, old cultural names and references, etc., pose linguistic and aesthetic challenges to understand and translate. I spent a considerable amount of time searching for good translations, and sometimes, not finding any, I translated classical Arabic poetry into modern English prose. I have tried to be as faithful to the original meaning as possible, through digging deep into the meaning and context of the poem and eliciting relevant information from the author of the book, and also through numerous footnotes.

Moreover, it was problematic to translate the subtly sarcastic tone embodied in the author's style when he is commenting on those medieval scholars and writers' offensive theorization and representation of black people. I had to spend a long time wrestling with words and structures to make it clear to the English-speaking reader that the author is being sarcastic and not in any way supportive of those anti-black arguments and representations.

The other issue is dealing with Arabic translations of sources written in or translated into English or French. Based on my research, access, and convenience, I quote sources available in English (or written in English) from the English originals, or from standard translations into English (e.g., Freud, Durand); when unable to find any, I translate the Arabic into English myself.

I hope this book contributes to the global awareness of anti-black racism and to an understanding of the cultural underpinnings of racism in Arab culture.

ACKNOWLEDGMENTS

This work would not have been possible without the financial support of the Bahrain Ministry of Culture. Also, I would like to acknowledge my indebtedness to my mentor and friend, Professor Robert Fothergill (1941–2022), for his constant willingness to consult and advise. Special thanks are due to my editor at McGill-Queen's University Press, Richard Ratzlaff, for his support and advice.

AFRICANISM

Introduction

I

When the first Arabic edition of my book *Tamtheelat al-Akher: Surat al-Sood fii al-Mutakhail al-Arabi al-Waseet* (Representations of the Other: The image of blacks in the medieval Arab imaginary) was published in 2004, a Bahraini feminist stopped me and shared with me her great admiration for the book. Then she suddenly said: "But if a black man proposed to marry my daughter, it would be impossible for me to agree!" I told her: "In principle, I do not interfere in anyone's personal convictions and attitudes, nor in this contradiction between a feminist like you who demands women's empowerment and equality with men, and at the same time interferes in her daughter's life to decide whom she can marry. However, I want to draw your attention to the fact that what you think of as a personal opinion (which I respect) is not the case." She replied: "I can't help it. I just can't accept it psychologically." I responded: "This confirms that it is not a personal opinion, because you haven't formed this opinion in the first place. It was developed before you, and you are a victim like others who are controlled by those stereotypes that were created about blacks[1] in certain historical contexts." In that conversation, I realized how valuable this book is, and how much we need to further deconstruct the negative representation of blacks that has formed in our history over many centuries and is so deeply embedded in our subconscious that we think we cannot break free from it, or think we cannot accept it psychologically, as in the words of the Bahraini feminist.

It is strange that this negative representation was not dismantled in the modern era by the pioneers of the Arab Renaissance (*al-Nahda al-Arabiyya*). These pioneers constantly reproduced this representation, despite being inspired by notions of universal human values and rights from the West. Neither Rifa'a al-Tahtawi, who initiated the Arab Renaissance, nor even Salama Moussa, the most anti-Arab of all, refrained from reproducing this pejorative representation.

In February 1910, Salama Moussa, a well-known Egyptian writer, began a racist polemic that continued until August 1910. The story of this polemic reveals the extent to which racism towards blacks is rooted in the Arab imaginary from the Middle Ages until the modern era. Salama Moussa wrote an article, published in *Al-Muqtataf*, about an English writer named H.G. Wells. In the article, he praised the writings and novels of the latter, and presented Wells's most famous books and novels, among them a book called *The Future in America*. Wells was a socialist writer ("*sociali*" in Salama Moussa's words) who visited the US and wrote about the wealth of the country, the American obsession with wealth, and their racism towards blacks, where any mixing of white people with blacks in public places (restaurants, hotels, etc.) was forbidden. As a socialist, Wells thought that racism was unjustified, rooted in old customs, and no longer necessary; thus, he demanded equality between whites and blacks.

Up to this point, Salama Moussa had made no personal comments about blackness or racism; he was just a writer reviewing the ideas of another writer. However, Salama Moussa refused to let this topic pass without comment, and he wrote in response to Wells's request for equality between whites and blacks: "I disagree. I cannot understand how blacks, whose ancestors were eating each other a hundred or two hundred years ago, can be reformed and mix their blood with the blood of the white people; no matter how civilized a black person pretends to be, his brutality is deeply rooted." He closes with his shocking, racist conclusion: blacks are savages and there is no hope of reforming them. Yes, we can be kind to them: "... we treat them humanely, but they must be prevented from reproduction, even by castration."[2] *Al-Muqtataf* magazine was alerted to this intolerable racism, and wanted to lessen its impact on readers, so in a footnote, it added this comment: "Many blacks have exceeded white people in their good manners and morals, even in the United States."[3]

However, this statement did not deter Moussa, so in March 1910, he returned to complete his racist attack against blacks. He could not accept the magazine's comment on his opinion, so he wanted to present his "definitive" evidence of the "inferiority of blacks."[4] He began by presenting simple evidence: unlike other nations in the world, blacks had not established a civilization of their own, and even external attempts to civilize them (by colonialism or Christian missionaries) all ended in failure. Here, he tells us this racist story: A preacher wanted to convince a *zinji*[5] of the value of monogamy over polygamy. "The zinji showed his piety to the missionary, except that he ate all his wives and left one!"[6] What can we conclude from this story? Blacks are wild beings with no hope of civilization. Then he turns to his second piece of evidence: American zinj did not take advantage of the rights granted to them in the United States of America, and they remained barbarians. He quotes an American doctor with whom he shares his racism: "There is no need to castrate him [that is, the zinji] because his animalism will destroy him." As for the third evidence, it is the most extreme of all, after which there is no hope for all those who demand equality between whites and blacks. Here, Moussa uses science (biology in particular), like many stubborn racists in the modern world. Biologists, he says, assert that "the activity of the zinji brain is closer to that of the monkey brain than to that of the white human brain."[7] It seems that this "scientific" evidence was convincing at the time, as Moussa was writing in the name of science at a time when science was raised to the level of "religion." It seems that the language of science was what made *Al-Muqtataf* recant its previous footnote, stating that it "does not disagree with the writer that blacks are lower than white people, and that white people are superior to blacks in general."[8]

Other writers got involved in this battle, some of them objecting to Moussa's racism, and others supporting him and taking his side. Among them was a medical student named Dalawer Salman who went further than his master in racism. As a medical student he could show medical and scientific evidence of the inferiority of blacks. He started speaking in the language of skulls, skins, and noses, and thought that the narrow skulls of blacks did not respond to education or reform. For him, the process of changing blacks is against nature, which takes hundreds of centuries to change. Whoever wants to change blacks can do so, but only "if he can change their black skin, their narrow skulls, and their flat noses, to a tender white skin, delicate narrow noses, and larger skulls."[9] For several months, Moussa relentlessly defended his racist ideas, imagining himself to be the new Nietzsche, and demanding that all the "lazy and inferior people" who hinder the victorious progress of white humanity be punished without mercy.

Where did Moussa and the medical student get this racism towards blacks? It is clear that the pseudo-racist science (biology in particular) that both used played a role in deepening this vile racism; however, the truth is that this pseudo-science did nothing but present an old and rooted racism in a new language. Although Moussa called for abandoning the ancient Arab heritage, he remained in the grip of this heritage and its negative perception of blacks. Today's racism is the result of a marriage between old racism rooted in the Middle Ages and modern racism, with its blind faith in racist pseudo-science and morbid obsession with the superiority of white people.

2

The Tunisian thinker Abd al-Wahhab al-Mo'dab had previously identified the illness of Muslim societies in the modern era through a collective psychological diagnosis. He believes that modern Muslim societies have a pathological condition characterized by grief over the loss of their supremacy, as most Muslims suffer from an unhealed wound because their civilization has changed "from a victorious civilization to a defeated one." This has generated a complex emotional combination: a feeling of hatred towards the West; a morbid denial of the misery of its reality, including civilizational and scientific backwardness and its subjugation to the dominant colonial West; a struggle to acknowledge the West's scientific and technical superiority; and an illusion propagated by political Islam that dreams of restoring the glory of the early Islamic civilization.

The issue of Otherness, and questions of identity and difference in the Arab world with in this tragic and schizophrenic context, is described through the self's struggle between the present, where the Western Other appears as a colonialist and civilized superior, and the past, of the prosperous Islamic era that is gone. Those past ages represent the historical and cultural contexts within which the representations of the black Other are to be studied. At that time, Arabs and Muslims were the masters of the world, conquerors of lands, world travellers. In the modern era, the situation has been reversed: the ancient conquerors have become the conquered, to be subjected, as the others were before, to a negative representation.

The different contexts of the medieval and modern eras reflect a clear difference in the image of the Other in Arab culture. While in the modern era, the Other is solely embodied in the West, in the

Middle Ages, it was portrayed in various and multiple ways in Arab and Muslim culture.

Blacks were among many Others that Arab culture knew and sought to represent in various ways. However, what distinguishes the representations of blacks is the enormity of the representation produced by Arab culture, and the repetitive stereotypes of their animal nature and hypersexuality for such a long time and in various fields of knowledge.

To support and buttress those stereotypes, a network of interpretive knowledge was needed. It was not at all easy to describe, for example, the putative brutality of blacks, their barbarism, and the corruption of their morals and deformation, without relying on an arsenal of knowledge circulating at the time and provided by medicine (theory of the four humours), geography (Ptolemaic seven climes), astrology (the influence of the celestial bodies and the constellations on humans and regions), history (the conflict between the Abyssinians and Arabs), Biblical stories (the story of Noah and his three sons: Shem, Ham, Japheth), and other so-called "knowledge" circulating at that time. To examine the nature of this representation process is to understand the history of its formation and its determinants, and to explore the underpinnings and patterns that have governed and directed this process "unconsciously," i.e., it imposes itself on individuals and groups without necessarily being filtered by their critical awareness.

Almost no culture is devoid of representation of itself or the Other. Representation is what gives the group a certain image of itself and the Other, and it is what creates for this group an equivalent that Paul Ricoeur calls the group's "narrative identity." To represent is to assume the responsibility of speaking on behalf of the represented Others. This claim to agency did not exist before Islam in the Arab community. When Islam emerged, it pushed Arab culture to the fore, allowed it to expand and extend in the world, and provided it with a great capacity to embrace and absorb those different Others and their diverse cultures.

From this capacity to absorb different Others, Arab culture derives its distinctive cultural identity, where identity is an incomplete or unfinished project; it is a developing process that is magnified by the diversity of those entering Islam. Since cultural identity is neither defined nor framed by borders, Otherness has also remained open without a definitive delineation of its borders. The question about who is the Other in this culture is a question that cannot be answered easily except in a negative way, meaning that the Other is the "non-Muslim," who may embrace Islam and become a Muslim and therefore be included in the Arab cultural identity. And it is possible to speak of an Arab identity without the need to associate it with Islam. In this book I will draw on texts that were originally written in Arabic, and not in other languages used in Islamic societies at the time. Also, an important component of this culture is that "whoever was born in Islam, He is an Arab," and "He who speaks Arabic is an Arab, and he who has two [parents] in Islam is an Arab."[10] These sayings express the openness of cultural identity and its ability to embrace Others, as they express the tolerance of Islam and its remarkable transcendence of barriers of colour and race, but at the same time they include a national and ethnic centrality that made the diverse and extended societies of Islam, spread in all parts of the world, tightly tied to the centre, to Arab culture that won, conquered, and made itself the central and reference power of Islam.

Arab culture has clashed with other "enemies" because they are non-Muslims or hostile to Islam and Muslims. Every culture has its Other, the enemy, but the strange thing here is that Arab culture has been hostile to other non-Muslims who were not hostile to Islam, or who converted to Islam. The depth of difference and contrast between this culture and blacks was greater than the tolerance that this culture derived from Islam. This black Other is characterized by bestiality, brutality, excessive sensuality, corruption of morals, deformation of physical appearance, derogatory representations, and distorted and prejudiced stereotypes, which have been embedded in the Arab imaginary and reinforced by various discursive and non-discursive representation practices. These practices clearly have reflected the extent of the predominance of hegemonic policies and the immunization of identity against the inclusion of the foreign and culturally foreign Other.

We can say, therefore, that this culture has two mechanisms that work together but in contrast with each other: The first mechanism is that of attracting, integrating, and embracing, which was made available in this culture, thanks to Islam and its universal principles of inclusiveness. The second mechanism is that of excluding, which indicates the desire of this culture to fortify its own identity against the different Others. Thus, while the first mechanism creates an open and tolerant cultural identity, the second mechanism creates a closed, "aggressive" identity that is in conflict with Others.

As a result of this conflict between the two mechanisms, the practices of representation and learning about the Other in this culture have witnessed many paradoxes, perhaps the most important of which is the paradox of the equivocal position of the black Other in the medieval Arab imaginary. Islam has allowed blacks to integrate into the cultural identity of the Arab Muslim community, for example, Bilal al-Habashi and Wahshi bin[11] Harb after they embraced Islam; however, the expulsion mechanism distinguished those blacks, and made their blackness a distinguishing mark that prevented them from fully and truly assimilating into this culture and its identity. Perhaps the strong presence of blacks during the era of the Messenger gives evidence of what we call here the mechanism of integration and embracing; their diminished role in public life after the death of the Messenger clearly reflects the extent of the predominance of the expulsion mechanism in this culture.

This contradiction is the result of the conflict between the two mechanisms, and it is the conflict that governed the path, scope, and extensions of this identity. When the mechanism of integration dominates, identity opens to and absorbs the Other, not to subjugate and dominate, but rather to assimilate and coexist peacefully with all differences. But when the expulsion mechanism prevails, which mostly happens, identity closes in on itself, narrows its members, and alienates the Other, an aversion that pushes it to isolation, or to seek to subjugate, dominate, and possess the Other.

The concept of Otherness is relative because the Other is determined only by comparison to a central point, which is the self. The self is a relative concept as well, since it is not stable. The Other may be identified individually in comparison to me as an individual, or to a specific internal group such as women in comparison to men, and the poor in comparison to the rich, or external in comparison to society in general. The Otherness of blacks in Arab culture is explored through the following question: Is their Otherness an external Other that is limited to those of Abyssinia, Nubia, Zanj, and the countries beyond the desert? Or is it an internal Other that is connected to this culture by the bond of religion, language, place, and sometimes Arabism as a national and ethnic affiliation? Blacks have played the role of both Others. They are both external and internal at the same time. There are black Arabs, as in the offspring of Salim bin Mansour, who were distinguished by their dark skin; there are Arabs who are from an Arab father and a black mother; and there are also blacks who were brought from unknown areas of Africa south of the desert.

Black in this sense implies a double Otherness that could have made the relationship of the self with the black Other go in three directions: (1) fluctuation between rejecting and accepting the black Other; (2) acceptance of the black Other by virtue of its connections to the identity of the self; and (3) rejection of black Other and a severing of all existing or imagined ties. The third direction seems to be the one that has dominated and in which rejection was not limited to the black as an external Other, but applied to the internal black as well.

3

The problem described above is the subject of investigation and analysis in this book. It is a very sensitive topic, and it requires sensitivity and deep familiarity with many fields of knowledge that were common in the Middle Ages as well as great accuracy and caution to avoid the slippery slope of bias. Studying this issue may deviate from critiquing to accusing culture of racism, or from analysis to fanaticism and prejudice. I hope that my methodological and theoretical premises in this book will allow me to avoid falling into the trap of accusation and prejudice. Among the theories that will be utilized are cultural criticism and neo-historicism (or cultural aesthetics), which intersect with cultural materialism, cultural pluralism, cultural studies, postcolonial studies, and postmodernism, which Patrick Brantlinger called "Post-Poststructuralist" theories. Those theories go beyond the focused interest in analyzing text structures. Instead of merely exploring a text's aesthetic and literary aspects and significance, post-poststructuralist theories are more interested in analyzing discourse and its patterns, and in questioning its cultural connotations and ideological biases, revealing its dialectical relationship with its historical and cultural context, and clarifying its role in shaping the cultural identity of society. These theories were a reaction to formalist structuralism and post-structuralist textuality. Post-poststructuralist theories combine an interest in texts, histories, cultural patterns, and discursive and non-discursive practices, and this is what enabled it to transcend the boundaries between literature, criticism, history, sociology, anthropology, and politics.

Arabic literary and cultural theory has excluded studies of the imaginary, its representations, and its importance in shaping cultural identity, and crystallizing the relationship between the self and the Other, all under the pretext of objective scientific research, which is influenced by rationalism and Marxist materialism. The imaginary was viewed as the counterpart of rationalism and materialist reality. Due to the excessive modern interest in reason and rationality, the imaginary has been neglected as a product of the imagination, which has been described, since Descartes, as the master of deception and an offender against reason, a faculty that disrupts the work of the mind or does not respond to its standards and principles. On the other hand, the imaginary was excluded as being a weak kind of superstructure with no autonomy or "history," and thus being materially governed by the infrastructure and the economic factor.

Under the influence of modern rationalism and Marxist materialism, a great obsession with rationality and materialism emerged in modern Arab thought. This necessitated vigorous work to strip the "Arab mind," "Arab reality," and "Arab history" of the impurities of the imaginary, which was associated with imagination, legends, myths, and illusions. Moreover, due to the preoccupation of modern Arab thinkers with *al-Nahda* questions (the Arab Renaissance) and with the reasons for our backwardness and others' progress, most thinkers, despite their different methodological and ideological premises, agreed that the reason for our backwardness was a lack of awareness and the domination of the medieval mythical mentality over the modern rational mentality. If this diagnosis is correct, then the solution lies in liberation from the hegemony of the medieval mentality and in the breaking with "heritage," its creations, manifestations, and imaginaries.

This commitment to reason, rationality, realism, and materialism has prevented criticism from thinking seriously about the imaginary. The opportunity to study the imaginary and its representations was made possible only by the theories of post-poststructuralism, new historicism, sociology of knowledge, and cultural anthropology, as well as the contributions of such thinkers and scholars as Gilbert Durand, Paul Ricoeur, Clifford Geertz, Pierre Bourdieu, Hayden White, Edward Said, Mohamed Arkoun, and others. Among the valuable Arab writings in this field is Muhammad Abed al-Jabri's *al-'Aql al-Siyasi al-Arabi: Muhadidatah wa Tajaliyatah* (The Arab political mind: Its limitations and manifestations). Unlike his previous writings (*Takwiin al-'Aql al-Arabi* and *Bunyat al-Aql al-Arabi*), which were biased towards rationalism in understanding the epistemological systems in Arab culture, in *al-'Aql al-Siyasi al-Arabi* (1990), al-Jabri returns to the imaginary and popular culture, focusing this time on the importance of the imaginary or what he called "al-Mikhyaal al-Ijtima'i" (social imaginary) in approaching and analyzing the Arab political mind.

For al-Jabri, the imaginary is a symbolic reservoir filled with cultural capital and a set of personalities, events, perceptions, symbols, connotations, standards, and values that give political ideology its "unconscious structure" in a specific historical period. It is this structure that exercises its authority over individuals and groups, not only in the field of perception but also in the field of social action. On the other hand, in *al-Arab wa al-Barabira* (Arabs and the barbarians) (1991), Aziz al-Azma investigates cultural perceptions that have governed the knowledge of other civilizations such as the Chinese, Indian, African, Turkish, Slavic, and European in medieval Arab culture. Examining those perceptions from the dialectical perspective of civilization versus barbarism, al-Azma highlights the reliance of that knowledge on the literary, geographical, and historical heritage that transformed it into a mere process of "acquaintance," but nothing more.

Muhammad Nur al-Din Afaya, in *al-Mutakhayal wa al-Tawasil* (The imaginary and communication) (1993) and *al-Gharb wal Mutakhayal* (The West and the imaginary) (2000), attempts to uncover the Arab Muslim discursive mechanisms in representing the Latin European in particular. Afaya highlights the imagined dimensions in this representation governed by a network of images, judgments, and attitudes that flow from a huge symbolic, emotional, and ideological reservoir called "the imaginary."

Another scholar is Abdullah al-Ghathami, whose project is devoted to analyzing and interpreting Arab cultural patterns and their role in determining the nature of the relationship between the self and the Other. His interest was initially focused on the problem of the internal Other, represented in the image and voice of women, as in his books *al-Mar'a wa al-Lugha* (The woman and language) (1996), *Thaqafat al-Waham* (The culture of illusion) (1998), and *Ta'neeth al-Qasida wal Qari' al-Mukhtalif* (Feminization of the poem and the different reader) (1999). Later, however, he has expanded the scope of the Other in his book *al-Naqd al-Thaqafi: Qira'a fil Ansaq al-Thaqafiyya* (Cultural criticism: A reading of cultural patterns) (2000) where he explores the defects in the Arab "poeticized" personality patterns and their constructions of an exaggerated masculine self that denies the Other, be it woman or otherwise.

Finally, there is the work of Abdullah Ibrahim, which focuses on dismantling cultural centralities, starting with Western centricity in *al-Markaziyya al-Gharbiyya* (The Western centricity) (1997), then Arab centricity in *al-Thaqafa al-Arabiyya wal al-Marja'yat al-Musta'ara* (Arab culture and the borrowed references) (1999), to Islamic centricity in *al-Markaziyya al-Islamiyya* (Islamic centricity) (2001), in which he studies the image of the Other in the Islamic imaginary during the Middle Ages, and critiques those cultural narratives that included semi-constant representations of other races, cultures, and religions.

The premises of these scholars rely on shared perceptions and conceptions within the cultural text instead of the literary text, which also questions the authenticity and credibility of representation, but at the same time does not deny its role in determining the nature of the relationship between the self and the Other. They ascribe to cultural patterns and the imaginary a major role in fabricating the cultural identity narratives, and in shaping the image of the Other as a subject over which power relations and mechanisms of domination are exercised.

Hence, this huge archive of texts, narratives, and poems that Arab culture has produced about other cultures and identities is not an objective or neutral description of the Other. Rather, it is a representative discourse that includes desires, perceptions, assumptions, and prior value judgments; it is an arena that mixes the imaginary and fictional with the real and actual. In addition, this huge archive should not be neglected and left without examination, analysis, and critique, nor should it remain "untouchable," forbidden to approach, criticize, and dismantle.

4

This book presents a critical study of the images of blacks in the medieval Arab imaginary, and their relevance to the Other and identity. It consists of four chapters, each of which investigates the cultural representation of the imaginary in both forms, fictional and non-fictional, where blacks are represented as an external Other that lurks in the remote jungles of Africa, and as an internal Other distinguished by black colour, despite the fact of being born and raised in the vicinity of Arab culture. By examining the Arab imaginary, the book digs deep into the cultural constructions of blacks in all aspects of the Arab imaginary, including language, religion, philosophy, literature, geography, and history.

The first chapter explores those foundations that animate, support, and reinforce those representations of blacks in the Arab imaginary. The focus of this chapter is on two main underpinnings: history as a set of significant and residual events in the Arab collective memory of the relationship with Abyssinians and blacks before and after the emergence of Islam; and cultural patterns, which include religion as a cultural pattern, language as a socio-cultural institution, and symbol as a cultural significance-bearer.

The second chapter seeks to dismantle the contents of the non-fictional cultural imaginary, and its derogatory stereotypes about blacks. It shows the cultural power of this representation, whose formation has been informed by various discourses and narratives of traveller dairies, geography, astronomy, astrology, history, theology, hadith, marine science, philosophy, natural sciences, and ancient medicine. Because of this active and proliferating representation, the Arab imaginary has ended up forming a cultural identity specific to its members. This identity is intended to be pure, impregnable, and impervious to the infiltration of other identities, most notably that of the black Other, who was presented as different in everything (religion, race, colour, language, and geography): the "absolute Other" and the "multiple difference" or the "compound difference."

The third chapter analyzes those great medieval narratives in Arab culture. I have chosen five narratives in which blacks had a remarkable, distinctive, and significant presence. These are: *Sirat bani Hilal, Sirat al-Amirah Dhat al-Himma, Sirat Antarah bin Shaddad, Sirat Saif bin Dhi Yazan*, and *Alf Laila wa Laila (One Thousand and One Nights)*.[12] These narratives share some common features: they are popular folk narratives, they are transmitted orally, and they are written anonymously. These reasons made them a fertile ground for the collective cultural imaginary to implant its derogatory representations of the black Other without supervision or questioning.

The fourth chapter, utilizing Edward Said's "contrapuntal reading," examines Arab poets' representation of blacks and black poets' counter-representation in Arabic poetry. The first part of the chapter focuses on the depiction of blacks in the poetry of Ibn al-Rumi and al-Mutanabbi. The second part studies the resistance and counter-representation of blacks in the poetry by black poets. Black poets are divided into those who were assimilated within Arab culture, such as Antarah bin Shaddad, and those who rebelled against representation of blacks by the host culture, such as Suhaim Abd Bani al-Hashas.

PART ONE

Cultural Representations and the Imaginary Underpinnings

AL- ISTIFRAQ AL-ARABI (ARAB AFRICANISM): IMAGINARY, REPRESENTATION, AND DUAL NATURE

Studying the underpinnings of the imaginary means researching the backgrounds on which this imaginary is based as well as studying the drives that guide it and the "tribal" premises that allowed it to appear in a particular culture and in specific historical contexts. However, it should not be understood from this that the imaginary is governed through those backgrounds in an absolute manner. Rather, it is true that the relationship between the imaginary and its underpinnings is not stable, nor is it conclusively defined. This imaginary is found only in a culture, or in a certain human group, that resorts to it in an attempt to identify itself through comparison with others. No culture and human group can dispense with an imaginary; it always needs one in order to establish its existence, and to give this existence a value and meaning. The imaginary does not mean illusions or images in the material sense of the word. It refers to the major significations that make society seem coherent as a whole and enable it to give meaning to the lives of individuals who belong to it. It is those significations that direct the effectiveness of human beings, and thus give value to things and actions or reduce their value.[1] Cornelius Castoriadis says that the imaginary has two dimensions: it both creates and is created at the same time.[2] It creates the identity of a society; Castoriadis says that society is founded on the imaginary. It is also created in a particular society, by virtue of certain underpinnings, and multiple and overlapping historical contexts. The question raised here is: What did constitute the imaginary and reinforce the web of images about blacks in Arab culture? Furthermore, is it the external historical economic, political, and social contexts? Or is it the cultural patterns that the Arab Muslim person embodies, such as religion, language, and symbols? Or is it the result of these historical contexts and cultural patterns together?

The subject of the imaginary, its symbolic connotations, and its relationship to external contexts has attracted the attention of many thinkers, such as Jean Piaget, Gaston Bachelard, Sigmund Freud, Alfred Adler, Carl Jung, Mircea Eliade, Ernst Cassirer, Jacques Lacan, and others. However, their approaches deal with the imaginary in opposing ways, and mostly focus on one of its dimensions. The imaginary is reduced either to its internal subjective psychological dimension or to its external social dimension. The first tendency is represented by Sigmund Freud, who considers that the stimulator of symbols is the "center of desire" or sexual energy.[3] As for Adler, the stimulator of these symbols lies in the "inferiority complex" that drives a wide range of symbols through a compensatory mechanism that aims at removing feelings of inferiority.

In his description of the child's three stages of development, Lacan used the term "imaginary" as a distinction between the symbolic and the real. Lacan uses the concept of the imaginary, or the field of the imaginary, to denote the "image of the ego" of the child in an imagined moment, which he calls the "mirror phase," ranging between six and eighteen months. The *self*, from Lacan's perspective, does not appear to exist until after it acquires self-awareness, which is what happens in this stage that precedes the Oedipal stage, and that is based on what the child perceives as an imaginary match with their image reflected in the mirror, a stage that does not indicate a clear distinction between the self and the subject. Also, in this stage, there is no real understanding of the self, since this knowledge is acquired by the child only in the "linguistic stage" when the self enters the symbolic system (language) that provides it with the general concept of the "I," which makes the child a member of the social construction. It is a system where "the I is precipitated in a primordial form, before it is objectified in the dialectic of identification with the Other, and before language restores to it, in the universal, its function as subject."[4]

On the other hand, Carl Jung considers that the primordial images, prototypes, or symbols are older than the historical humans, that they have been ingrained in humans since the earliest times, and that it is wise to return to them.[5] The issue is not a matter of faith, nor a matter of spirituality, but rather an agreement of thought with the primordial (unconscious) forms. It is the source of all hidden thoughts. This tendency also appears in both Dumézil and Piganiol: "one stressing the functional and social nature of the motivations of ritual, myths, and terminology itself; and the other the difference in modes of thought and symbolisms which derive from the historical and political status of the occupier or the occupied."[6]

The above disagreement is based on a larger disagreement between two schools in philosophy and the humanities and social sciences, namely Materialism and Idealism. The former emphasizes the primacy of material substructure (the forces of the economy and the relationships of production) and their inevitable role in influencing the superstructures that depend on and are determined by the former. Idealism stems from the belief that mental phenomena or awareness and "ideas" define or shape material reality, as well as human existence and various social phenomena. It has become a given that traditional Marxism (some call it vulgar Marxism) believes in a single pattern in analyzing the relationship between substructure and superstructure, that is, substructure is the foundation of superstructure, and that since the latter is "determined by forces outside itself, it does not have autonomy in a causal sense."[7] Thus, it is not human consciousness that determines their social existence, but social existence that determines consciousness. According to Marx and Engel's famous statement: "Life is not determined by consciousness, but consciousness by life."[8] This is a timely revolutionary statement opposing Hegelian philosophy, in which the world is dominated by reason, and the history of the world is therefore represented as a mental path. If this Marxist idea was revolutionary in the past, it has become "vulgar" since it sees only an automatic and exclusive pattern of the relationship of social existence with consciousness. Hence, many thinkers have said that the failure of Marxist theory lies in its reduction of the social world to the economic dimension alone:

> Marxism imagines the social world as if it were one-dimensional, as simply organized around the opposition between two blocs ... In reality, the social space is a multi-dimensional space, an open set of relatively autonomous fields, fields which are more or less strongly and directly subordinate, in their function and transformations, to the field of economic production.[9]

Some neo-Marxist thinkers in the Frankfurt School, cultural materialism, and cultural studies have tried to provide different interpretations of the nature of the relationship between substructure and superstructure. It suffices here to recall the position of the French Marxist thinker Louis Althusser, who emphasizes that the economic, political, ideological, and other fields enjoy relative autonomy, and that the infrastructure does not determine the nature of the entire entity of society, except "in the end" only. Hence, Althusser rejects Marx's definition of ideology, as well as the claim that ideology is absolutely subordinate to the substructure. He therefore also rejects the pattern of unilateral relationship between different factors in favour of a multiple type of possible relationships that Althusser calls "overdetermination."

Althusser reconsiders the concept of ideology, its effect on individuals, and the formation of their selves, identities, and consciousness. Formerly, ideology was conceived as a "false consciousness," "ghosts forming in people's heads," and "imaginary dreams," but now "ideology has a material existence."[10] Althusser insists that we need to recognize the materialism of ideology if we want to progress in analyzing its nature. The material existence of ideology appears in material practices that are determined by what Althusser calls the "Ideological State Apparatus." Unlike the materiality of stone or iron, the materiality of ideology is evident in its effect on individuals, and in the formation of their consciousness and cultural identities.

In short, ideas and beliefs (ideology) – and from now on I will use "imaginary/imaginaries" – are hidden in the collective memory, but they clearly impact individuals and groups through material practices determined ritualistically by the social-ideological apparatus. The first attempt to study the imaginary as an area of exchange and interaction between the representative psychological dimension and the external social dimension dates back to the French anthropologist Gilbert Durand and his book *Anthropological Structures of the*

Imaginary (1960). Durand criticizes the two previous approaches to the study of the imaginary, partly because they reduce the imaginary to either external or internal knowledge. Hence, Durand proposes a different approach to the study of the imaginary, which he calls the "anthropological dialectic," which is defined as "the ceaseless exchange taking place on the level of the imaginary between subjective assimilatory drives and objective pressures emanating from the cosmic and social milieu."[11] In this way, the old fruitless dispute over the ontological primacy of either dimension over the other can be disposed of. The imaginary has a dual nature, external-social and internal-psychological at the same time, and it provides us with general forms that organize our knowledge of the external world, as well as affecting the internal sphere of our psychological life.

The imaginary is formed in a culture as a result of multiple historical circumstances and contexts, and it also contributes to the formation of the identity of that culture, and acts as a catalyst and motivator for action in those circumstances and contexts. Therefore, it represents an area of permanent exchange and interaction between the internal representative components and the external drives and underpinnings. It is necessary to note that the reference to the internal representational dimension in the imaginary does not confuse between the individual psychological imaginary and the collective cultural imaginary. This is because "current psychological theories focus on peculiarities of individual personality to the neglect of social and cultural patterns."[12]

In modern cultural studies, the concept of the "imaginary" is used beyond individual psychological dimensions to include collective cultural dimensions, where the imaginaries of individuals are connected to "recognizable patterns in cultural systems"[13] that govern the behaviour of individuals and regulate their psychological and social processes alike. Accordingly, the imaginary is used to describe those mediations that images and discourses make, not in the Lacanian child's "mirror stage," but rather in the mirror of groups/societies that strive to paint a clear and coherent picture of their cultural identities. That is why the term "cultural imaginary" is used here as a collective memory, a symbolic reservoir, and a wide network of images, themes, narratives, discourses, values, and symbols that are intertwined, which constitute the frame of reference for the cultural identity. As for the process by which the imaginary is formed and reinforced, I would refer to it as "representation."

According to Michel Foucault, representation is not merely an object for human sciences; rather, it is "the very field upon which the human sciences occur, and to their fullest extent; it is the general pedestal of that form of knowledge, the basis that makes it possible."[14] The representation that Foucault means here is the most common strategy in the production of knowledge, and it is based on the idea of dispensing with the object by using its image, or the represented image (external reality, for example). As for representation as one of the mechanisms of domination and a tool of discipline, control, and punishment, it is based on this same idea that the punishment power depends on representation to impose its hegemony. If the motive for crime is the expected gain, then the effectiveness of the punishment is in the expected harm, or in the form of punishment and pain, not in the feeling of torment and bodily harm. Thus, punishment is more concerned with its representation. Or rather, if the punishment extends to the body, it is not torment as much as it is the object of representation: the memory of the pain can prevent recurrence, because the representation of punishment can be more frightening than the most severe physical punishments. The power of punishment is not realized in its physical reality, but in its representation.

Representing the Other is a mechanism of domination and subjugation, and is an integrated part in institutional discipline, surveillance, and punishment. Yet, representing the Other is a quite difficult task. It requires advanced knowledge and means, and it is governed by cultural, social, political, and linguistic determinants. Therefore, the ability to represent Others, in addition to being a painstaking process, is not available to any culture unless it has advanced on two levels: dominance at the political level with an expansionist tendency, and cultural urbanization or knowledge development that colludes with the tendency of political expansion. Hence, Arab cultural representation of blacks gained its strength and consolidation from the strength of Arab civilization and its hegemony in the medieval world. This power has also been reinforced through the extension of this representation over a vast area of Arab cultural production, as this representation is supported in various fields of knowledge: religious scripts, traveller chronicles, books by geographers and astrologers, medicine, poetry, wonder and fantasy literature (such as *One Thousand and One Nights*), historical narrations, folklore narratives (such as the biography of Antarah, Seif bin Dhi Yazan, al-Hilaliyya, and Princess Dhat al-Himma), and other influential books (such as *Rasa'l al-Jahiz*, *Uyoun al-Akhbar* and *Kitaab al-Ma'arifa* by Ibn Qutayba, *al-Imta' wal Mu'anasa* by Abu Hayyan, *Nihayat al-Arab* by al-Nuwayri, *al-Mustastari* by al-Abshihi, and *Subh al-A'sha* by al-Qalqashandi). Thus, the Arab imaginary about blacks was endorsed and nourished by a huge epistemological network circulating at the time, including geography, astrology, medicine, history, literature, etc.

Arab culture was able to represent Others due to the political and knowledge production power that it had in the Middle Ages. In the modern era, "representations of what lay beyond insular or metropolitan boundaries came, almost from the start, to confirm European power,"[15] and to prove the industrial, military, and scientific progress of this culture. Culture is capable of representation when it possesses power and the means of imposing hegemony. "There is an impressive circularity here: we are dominant because we have the power (industrial, technological, military, moral), and they don't, because of which they are not dominant; they are inferior, we are superior."[16]

When such representations of Others are propagated, those Others may be persuaded of the image formed of them, and that their representations in the discourses of Others are true. Consequently, representation is often capable of maintaining the same pejorative image (slave, inferior, ignorant). If "we try to convince people that they are slaves, they believe it in the end."[17] Hence, we can discover the destructive and inhumane consequences that this dubious collusion between power (for example, the military) and knowledge (the advancement of science and knowledge, for example) can lead to.

Representations, then, include two dimensions, and they are similar to the dimensions of the imaginary in that they create and are created, or form and are formed, and are both a cause and effect. Representations are a means of subjugating and dominating Others, and thus maintaining the continuity and perpetuation of power and domination. Some scholars go on to say that these representations and the total images that the imaginary creates about Others "do not so much have power: they are power."[18] They are perceptions in the collective conscious or unconscious. They have a strong impact on the course of events, on relationships among groups, and on shaping and transforming reality.

Knowledge, as we have come to know from Michel Foucault, Edward Said, and others, is not necessarily innocently constructed. As for knowing the Other, it is far from innocuous. The genealogical analysis of knowledge, as Foucault postulates, shows that knowledge is always entangled with the will to power and domination, and that "all knowledge rests upon injustice; there is no right, not even in the act of knowing, to truth or a foundation for truth; and the instinct for knowledge is malicious,"[19] and may seek the misery and annihilation of humanity:

> knowledge is an illusory effect of the fraudulent assertion of truth: the will that brings both of them has this double character: (1) of not being will to know but will to power; (2) of founding a relationship of reciprocal cruelty and destruction between knowledge and truth.[20]

Accordingly, we seek to know Others and write about them not only for the purpose of pure knowledge, nor is it only in response to the impulse of free and innocent curiosity, but also to pursue and maintain domination over those Others. Hence, "all cultures tend to make representations of foreign cultures, the better to master or in some way control them." And when these representations multiply and are characterized by great consistency and intensification, then these representations have a physical presence in the form of practices or institutions, as is the case of Orientalism, that Edward Said interprets as "a system of representations framed by a whole set of forces that brought the Orient into Western learning, Western consciousness, and later, Western empire."[21] Orientalism, as a system of representations, is a product of political power, and a consequence of the scientific and military advancement of Europe in the modern era. It is therefore an epistemological discourse governed by power and external material institutions. On the other hand, Orientalism represents the West's epistemological discourse that is concerned with studying, describing, teaching, and producing judgments about the Orient, with the aim of invading, possessing, and recreating it.[22]

Similar to the Western interest in the study of the Orient, Arab culture too had a strong interest in studying the cultures of other people of the north, south, east, and west. This Arab interest did not have research institutes and universities behind it, but it did create a huge heritage and a very rich archive on "the black" or "al-Zanj," and its culture, customs, traditions, and religions (though most Arab travellers assert that blacks have no religion or Sharia), its clothing, its food, etc. All of this was achieved in the context of the cultural and political dominance that Arab civilization had throughout the first five centuries following the rise of Islam. In the context of this predominance, the discourse of what I call "Arab Africanism" (*al-Istifraq al-Arabi*) emerged. The term refers to the Arab representations of blacks, and their intense interest in learning about the various races and cultures of the Sudan, al-Zanj, and Africans, comparable to the West's interest in Orientalism and its relationship with the Orient.

The aims and intentions of Western Orientalism are not necessarily identical with those of Arab Africanism; however, both arose and flourished in the context of the cultural, political, and military predominance of the studying and observing self. Although Arab Africanism does not reach the dangerous extent of Orientalism in its political, economic, and institutional power, it still resembles Orientalism. The discourse in which the political and cultural will to power was reinforced in Orientalism by colonialism is paralleled in Arab Africanism by the Islamic conquests and the rush of "will-to-know" discoveries and explorations. Both Orientalism and Africanism were active and aggressive processes of representing an external Other that was different from it religiously, culturally, and linguistically. This has led to the formation of imaginary and fabricated representations of the Other. Just as the Orient, from Edward Said's perspective, was an entity formed by Orientalism, so the black/African was a creation of Arab culture. Both Orientalism and Africanism formulated a comprehensive and rich discourse about the Other. This discourse is formed of images, representations, and prejudices that acquired their so-called self-evident nature from contexts that draw lines separating them as "pure" from those Other "polluted" races and cultures.

I

Blacks in the Arab Imaginary

THE UNDERPINNINGS AND THE IMAGINARY

In 1803, Muhammad bin Umar al-Tunisi (1789–1857) went to Darfur (Sudan) to look for his father, who had moved there following the departure of his father (Muhammad's grandfather). Muhammad bin Umar had met a friend of his father, Sayyid Ahmed al-Badawi, one of the great merchants of Darfur, and he travelled with him after he told Muhammad that his father was one of the greatest and most honourable people for the sultan. When Muhammad bin Umar boarded the ship to travel to Darfur, at the age of fourteen, he was overwhelmed with great fear and panic:

> When we set forth, I remembered the troubles and dangers of travelling, especially for those whose condition was like mine, destitution and disguised hardship, so I became skeptical and annoyed. The hardship continued as I found myself among people who were not like my people, among 40 nations whose conversation I knew little, and I could not see in them a beautiful bright face [sic]. So, with tears in my eyes, I said:
> Your bodies, your clothes, and your faces,
> Are black, black, and black.
> So, I regretted being with the sons of Ham, as I remembered the enmity between them and the sons of Shem. I cannot describe how terrified I was, as I almost decided to go back home.[1]

Why all that panic felt by Muhammad bin Umar al-Tunisi? It seems that fear was present in his inner self as he travelled from Fustat

(Egypt) to Darfur. What increased it and brought it to the point of "panic" was his presence among people who were "different from his people" – Ham's descendants. Then, he remembered the hostility between Ham's black descendants and Shem's white offspring. Frightened, al-Tunisi thought of going back home to be among people of his own kind whose faces were bright and beautiful.

Al-Tunisi had had no direct contact with those people in Sudan before. He became aware of them through his father and grandfather, who travelled to Sennar (Sudan) and who preferred to stay there, leaving their families behind in Tunisia. What he learned through his father and grandfather living in Sudan, as well as from his direct experience with the people of Sudan, strongly contradicted his panic. He had not dealt with them directly before that moment, and when he did, through Sayyid Ahmed al-Badawi, he found nothing but kindness, nobility, and generosity. His panic was triggered by a narrative that infiltrated his mind and imaginary from books, stories, stereotypes of the people of Sudan, and the imagined relationship between the sons of Ham and the sons of Shem. In short, it is this imaginary that the collective Arab consciousness has preserved about blacks. This imaginary has been shaped and fed through various underpinnings, making everyone assimilate and comply with it, even in irrelevant personal situations, as in the case of Abu Hilal al-Askari when addressing annoying fleas:

> They are taking revenge on me for a reason I know not,
> Except for the enmity of blacks against whites.[2]

HISTORY AS NARRATIVE

History is a discourse about events that occurred in the past. However, approaching this discourse does not mean grasping those historical events as they actually occurred in that past, because history, in the end, is a sort of narration or storytelling. Those events can only be accessed through a medium that is often a historical text. Hayden White argues that a historical text is comparable to a literary text, since all historical writings depend on an undeniable aspect, the "form of the narrative itself," that is, the order of events in a plot. History is perceived or formed as a story consisting of events, facts, and personalities. This story, or narrative, is not present in real events; the historian has to invent it. In order for historians to narrate their history, they have to extract a story from a heap of discordant, unconnected, heterogeneous, or not necessarily opposite events; they have to put certain events in a cause-and-effect structure; they have to highlight one event and omit another, just as they have to make one character a hero, and the other a villain. This process is what Hayden White and Paul Ricoeur call "plotting" or "emplotment"; Homi Bhabha calls it "narrating."[3] Historians follow this process, so their narrative appears as a coherent, clear, and understandable picture.

Accordingly, these histories have their own facts, as well as their own symbolic and imaginary dimensions. "To enter into history is to enter, if not into fictionality, then into unknowability."[4] These are histories that come to us from the past; they are formed at a certain moment, then developed, and then transmitted to us through a medium and not directly. This makes the formation of histories not only a process of "emplotment" or "narration" but also a process of interpretation or misinterpretation of the past, history, and culture. The past continues as long as it speaks to us, and this conversation is not a simple process between a completely present self and a real past, but rather, it often occurs through the corridors of memory, fantasy, narrative, and myth. The past is not necessarily imaginary and unrealistic, but it remains an unverifiable subject, because, in short, it no longer exists. Therefore, the discourse of history or the historical narrative can only be approached indirectly, and hence, one can realize the connection between history and the imaginary narrative. The reconstruction of the past, as Collingwood emphasizes, is an act of the imaginary. History seeks to harmonize the narrative coherence with its documents. This complex relationship characterizes the significance of history as an interpretation as well as a narration, and the plot as the mediator between the event and the story.

Hence, when I investigate the historical drives of the Arab imaginary of blacks, I mean not to probe the events as they occurred or research the actual relations between Arabs and blacks but rather to explore the narrative discourse of the event. "Historical events, whatever else they may be, are events which really happened or are believed really to have happened, but which are no longer directly accessible to perception"[5] and without mediation by the written quotations about these events. This is because the historical past is "inaccessible to us except in textual form … it can be approached only by way of prior (re)textualization,"[6] whether in the form of documentary records, or in a form of statements and reports issued by the historians themselves.

Thus, the inability to access the historical past directly results from the fact that all records and reports on this past – and Stanley Fish adds the present as well – come to us as mediated. It becomes "the product of a process of linguistic condensation, displacement, symbolization, and secondary revision ... On this basis alone, one is justified in speaking of history as a text."[7] This is because history is shaped by language through its vocabulary, structures, and expressive aptitudes, where language "itself is not innocent of its involvement in forms of ideological vision,"[8] and that defines the historian's angle of view of events, as well as controls the appropriate method of interpretation corresponding to the pressures of historical circumstances and the constraints of cultural contexts. Thus, "history cannot directly give us objective facts, for the historian's ideology and verbal strategies will determine what he chooses to observe, as they will determine how he describes it."[9]

In this book, the focus is on significant and "believable" historical events in the collective Arab memory. The Arab historical discourse has presented extensive narrations and cultural connotations of those events. The Arab collective memory is full of historical events of the conflicts between Arabs and blacks/the Abyssinians: Abyssinia's invasion of Yemen, the recourse of Saif bin Dhi Yazan to Khosrau of Persia, Abyssinian Abraha's (Abu Yaksum) campaign to demolish the Kaaba, and the migration of the first Muslims to Abyssinia. It is noteworthy that Arabs' relationship with blacks, at that early historical moment, was limited to their relations with Abyssinia, which included large parts of Africa in the East, such as Nubia; Ethiopia or the country of Kush; and parts of Sudan.

THE INNATE WHITENESS AND THE IMAGINARY KINGSHIP

The formation of a cultural identity is associated with a group's sense of its own particularity on the one hand and its difference from Others on the other hand. While certain groups derive their own identity positively, other groups derive their sense of identity negatively. This entails that identity is not an objective, realistic, and fixed reality but, rather, an imagined reality, obtained through a process that Edward Said and Keith Whitlam call "invention,"[10] that Martin Bernal calls "fabrication," and that some anthropologists refer to as "symbolic formation" of the past and identity. One of the most prominent examples of this is the process through which an ancient history of Israel was fabricated after the Palestinian history was silenced.[11] Another example is how the history of Greece was "fabricated," by cutting off its Afro-Asiatic roots, to be purely European.[12] This process overlooks the origin and dismisses the belief that it is made by a human's fantasies, objective, and imaginary needs at a particular historical moment.

From Ibn Khaldun's[13] perspective, the imaginary kinship, which he calls "assabiyyah" (group consciousness and solidarity), is triggered when there is something threatening the group's entity, which necessitates unity between the members of this group. This natural tendency in humans is provoked by the presence of an external threat or aggression against the group entity and its common interest. People usually become more aware of their culture when they encounter other cultures. The provocation of this tendency among Arabs in the sixth century CE was due to the confrontation with a foreign threat imposed by the blacks of Abyssinia.

The battle of Arabs with the Abyssinians in 525 CE and the defeat of Dhu Nuwas (Jewish king of Himyar) in Yemen was not the first clash. The desire to find conformity between the Torah's account and the geographical distribution of human races led Arab chroniclers to write about other battles and conflicts between the Shemites (Arabs among them) and the Hamites (blacks). Al-Masudi mentions that after the birth of Ham's black son (Kush), Ham (Noah's son)

> wanted to kill his wife, but Shem tried to stop him by reminding him of his father's curse, so Ham became angry. Then Satan fomented discord between the brothers and pitted one against the other. In the end, Ham had to flee to Egypt; his children were scattered, and he continued his journey westward, till he came into the Sūs-al-Aqsa.[14]

While black Hamites scattered in the African continent, the Shemites dispersed in Arabia and Palestine, and Japheth's descendants settled in the north. But how did this happen? This is a question to which some historians have tried to find an answer. Arab historians have not paid much attention to the reasons for the division and the dispersion of the sons of Japheth. Instead, they have been more interested in the division and dispersion of the sons of Shem and Ham. In *Kitaab al-Ansab* (The genealogy book), the story tells us that after the Flood:

when the loneliness left the land, Ham and his sons travelled towards al-Maghreb then they settled in Palestine. He lived there with his sons until Satan fuelled discord between Ham's and Shem's sons, so Shem and his sons wanted Ham and his sons to leave their land for them. Ham's sons refused. So, the war broke out. The sons of Shem won the battle, so Ham and his sons left to al-Maghreb and settled in a place in the Far Maghreb, called Asilah, which is a place between Tangier and the palace of Masmouda, where Ham's grave is known to this day.[15]

This story shows a desire to explain the dispersal of races in accordance with the geographical distribution of races at that time, and in light of the Torah story (Genesis 10:1–32).[16] It was necessary to assume that Ham left Palestine for Morocco, and from there his descendants dispersed between Egypt (the Copts from Mizraim, Bansar's son) to the Middle and Far Maghreb (the Berbers and the children of Nesla, Qut's son) and to the south of the Sahara (the Zanj from Sudan, Canaan's son, and the children of Kush's son, Habash).[17] However, this theory conflicts with the difference in the lineage of the same origin. The children of Ham who migrated to the African continent were of various races, including Berbers, Copts, and Zanj. However, in order to match the Torah narrative with the dispersal theory, Arab historians had no choice but to merge these races into one, so that the Copts, Berbers, and Zanj are all offspring of Ham.

The Arab historical narrative seeks to delineate the boundaries of its ethnic identity by imposing the credibility of existing ethnic divisions, and the legitimacy of the dispute between Arabs and blacks, as an ethnic and ancient conflict represented in the wars between Ham's and Shem's sons. The Torah is filled with such epic battles. For example, it describes a battle that took place between the army of Asa, king of Judah, and Zerah the Kushite, where the first was victorious: "Asa and his army pursued them as far as Gerar. Such a great number of Kushites fell that they could not recover; they were crushed before the LORD and his forces. The men of Judah carried off a large amount of plunder" (2 Chronicles 14:12–13).

This dispute between the two races was employed when Arabs clashed with Abyssinia in the sixth century CE, in which religious differences had combined with ethnic and colour differences. The Arabic version tells us that the reason for the interference of Abyssinia in Yemen was caused by what happened to the "People of al-Ukhdood"

(People of the Ditch). The people in Najran, Yemen, were Christians, and the king of Yemen at that time was Dhu Nawas or Damianus (Jewish king). So, he dug a ditch, threw them in it, and set it on fire. A Christian man, called Dhu Tha'laban, escaped and went to Caesar (Qaisar),[18] King of Rome. He asked him for help, so Caesar wrote to the Negus (An-Najashi), the Christian king of Abyssinia, who was closer to Yemen. The Negus, hearing what Dhul Nawas did to those Christians, sent an army led by Ariat bin Ashama and Abraha. They defeated King Dhu Nawas and his army.[19]

While the Biblical story of the conflict between Ham's and Shem's sons highlights the racial difference, the story of the People of the Ditch underlines the religious difference between Jewish Arabs and Christian Abyssinians. Some historians point out that the People of the Ditch were converted to Christianity by the influence of the evangelical Abyssinian Christians. In a strange narration attributed to Abu Ja'far Muhammad al-Baqir, he said:

> Ali [bin Abi Talib] (PBUH) sent to the bishop of Najran asking him about the People of the Ditch, so he told him something about it. Ali (PBUH) said not as you mentioned, but I will tell you about them. God sent an Abyssinian prophet to Abyssinia, but the people denied him. So, he fought them, but they killed some of his companions, then captured him and the rest of his companions.[20]

Then their king dug a ditch, set it on fire, and threw them in it, and saved those who recanted.

In addition to the racial and religious difference, there is a colour difference, or "al-Jibla," according to Saif bin Dhi Yazan. After the suicide of Dhul Nawas, the last of the Himyarite kings, Yemen came under the rule of Abyssinia, where Ariat bin Ashama reigned for twenty years, then Abraha al-Ashram Abu Yaksum rose against him and killed him to rule Yemen. The Abyssinian Abraha was the one who marched with his army and the Companions of the Elephant to Mecca to destroy the Kaaba, which happened within a context of religious competition between the Christianity of the south and Abyssinia and the paganism of Arabs of the north in Mecca.

This event coincided with the birth of the Prophet Muhammad in 570/571 CE, the year that was called the Year of the Elephant (Aam al-Fil). The coincidence plays an important role in shifting the hostility between Jews and Christians (during the era of Dhu Nuwas), and between Christians and pagans (during the era of Abraha), to that between Abyssinian Christians and Arab Muslims later. This is seen as a "patching" strategy that the Arab imaginary has resorted to in order to merge Arabs and Islam on the one hand, and to instill the image of the invading black Abyssinian enemy on the other hand. This is done by bridging the gaps between the Arabs of the south and the north, where Islam emerged, and by deepening these gaps between Arabs and black Abyssinians.

"Bricolage" is one of the means to respond to the world around us to make it "meaningful" and "logical" from one's perspective. Levi-Strauss believes that "mythical thinking is a kind of intellectual bricolage"[21] that one resorts to in order to bridge the gaps between opposing phenomena or contradictory worlds in one's life. Regarding the story above, there are two contradictions that had to be resolved for the unity of Arabs at that crucial moment in their history. First, there was a deep rapprochement and tolerance between Islam and Christianity, as they are both monotheistic Abrahamic religions. Nevertheless, the Arab imaginary had endeavoured to deepen the dispute between these two religions at that moment. This was not the result of a feverish religious competition between Islam and Christianity. The gap between the Christianity of Abyssinia and Islam of Arabs was due to the fact that Christianity came from the land of Abyssinia, that is, the country of the black enemy, whom the Arab imaginary did not consider as having any cultural value.

Moreover, there was a simultaneous effort to bring together Arabs of the south and those of the north, as well as the assumption of an imaginary relationship between Arabs of the south with the Persians of the north. These two practices took place in the same historical context. After the death of Abraha, who reigned over Yemen for forty-three years and against whom God sent the feathered flocks of birds, his son Yaksum took over Yemen. He reigned for two years then died. He was succeeded by Masruq bin Abraha, whose tyranny and harm spread to all the people in Yemen and even exceeded the damage done by his father and brother. At that time, there emerged the Arab epic hero Saif bin Dhi Yazan, the hero of the well-known Arab biography. Saif bin Dhi Yazan was a descendant of the Himyarite kings of Yemen. In order to save his country, he had sailed to the Byzantine Emperor to seek his help and stayed at his gate for seven years. The Emperor refused to help him, saying: "You are Jews and the Abyssinians are Christians, and it is not licit that we help the religiously deviant against the religiously orthodox."[22]

Caesar's (i.e., the Emperor's) response had an influential impact on Dhi Yazan, for Caesar reminded him of the religious difference between Arabs and the Romans (al-Rum),[23] and also of the religious commonality between the Romans (Byzantine Greeks) and the Abyssinians. For Dhi Yazan, matters of disagreement and reconciliation between nations are not final or predetermined; rather, they are options existing within certain contexts, circumstances, interests, and needs of that time in history. Hence, the factor that brought together the Romans and the Abyssinians, despite their differences (colour, ethnicity, and location), could be the same factor that could bring together Arabs and other different nations. At that time, this idea arose in Dhi Yazan's mind to search for unifying aspects between Arabs and other nations, so that they would be able to unite and support each other in what Ibn Khaldun calls "Anna'rah wal Munasrah" (group allegiance and support).

Ibn Khaldun postulates that pedigree is imaginary and only useful in establishing blood ties that "eventually lead to mutual help and affection."[24] Dhi Yazan realized this wisdom from Caesar's response and decided to look for other forms of relationships with the Persians. He went to Khosrau Anushirwan and sought his help while claiming kinship. Khosrau asked him: "What is this kinship that you are claiming? He responded: O King, the innate colour, the white skin; I am closer to you than them (black Abyssinians), then Anushirwan promised him victory over the black."[25]

Dhi Yazan's discourse is clearly pragmatic. He is a king who is looking for someone to help him triumph over the black Abyssinians. After his failure with Caesar, Dhi Yazan found a king (Khosrau) with strength and a great army, but he had to be careful with his appeal. Hence, the first thing that Dhi Yazan did was to remind the Persians of their kinship with Arabs, which is the affinity of colour (white skin). Dhi Yazan was not as white as the Persians, but he was also not as black as the Abyssinians, and for this reason he was closer to the Persians than to the Abyssinians. And if Anushirwan had been evasive and skeptical, he would have said to Dhi Yazan that he was closer to the Abyssinians than to the Persians. Dhi Yazan's colour was neither white nor black, and for this reason he was equally close to the two.

This kinship that Dhi Yazan claimed was a fabricated kinship, specifically after he failed to obtain Caesar's help. Therefore, it was Dhi Yazan's brainchild. The idea of kinship had not been invoked before that moment, which is why Anushirwan was astonished by Dhi Yazan's claim. Although he was aware that kinship was imaginary, Dhi Yazan sought its benefit in that Anushirwan promised him victory. While some historians mention that Dhi Yazan was the guide and ally for the Persians in the war against Abyssinia, other historians indicate that Khosrau was preoccupied with the war with the Romans and never fulfilled his promise. Dhi Yazan died, and his son Ma'dikarb bin Dhi Yazan succeeded him. He stood before Anushirwan and said: I am the son of the sheikh whom the king promised victory against Abyssinia. Anushirwan responded by sending an army who scattered the Abyssinians, and rid Yemen of their rule.[26]

This victory and the return of Yemen to Arabs was an opportunity to rearrange the kinship balance between the Arabs of Yemen and their neighbours. The Arabs' disassociation from Abyssinia must have coincided with establishing kinships with its neighbours in the north, whether the kinship is related to lineage, race, language (Arabs of the south and the Arabs of the north), or to colour (Arabs of Yemen and the Persians).

Al-Masudi had a twofold hidden agenda behind narrating the wars between the Arabs of Yemen and Abyssinia: to cut the roots of the relationship between Arabs and black Abyssinians, and to restore cohesion between Arabs and the Persians, and also between the Arabs of the north with those of the south. For this reason, intentionally or unintentionally, he used three different calendars for the historiography of the Abyssinian Abraha Campaign against the Kaaba, none of which was a Roman or Christian calendar.

Although the Christian calendar was common in al-Masudi's era, he overlooked it in favour of other unfamiliar calendars when describing the Christian campaign against the Kaaba during Arab paganism. He wrote: "The arrival of the Companions of the Elephant to Mecca on Sunday, Muharram 17th, 832 of the Alexander era, and 216 of the Arab era, which commences with the Pilgrimage of Treachery."[27] Before that, he wrote: "And Abraha Abu Yaksum was the one who marched with the Companions of the Elephant to Mecca to destroy the Kaaba, which took place in the fortieth year of the reign of Kisra Anushirwan."[28]

The abandonment of the Christian calendar and the use of a Greek, Persian, and Arab pagan calendar shows al-Masudi's desire to identify with the event he is describing. The event was indicative of the severing of the relationship between Christian Abyssinians and Arabs on the one hand, and of creating kinship between Arabs and the Persians, and also between the Arabs of the south and those of the north (whose calendar starts with the Pilgrimage of Treachery). After the victory over the Abyssinians (around 570 CE), Arab delegations, including Prophet Mohammad's grandfather Abd al-Muttalib bin Hashim ibn Abd Manaf, went to Ma'dikarb and his father to congratulate them:

> Abd al-Muttalib spoke first and said: "O king, God in His majesty has elevated you into a high, difficult to reach, unassailable, exalted, and glorious station. He has caused you to have a pedigree of fragrant stock and splendid stem. This has taken root and spread its branches in the noblest soil and the sweetest homeland, since you, may you be free from all curses, are the chief of all the Arabs and the season of spring that brings forth fertility and prosperity. You, O king, are the pinnacle of the Arabs to whom they pay obeisance, the pillar around whom they rally and their place of refuge that shelters its subjects. Your predecessors are the best of predecessors, and you are, for us, their best successor. The memory of your predecessors will never fade and none whom you succeed will ever die. O king, we are the inhabitants of God's Sanctuary and the guardians of His House. What brought us here was our joy that the sorrow that afflicted us grievously is now dissipated. We are a delegation that offers its congratulations and not one that comes to condole." The king said to him: "Who are you, O speaker?" "I am `Abd al-Muttalib bin Hashim bin`Abd Manaf," he answered. The King Ma`dikarib bin Saif said: "Are you the son of our sister?" "Yes," he responded. The king said: "Bring him closer." He was brought near and the king leant forward and said to `Abd al-Muttalib and the delegation: "Greetings and welcome! A she-camel and a saddle! Let your camels lie down with ease! A kingdom of great importance and grants most generous! The king has heard your speech, recognized your kinship to him, and accepted your entreaty. You are the people of night and the people of day. You will be treated with honour if you stay and receive gifts when you depart."[29]

The congratulatory speech delivered by al-Muttalib is similar to the plea for help that Dhi Yazan presented earlier: a speech with one goal – a reminder of kinship, or an "imaginary kinship." While Dhi Yazan's speech succeeded in deceiving Khosrau with an imagined colour kinship between Arabs and the Persians, al-Muttalib's speech succeeded in recalling and introducing another kinship, that of race and lineage between the Arabs of the south and the Arabs of the north. The kinship is specifically represented between the Arab national hero Saif bin Dhi Yazan, who was summoned by the Arab imaginary when Arabs were defeated by the Abyssinians, and Abdul Muttalib bin Hashim, the noble northern Arab figure, the guardian of watering and delegation in Mecca, and the link between Arabs and Islam through his relationship with Muhammad. Thus, the unification has taken place between the Qahtanites and Adnanites on the one hand, and between Saif bin Dhi Yazan and Prophet Mohammad on the other hand.

Hence, the event is seen by some scholars as the first sign of Arab Nationalism. The victory over the Abyssinians "was behind the strong unity among Arabs, whose leadership was fought over among Arab tribes."[30] Arabs were threatened by the Abyssinians in the south and by the Abraha campaign against Mecca in the north.

For Ibn Khaldun, the tendency of "assabiyyah" is provoked in times of distress when a group and its common interests are threatened. When the Abyssinian threat began to approach from the north, "Arabs felt that they were in real danger, so they stopped their internal conflicts, and began to unite, feeling that they would be in real danger if they remained torn apart. The Arab awakening in the Arabian Peninsula emerged because of the Abyssinian threat,"[31] which represented a national and a religious threat to Arabs. In order to confront the national threat, Arabs had to unite. The call for unity is clear in Abd al-Muttalib's speech to Dhi Yazan and his son Ma'di Karb since the latter is seen as the "chief and pinnacle of the Arabs and their spring." As for the strategy to confront the religious threat (paganism in the north and Judaism in the south), it was through "sympathizing with Judaism in the face of Christianity coming from Abyssinia, and sharing an understanding of Hanifism[32] as the national religion."[33]

Within this context, there is another problematic story narrated by al-Masudi:

On the gate of Zafar was inscribed, in ancient script and on a black
   stone, the following verses:
The day Zafar was built, it was asked:
To whom do you belong? To Himyar the virtuous, it replied.
Later, it was asked the same question and replied:
My masters are the wicked the Abyssinians.
Later, it was asked that question and replied:
My masters are the free born The Persians.
Later it was asked that question and replied:
My masters are the traders of Quraish.
Later it was asked that question and replied:
My masters are the Himyar, the magicians.
A little time only will its people remain in it,
For since its foundation it was destined to be ruined,
By lions invading it from the sea,
Who will torch its topmost towers.
This inscription was written about the kings who would rule the city ... [34]

As for Yaqut al-Hamawi, he narrates the same story with a slight difference, which is that the stone "was found at the foundation of the Kaaba when Quraysh demolished it in the pre-Islamic era." This story refers to the succession of nations who ruled "Dhafar/Zafar" or "Sana'a" (Yemen), starting with the Himyarites, then the Abyssinians, then the Persians, then Quraishites after the victory of Islam. What is notable in this story are the attributes that are attached to each nation on the one hand, and the claim that this stone was written in the early time or found in the foundation of the Kaaba. This means that those attributes are predetermined and based on religious considerations since the stone/inscription was found in the foundation of the Kaaba/the Zabur. This story is a product of the historical conflict between Arabs and the Abyssinians. It clearly expresses the nature of the relations between Arabs and their neighbouring nations in the sixth century CE, when the Himyar, or the Arabs of the south, are good people; the Persians are free; the Abyssinians are wicked; and the Quraishites are traders. This comes in a historical context in which the relations between Arabs and Abyssinians, "the wicked," were severed, while at the same time, relations were consolidated with the "free" Persians and the traders of Quraish Arabs.

The call for religious and national unity among Arabs deepened at the end of the sixth century and the beginning of the seventh century CE when Islam triumphed. But after the Yemeni king (Ma`dikarib) was killed at the hands of black Abyssinians, the Persians intervened once again, not only to expel the Abyssinians and rid Yemen of their rule but also to annihilate them all, and eliminate every Yemeni of their lineage and every Arab whose blood mixed with a black Abyssinian's blood:

> Wahrez (a Sasanian general) informed the king who dispatched him by land with four thousand Persian knights and commanded him to restore order to the Yemen and to spare not one single remaining Abyssinian and not even anyone with curly woollen hair who was connected to them in kinship. Wahriz arrived in Yemen and resided in Sana`a. He left not a single black man or any of their kin alive. Anushirwan then appointed Wahrez as king over the Yemen and he eventually died in Sana`a.[35]

With this genocide, the conflict narrative between Arabs and black Abyssinians ends. However, another counter-narrative begins, starting with the reconciliation represented in the event of the first Muslim migration to Abyssinia (First Hegira to al-Habasha). But the old narrative of conflict remains in the background of the latter's narrative of concord, which later finds its most prominent expression in the slave trade, and in the treatment of blacks who are always seen as slaves and inferiors. The defeat of the Abyssinians by Arabs in Yemen made the Abyssinians, and later all blacks, among the weakest powers that Arabs dealt with in their regional and economic struggle.[36]

THE TENSION IN THE IMAGINARY: NARRATIVES OF CONCORD AND CONFLICT

The imaginary, like any form of individual or collective memory, represents an arena in which several narratives contend with each other, rendering the imaginary tense and constantly fluctuating. Accordingly, the dominance of a narrative does not necessarily mean the complete disappearance of other opposing and alternative narratives. In the early Islamic period, the Arab imaginary continued to propagate the narrative of concord between Arabs and the Abyssinians by "focalizing"[37] the narrative of the first Muslim migration to Abyssinia, and also by silencing the narrative of conflict and the Abyssinian oppression of the Arabs of the south for five decades in the sixth century CE. Nonetheless, there were cracks that allowed the conflict narrative to surface from time to time, often provoking feelings of hostility and hatred towards the Abyssinians and blacks in general.

In Sana'a, Abraha Abu Yaksum built one of the greatest cathedrals of that era, which the Arabs call "al-Qullays" or "al-Qalis," and his aim was to wrest the religious leadership from the honourable Kaaba of the Arabs of the north. Abraha wrote to the Negus (Christian King of Abyssinia): "I have built for you, O king, a church the like of which was not built for a king before you, and I am not finished until I divert the Arab pilgrimage to it."[38] This desire was reinforced when he launched his well-known campaign to demolish the Kaaba. Why, then, did the Prophet advise the first Muslims to emigrate to Abyssinia? Some modern scholars believe that the decision to migrate to Abyssinia was not random, but the result of a deep study, which resulted in an agreement to send a group to explore the country and feel the Negus's desire for a large number of Muslims to arrive in Abyssinia. Some old narrations tell us about the Prophet's emotional attachment to that land.[39] Ibn Saad narrates that the Messenger loved this land. The narration says that when the polytheists experienced an increase of torture against Muslims, the Messenger of God (PBUH) said to them: "Disperse in the land." They said: "Where do we go, O Messenger of God?" He said: "There," and pointed to Abyssinia, the most beloved land to him.[40] In addition to this reason, the Messenger indicates that in Abyssinia, "there is a king in whose presence no one is wronged, and it is a land of truthfulness."[41] According to al-Ya'qubi's narration, the Prophet said to his companions: "Leave as emigrants to the land of Abyssinia, to the Negus, for he is a good neighbour."[42]

These reasons (love, justice, and good neighbourliness of the Negus and virtues of the Abyssinians) were supported by many hadiths and by the Prophet's Companions who emigrated to Abyssinia. It was narrated from Umm Salma that "when we came to the land of Abyssinia, we were next to the best neighbour of the Negus, we were reassured to practice our faith and worshiped God Almighty. We were not hurt nor harassed."[43] In chasing those first migrant Muslims, the people of Quraish sent Abdullah bin Abi Rabia, Umarah bin al-Waleed, and Amr bin al-Aas to Abyssinia, carrying gifts for the Negus and his Patriarch, but their attempt failed. Later the Prophet sent letters to the Negus asking him to convert to Islam. Some narratives mention that the Negus embraced Islam, and even started preaching it. It was narrated that the Messenger, when he commanded Muslims to go to Abyssinia, and asked them to remember his hadith, the Negus said: "I bear witness that he is the Messenger of God (PBUH) and that he is the one whom Jesus, son of Mary, preached. Were it not for my kingship, I would have come to him to carry his sandals."[44] In another account, Amr bin al-Aas converted to Islam because of the Negus: "in the Battle of the Trench, Amr bin al-Aas fled with a group of the infidels of Quraish to Abyssinia, seeking protection, but the Negus asked him to pledge allegiance to Islam, so he did."[45]

In one of the stories, the Prophet wrote to the Negus proposing for him Um Habiba after her husband had died in Abyssinia. So, a delegation of Ja'far bin Abi Talib and migrant companions went to Um Habiba and carried out the engagement ceremony. The Negus sent her four hundred dinars as a dowry, and the Prophet asked the Negus to return the Muslim immigrants to Medina, so he sent them by boats at his own expense. When the Messenger learned about the Negus's death, he prayed for him, according to the narration by Abdullah bin Masoud. Another account says that when the Messenger heard of the Negus's death, he said: "There died today the pious servant of Allah, Ashama. So he [the Prophet] stood up and led us in (funeral prayer) over him."[46] It is narrated by Aisha that she said: "When the Negus died, we used to speak about the ongoing light seen on his grave."[47] Also, in a hadith attributed to Ibn Abbas, the Prophet said: "Emulate the blacks, for among them are three lords of the people of Paradise, Luqman the Sage, the Negus [Emperor of Abyssinia], and Bilal the Muezzin."[48] In another hadith, the Prophet said: "Whoever enters his house an Abyssinian, God will bless his house."[49] All of these narratives show that there was a strong relationship between the Messenger and the Negus, and between Muslims and the Abyssinians. More importantly, they also indicate the need for the Arab imaginary in that period to increase the number of narrations that deepen the bond of kinship between Arabs and the Abyssinians and overshadow the past events of hostility and hatred between the two parties.

Those narratives multiplied to the extent that some treatises and books were written on the virtues of the Abyssinians, such as *Manaqib al-Najashi* (Virtues of the Negus) and *Manaqib al-Habshan* (Virtues of Abyssinians), which are similar to Jalal al-Din al-Suyuti's *Rafi' Sha'n al-Habshan* (Raising the status of the Abyssinians); *al-Tiraz al-Manqush fi Mahasan al-Habush* (The coloured brocade on the virtues of the Abyssinians); and Muhammad al-Hafni al-Qana'i's *al-Jawahir al-Hisan bima Ja'a min Allah wal Rasool wa Ulma al-Tarikh fil Hibshan* (The fine jewels in God's, the Messenger's, and the historians' words on the Abyssinians). This proliferation and prolongation in the narratives managed, at least in part, to push the narrative of conflict and hostility between Arabs and the Abyssinians into the background and highlight the narrative of concord. The migration to the land of Abyssinia was an important event in the history of the first Muslim migrants, since "this group protected Islam in its early years or contributed to protecting Islam later."[50] It seems that all those narrations and books were written to return the favour.

No narrative is immune to the fissures that allow counter-narratives to infiltrate. This narrative of concord and acceptance was the first and most prominent in the collective memory, but it was not the only narrative. Like any form of hegemony, this dominant narrative has been crowded out by other narratives. According to Raymond Williams's theory, the dominant narrative remains in perpetual conflict with two other narratives, namely, residual narrative from an old narrative and emergent narrative.[51]

Thus, despite the dominance of the new narrative of concord, the old narrative of conflict, hostility, discord, and exclusion has not been completely forgotten, but rather remains as a repressed residue in the unconscious that emerges occasionally. Let us look at the conversation below between Umar bin al-Khattab and Asma bint Umais, Ja'far bin Abi Talib's wife. It is known that Umar did not migrate to Abyssinia, but Asma did:

> Abu Musa reported: We were in Yemen when we heard of the migration of Allah's Messenger (may PBUH). We also set out as immigrants to him. And I was accompanied by two brothers of mine, I being the youngest of them; one of them was Abu Burda and the other one was Abu Ruhm, and there were some other persons with them. Some say they were fifty-three or fifty-two persons of my tribe. We embarked upon a boat, and the boat sailed away to the Negus of Abyssinia. There we met Ja'far b. Abu Talib and his companions. Ja'far said: Allah's Messenger (may PBUH) has sent us here and has commanded us to stay here and you should also stay with us. So we stayed with him and we came back (to Medina) and met Allah's

Messenger (may PBUH) when Khaibar had been conquered. He (the Holy Prophet) allocated a share to us and in the ordinary course he did not allocate the share to one who had been absent on the occasion of the conquest of Khaibar but conferred (a share) upon him only who had been present there with him. He, however, made an exception for the people of the boat, viz. for Ja'far and his companions. He allocated a share to them, and some persons from amongst the people said to us, viz. the people of the boat: We have preceded you in migration. Asma' bint 'Umais who had migrated to Abyssinia and had come back along with them (along with immigrants) visited Hafsa, the wife of Allah's Apostle (may PBUH). (Accordingly), Umar had been sitting with her (Hafsa). As Umar saw Asma, he said: Who is she? She (Hafsa) said: She is Asma, daughter of 'Umais. He said: She is an Abyssinian and a sea-woman. Asma said: Yes, it is so. Thereupon Umar said: We preceded you in migration and so we have more right to Allah's Messenger (may PBUH) as compared with you. At this she felt annoyed and said: "Umar, you are not stating the fact; by Allah, you had the privilege of being in the company of the Messenger (may PBUH) who fed the hungry among you and instructed the ignorant amongst you, whereas we had been far (from here) in the land of Abyssinia amongst the enemies and that was all for Allah and Allah's Messenger (may PBUH) and, by Allah, I would never take food nor take water unless I make a mention to Allah's Messenger (may PBUH) of what you have said." We remained in that country in constant trouble and dread and I shall talk about it to Allah's Messenger (may PBUH) and ask him (about it). By Allah, I shall not tell a lie and deviate (from the truth) and add anything to that. So, when Allah's Apostle (may PBUH) came, she said: "Allah's Apostle, Umar says so and so." Upon this Allah's Messenger (may PBUH) said: His right is not more than yours, for him and his companions there is one migration, but for you, i.e., for the people of the boat, there are two migrations. She said: "I saw Abu Musa and the people of the boat coming to me in groups and asking me about this hadith, because there was nothing more pleasing and more significant for them than this. Abu Burda reported that Asma said: I saw Abu Musa, asking me to repeat this hadith to him again and again"[52]

The dominance of the concord narrative did not prevent the old narrative of hostility from appearing twice in this story. Umar refers to Asma with mockery as "an Abyssinian and a sea-woman." Provoked by Umar's remarks, Asma responds with expressions that expose the hidden prejudice in Arab memory. The narrative of hostility was waiting for the opportunity to appear, which makes it, according to the Freudian interpretation, an expression of the tendencies and intentions we want to hide from ourselves and our feelings, whose source lies in repressed desires and complexes.[53]

Asma found herself in a challenging position, obliged to defend herself, and then all those who crossed the sea, migrating to Abyssinia. Asma's defence strategy was to turn the source of shame and inferiority into a source of pride. If Umar was proud of his precedence to migrate with the Messenger to Medina, then Asma migrated twice, once to Abyssinia, and the other time to Medina. Asma was aware that the source of pride here lies in the emigration with the Messenger to Medina in particular, the country that witnessed the first Muslim inauguration. Hence, Asma had to reverse these two sources of pride. As for emigrating with the Messenger, it is not a source of bragging, because whoever emigrated with the Messenger was in safety and security. Emigration to Abyssinia was a source of pride, because the one who migrated to Medina had migrated to the land of the relatives and friends "Ansar," while the one who migrated to Abyssinia had migrated to the land of enemies and hostility. Here, the repressed imaginary of the black Abyssinians as hostile and as enemies emerges. This contradicts the narratives of harmony that praise the Negus and the Abyssinians and the pleasant experience of the first Muslim migrants to Abyssinia.

In another context, it was narrated that the reason for the revelation of the Quranic verse, "And indeed, among the People of the Scripture are those who believe in Allah and what was revealed to you and what was revealed to them" (Quran 3:199)[54] was that when the Negus died, Gabriel mourned him to the Prophet who said to his Companions: "Stand and pray for your brother the Negus." They remarked to one another, "He commands us to pray for one of the Abyssinian *Ilooj*!" Then Allah revealed this.[55] It seems that those objectors denounced the prayer for a black Abyssinian, while rejecting shared brotherhood. In their precipitated imaginary, a black Abyssinian is not equal to them, and that is why they said about the Negus that he was one of the Ilooj of Abyssinia. *Ilooj* (singular *Ilj*) refers to either a Persian infidel or to a thick and wild zebra/ass.

Another incident occurred between Imam Ali bin Abi Talib and his brother Aqil. When Imam Ali became the caliph, he preached to the people of Medina and indicated that, in distributing the money, he would not discriminate between any Muslims, Muhajireen (migrants), and Ansar (supporters) and any Quraish or others, except on the basis of piety. There was nothing in this speech that provoked anyone, but when he said: "And I shall treat the black and the red equally," Aqil stood up to him, and said: "How can you make me equal to one of the Medina blacks, and Ali said to him: Sit down, may God have mercy on you. Is there anyone else to speak here? You are not better than him [black] but by a good deed or piety."[56]

Aqil's response implies a desire to emphasize the difference between Arabs and blacks, even if Islam is what unites them. In the same context, it is narrated that on the conquest day of Mecca, upon the Messenger's order, Bilal climbed the wall of Kaaba and called for prayers. Seeing Bilal calling for prayers, 'Attab bin Usayd said: "Praise be to God who took my father's soul, so he does not see this day." Then, al-Harith bin Hisham said: "Couldn't Muhammad find someone better than this black crow."[57] Then God revealed: "O mankind, indeed We have created you from male and female and made you peoples and tribes that you may know one another. Indeed, the most noble of you in the sight of Allah is the most righteous of you. Indeed, Allah is Knowing and Aware" (Quran 49:13). Once again, a black person is compared to an animal, and here, to a crow, which is an ominous bird in Arab culture. Thus, words such as "ass," "crow," "black slave," and "son of black mother" erupt like sparks in cases of tension and provocation, as if they were released from the suppressed unconscious.

In another similar incident, Ibn Habib mentions that the Umar's mother (Hayya) was Abyssinian, so he called Umar "O Ibn al-Sawda!" (son of a black woman), then God revealed:

> O you who have believed, let not a people ridicule [another] people; perhaps they may be better than them; nor let women ridicule [other] women; perhaps they may be better than them. And do not insult one another and do not call each other by [offensive] nicknames. Wretched is the name [i.e., mention] of disobedience after [one's] faith. And whoever does not repent – then it is those who are the wrongdoers (Quran 49:11).

With early Muslim/Arab conquests and their consequent domination of the medieval world, and with the trade in the Indian Ocean and on the East and West African coast, a new narrative emerges. Muslim Arabs were "the most important trade force that contributed a great deal to the movement of trade exchange"[58] in that part of the world. Islam had "quickly crossed the Sahara into Western Africa. The men who brought their Islamic faith with them to West Africa were mostly Arab merchants"[59] who discovered great African empires such as the empires of Ghana and Mali. On the East coast, there were trade cities built by the Swahilis (inhabitants of the coasts of Kenya, Tanganyika, and Zanzibar Island) who used the Arabic language. Those cities played an important role in the trade exchange with Arabs at the time. Trade flourished until 1497, when Vasco de Gama sailed down the western coast of Africa and rounded the Cape of Good Hope.

While the discriminatory and racist narrative was gradually disappearing throughout the Prophet's time,[60] narratives of exclusion and enslavement started to dominate during the Arab conquests. Some scholars explain this phenomenon as a historical punishment for black Abyssinians who stood in the way of the rise of the Arab nation in the pre-Islamic era. With the flourishing of the slave trade between the Arab world and the coasts of Africa, the image of the noble Abyssinian and the virtuous Negus began to fade and disappear, and words like "Ahbash" or "Huboosh" (Abyssinians) were gradually replaced with the word "Zanj" or "Sudan"[61] (blacks), which was used to describe blacks in general.

Perhaps this is what made al-Tabarani comment on the Prophet's hadith on Sudan (praising Sudan and commanding people to follow them), indicating that by Sudan, the Prophet means "Abyssinian" and nothing else. Thus, whereas the praise of Sudan is only specific to "Abyssinians," criticism would be specific to the "Zanj." Distinguishing between the races of Sudan (Abyssinians and Zanj), some scholars find a way out of the contradiction in the hadiths. Addressing the contradiction between the pro-Sudan hadiths and anti-Sudan hadiths, al-Manawi comments: "If you say this is contradicted by the hadith of 'Be aware of the Zanj, or stay away from the Zanj for they are deformed creation, and that blacks are beholden only to their stomach and genitals,' I said no, because blacks (Sudan) are divided into Zanj and Habashi (Abyssinian); the Abyssinian is desired but the Zanji is not."[62] Al-Ahbash (Abyssinians) are singled out, which is why the Prophet commands people to follow three of the Sudan (Abyssinians): Luqman, al-Najashi (the Negus), and Bilal.

In the pre-Islam era, *Sudan* (Abyssinians) were equal and contenders to Arabs, and even defeated and prevailed over them in some areas. The extensive narratives about good and equal relations between Arabs and Abyssinians during the Prophet's mission did not last long. Shortly after the Mission era, there were extensive narratives of tense and hierarchical relations between Arabs and blacks or undesirable Zanj. In this regard, al-Jahiz says: "The Zanj said to Arabs: because of your ignorance, you regarded us as your equals, during Jahiliya, to marry Arab women, but when the justice of Islam came, you deemed this practice as bad … Yet the desert is full of Zanj married to Arab wives, who have been leaders and rulers, and have protected your honour and safeguarded you from your enemies."[63]

After the death of the Prophet, the dominance of the slavery and subjugation narrative over the narrative of concord and acceptance that prevailed during the life of the Messenger resulted in the withdrawal of black Muslims from mundane life and people, and consequently into solitude and solitary death. For instance, Bilal bin Rabah went to Sham (Damascus) and led a life of solitude there until he died in 20 or 21 AH. It was also narrated that Aba Bakra bin Kalda al-Thaqafi went to Basra and died in isolation, similar to Wahshi bin Harb who went to Homs and died there.[64]

The relationship between Arabs and blacks was limited to the slave trade, a relationship between the Arab master and the black slave. Black slaves and their communities were at the bottom of the social stratification. In a desperate and indistinct attempt to do justice to blacks, al-Jahiz, in his treatise *Fakhr al-Sudan 'ala al-Bidhan* (The pride of blacks over whites), outlines the difference between black slaves and honourable blacks. He believes that Arabs have never seen the genuine Zanj, but rather they only saw

> captives who came from the coasts, jungles, and valleys of Qanbalah, from our low professions, our mean people, and slaves. The people of Qanbalah have neither beauty nor reason. Rather, beauty and reason are in the people of Nanjuyah. In this way, Zanj is divided into two types: Qanbalah and Nanjuyah. Just as the Arabs are of two types: Qahtanites and Adnanites.[65]

Nevertheless, Arabs did not see those genuine Zanj, nor were they ready to accept such a description. For Arabs at that time in history, blacks were all of the same race: black skin with ugly faces, naked and neglected like animals, and savage like beasts.

At a later period in the third century AH, the longest lasting and most damaging stereotype of blacks was formed in Arab culture: blacks as roaming animals or raging beasts, creatures ranked between humans and animals, or subhumans with enormous sexual energy. According to Nasir al-Din al-Tusi's opinion, blacks "do not differ from monkeys except in their straight stature, and some even saw that monkeys are more receptive to learning and training than al-Zanj."[66] Arabs did not look at blacks except from the perspective of slavery in the slave market (*Sooq al-Nikhasa*). Nikhasa (slave-trading) is originally the selling of animals, and the seller is called *Nikhas*, which, according to Ibn Manzur, refers to the person who prods animals with a stick to make them stand erect and look healthy, so customers buy them. Like the Nikhas of animals, the slaver deceives customers by, for instance, reddening (bringing pink colour to) yellowish cheeks; yellowing the white spots caused by eye sores, leprosy, and vitiligo; adding eyeliner to blue eyes; fattening skinny and withered faces; removing beard hair from cheeks; dyeing, curling, and straightening hair; bleaching brown faces; increasing the flesh of thin legs; removing traces of smallpox, tattoos, freckles, and itches; etc.[67]

As the buyer inspects the slave to find the best product, the Nikhas (slaver) moulds the slave into a desirable product. Thus, the slave is an object shaped by the slaver and examined by the buyer. Both the slaver and the buyer need an expert in deceit, concealment, and inspection. This person is called "dallal" or "simsar" (middleman) who works as a mediator between the slaver and the buyer. On the one hand, the dallal/simsar helps the seller with concealing the undesirable features in the commodity (slave) and with promoting the commodity in the market; on the other hand, he helps the inexperienced buyer in discovering the hidden flaws in the commodity. In order to assist customers in buying and inspecting slaves, Ibn Butlan wrote *Risala Nafi'a fi Shray al-Raqiq wa Taqleeb al-Abeed* (A useful treatise on buying and inspecting slaves) and after him, Muhammad al-Ghazali authored *Hidayat al-Mureed fi Taqleeb al-Abeed* (Guiding the follower in inspecting slaves). Those books are written for the slave buyer who wants to identify in the slave "the healthy parts from the unhealthy ones, the good manners from the bad ones, and whether those female slaves are for service or for pleasure, and whether those slaves are obedient and loyal or arrogant with pride, and which of them are only suitable for labour and whipping, so he [the buyer] chooses from each type what is suitable for his purpose."[68]

The slave trade flourished with the expansion of the Islamic conquests, which brought with it several roles and professions to facilitate slavery transactions. For example, there was a group of people called *al-Khatafoon* (the kidnappers) whose job was to kidnap potential slaves from their country and export them to slavers. Another example is *al-Qayim* (the supervisor) who supervised the transaction. With this rise in the slave trade, slavery transgressed the Islamic conception of slavery, which is, according to Muslim scholars, "a judgmental inability that afflicts whoever is captured in a legitimate war ... a temporary inability eliminated by emancipation and redemption."[69] However, what was happening in Arab societies was not slavery in the Islamic sense; it was kidnapping and slavery trade, characterized by the objectification and commodification of slaves.

Slavery was a historical phenomenon with economic, social, and political dimensions. This phenomenon acquired a religious dimension due to the fact that Islam was forced to deal with a phenomenon that was widespread among Arabs at the time. Since Islam did not prohibit slavery but rather approved it in a way that leads to its abolition, this has caused a dilemma in Arab culture that did not exist before. Slavery before Islam did not raise any human or moral questions, and that is why Arab societies were not concerned with justifying slavery, as it was a natural phenomenon that did not need to be justified. Nonetheless, the need for justification appeared when Islam introduced the principles of human brotherhood and equality between human beings, so Arab culture had to derive its justifications of slavery from those stereotypes of blacks and Zanj, permitting Arabs to enslave them. Those stereotypes were supported by various fields of knowledge such as geography, literature, medicine, astronomy, and history, where the correlation between slavery and barbarism or savagery is underscored in a way that the former (slavery) is justified by latter (barbarism). Since blacks are seen as roaming animals or wild beasts, then they are among those blessings of God who are created to serve humans. Therefore, their enslavement becomes an obligatory human task that does not differ from cultivating the soil or benefiting from the livestock, which is a misinterpretation of these verses in the Quran:

"Lawful for you are the animals of grazing livestock" (Quran 5:1) and "The grazing livestock He has created for you; in them is warmth and [numerous] benefits, and from them you eat" (Quran 16:5).

RELIGION AS A CULTURAL SYSTEM

Analyzing religion as a cultural system does not mean isolating it from its larger context, which includes what Vincent Leach calls "regimes of reason/unreason," a concept that refers to an interwoven network of systems, practices, and institutions operating in a culture. To analyze and critique cultural texts and patterns in light of "regimes of reason/unreason" requires confronting "all historically formed, politically weighted, and institutionally situated, enacting inclusions and exclusions and privileging some things over others."[70] Perhaps the most important of these institutionalized practices that created distinctions between human beings is the institution of slavery, which has been one of the most discriminatory and effective institutions and practices in Arab culture before and after Islam.

By examining how Islam deals with a prejudiced phenomenon such as that of slavery, I will investigate the systemic nature of Islam and its dominance over other cultural systems. While Arabs before Islam did not have to justify slavery in their culture, they were compelled to do so after Islam. The justification was not an arbitrary act. Rather, it stemmed from the centrality of Islam in Arab culture, or what Clifford Geertz calls "the power of the cultural system," i.e., the centrality of a cultural system (religion, art, ideology, politics, science ...) in the lives of the individuals who adopt it. The power of this centrality differs from one individual to another, and from one society to another. "For one man, his religious commitments are the axis of his whole existence, his faith is what he lives for and would quite willingly die for."[71] In Arab society, religion is not "a marginal activity in the daily life ... Rather, it is a fundamental activity and a basis for the values-representation of the individual, who strives to preserve it, and rejects whatever contradicts it in thought and action."[72] Islam has its own view on slavery, and every (Arab) Muslim is supposed to embody this view and reject what contradicts it.

Studying the role of the religious system in shaping the Arab imaginary of blacks requires attention to two issues: (1) the Islamic view of the Other, and blacks in particular, and its representation and application in Muslims' lives; and (2) the Islamic view of religion as a cultural system. A culture with a religion has been viewed by Arabs as superior to a culture that has no religion or Sharia. Accordingly, "belief and disbelief, civilization and barbarism represented the foundation through which Arab elites passed their judgments on others."[73] Hence, understanding the concept of religion from the point of view of Arab culture will be very helpful in explaining Arabs' view towards Others, and towards blacks in particular.

Associating religion (and other cultural forms such as language, clothes, political governance, and trade exchange) with human beings is common in most cultures characterized by an exaggerated self-centric sense and religious centrality. In such cultures, their values are presented as comprehensive and universal values. This results in categorizing those who represent these values as humans, and those who do not as animals or subhumans. For instance, for Christopher Columbus and the Spanish explorers, Indigenous people seemed beastly, savage, and like animals, and the reason was that they lacked aspects of Western Christian civilization such as language, customs, norms, and religion; in the eyes of the conquistadors, Indigenous people did not have language, religion, weapons, laws, and clothes.[74]

When Muslim Arabs dominated much of the world and began their conquests and journeys to discover or proselytize the Other, a particular idea of religion and humans began to crystallize. A close relationship between religion and humankind was established, in which the first is the cause of the second, and the second is an essential element in the formation of the first. A person without a religion is not considered a human being, just as a person is an essential pillar of religion. Religion provides not only a universal vision for its believers but also the basis for their humanity. Hence, a human being is not determined by shape or colour, but by the extent to which they represent cultural norms and systems. Being a human means developing or having a cultural system such as religion and Sharia. As for the people who have neither religion nor Sharia, they are not necessarily among human beings. They are closer to animals and beasts. Therefore, religion is the distinguishing factor or boundary between humanity and animality, or between civilization and barbarism. And, since barbarism is defined as deviation from human norms and cultural systems, religion sits at the top of these norms and systems.

For al-Ya'qubi, who had never travelled outside the Muslim lands, the Sudan (blacks) and the Zanj are creatures who do not have law, and "they worship an idol they call Hahakhwa."[75] As for al-Masudi, blacks have no "sacred law to which they refer but merely certain regulations and policies instituted by their kings according to which they rule their subjects."[76] While al-Ya'qubi highlights the belief aspect of Sharia, al-Masudi underscores its legal and political dimensions. Consequently, Shams al-Din al-Dimashqi, known as "Sheikh of the Rabwah," describes blacks as "savages who do not have a religion, and they hardly understand a word ... they are more like animals than they are to humans."[77] The link between no religion and savagery is clear here: having no religion make blacks closer to animals than to humans. Human beings are not defined by their shape, but by the cultural systems they embody, such as religion.

The emphasized connection between religion and human civilization is common in Islamic Medieval history, which might have found support in the Quran and the Sunnah,[78] but does not fully comply with the comprehensiveness of the Islamic Mission and the values of tolerance and brotherhood that were promoted by the Quran and the Sunnah. Before I explain this paradox, I would like to tackle the following questions: What is the reason for this close relationship between religion and human civilization? Is it because religion as a cultural system occurs in societies that have achieved a certain degree of progress and have passed the primitive magic stage? From the perspective of Frazer's evolutionary anthropology, or Malinowski's functionalism, or Geertz's symbolic and interpretive anthropology, the answer could be "yes." But this is not accurate from the perspective of Islamic culture. Religion in this culture may be a cultural system, but it is not a subsequent system that follows a primitive stage. Rather, in Islamic culture, religion is the basis of human existence, and it is a cultural system that is closely related to humankind. Humans were created with religion and commanded from the first day of their creation to worship and obey the Creator. "And I did not create the jinn and mankind except to worship Me" (Quran 51:56).

In Islam, the first human being may be simple, but cannot be described as primitive and barbaric, because the first human had a religion, and he was a guiding prophet. He is the first of the twenty-nine prophets whom God mentioned to Muhammad. Adam is the father of humankind, and he is the first prophet in Islam. "Abu Dharr asked the Prophet (PBUH) about the first of the prophets and he said: 'Which of the prophets was the first?' He said: 'Adam.'"[79] Islamic culture does not believe in the existence of a primitive society since religion is the basis of humans' humanity and existence. Hence, Islamic culture does not endorse the evolutionary perspective in humans' progress: whoever was before Islam is not necessarily more backward, barbaric, and primitive. Yet, the era before Islam was described as "al-Jahiliya" (the ignorance age).

The previous conception assumes that humans are necessarily religious beings, and that there is an inextricable relationship between religion and humankind. Moreover, if Allah Almighty had "created Adam (humans) in His Form"[80] in the best form, and honoured him over many of His creation, then how to justify the derogatory image of blacks in the Arab imaginary? In a narration, the Messenger "passed by two men arguing and heard one of them cursing the other: May God disfigure your face and whomever looks like you! Then, the prophet (PBUH) said: O Allah believer, do not say this to your brother, for Allah Almighty and Majestic created Adam in His Image."[81] In another narration, the Messenger said: "If one of you strikes, let him avoid the face and do not say, May Allah disfigure your face and whomever looks like you for Allah created Adam in His Image."[82] If so, then how can this cruel and immoral treatment of blacks be explained? How then was it possible for the Arab imaginary to disfigure blacks' faces and include them among beasts and animals? What the Arab imaginary had to determine was whether those blacks deserved to be included among humans. Are they humans who deserve human treatment or they are roaming animals and predatory beasts? Those blacks possess a human figure: they stand straight and walk on two legs. However, this feature is not sufficient to include them among humans whom God has honoured and created in the best and most proper form. In this culture, the humanness or humanity is not realized in the form, but rather in adhering to a cultural system with a divine source.

As for Ibn Hawqal, he does not mention black kingdoms in the Maghreb, Beja, and others, and the reason is that in those states chaos reigns and there is no order, due to the absence of religion, since "the organization of kingdoms is based on religions, morals, and governance. blacks lack these qualities, so their kingdoms do not deserve to be mentioned along with other kingdoms."[83] In addition to not having a religion, Shams al-Din al-Dimashqi adds that "they don't have dualisms such as trust vs. betrayal, loyalty vs. disloyalty. They have no laws, and no prophets are sent to them, because they are unable to formulate dualism, and Sharia is command and prohibition, and reward and punishment."[84] They are unable to distinguish between good and evil nor between good and bad.

The lack of order in the lives of blacks is due to the lack of religion, and the lack of religion is due to their mental deficiency. Their minds are ridiculous, their thoughts are deficient, their brains are rigid, and their morals are close to "what is found in animals."[85] Evidence of inability, shortcomings, and animality appear in that they are unable to distinguish between a thing and its opposite, command and prohibition, good and evil, and "whoever does not distinguish good from evil is in the status of an animal,"[86] as Imam Ali bin Abi Talib said. Therefore, they are not mentally qualified to receive religion or Sharia, considering Sharia as the legal and jurisprudential codification of God's commands and prohibitions. It is this mental deficiency that makes them unfit to accept religion, and thus they are to be included among animals, or "astray donkeys"[87] as Al-Maqdisi states.

The relationship between religion and humankind is inseparable, and is therefore behind the justification for the animality, barbarism, and inhumanity of blacks in the Arab imaginary. References to the existence of pagan religions, drawings, and worldly policies in those black communities were not able to change derogatory images of blacks in the Arab imaginary. This means that religion, from the perspective of Islamic culture, is limited to the monotheistic religions only, and all other earthly and pagan forms of religion are not worthy of being called a religion. Accordingly, the concept of human/humanity is limited to the believer in the Abrahamic religions only, and this is what makes Ibn Hawqal ease off his harsh judgment of black communities bordering the home of Islam, such as Abyssinia and Nubia. In contrast to Shams al-Din al-Dimashqi's generalization of all blacks, Ibn Hawqal excludes Abyssinia and Nubia. Despite their black skin, they (Nubians and Abyssinians) are Christians. Regardless of this exception, Ibn Hawqal was attached to the Islamic centralism: the kingdom of Islam is the heart and centre of the civilized world. These countries, namely Abyssinia and Nubia, used to be Christian, but they were more "honoured and glorified" by Islam.

THE OTHER IN THE ISLAMIC PERSPECTIVE

The Quran and Sunna incorporate a conception of humankind in general on the one hand, and the Muslim person on the other hand. As for the Others, they are of three types according to al-Shahristani's division: those with "a verified revealed book, such as the Jews and Christians; those who have a questionable book, such as the Magians and the Manicheans; those who have jurisprudence and rules without a book, such as the early philosophers, materialist atheism, planet and idol worshippers, and the Brahmins."[88] The most prominent of these are the polytheists from Quraish, and the People of the Book (Jews and Christians).

The Quran and the hadiths of the Prophet show a tolerant view of the Other in general, based on the Islamic conception of humans as the best and most honourable of all creatures. God, according to the Quranic conception, has honoured humankind regardless of their civilization, colour, language, or religion: "And We have certainly honoured the children of Adam and carried them on the land and sea and provided for them of the good things and preferred them over much of what We have created, with [definite] preference" (Quran 17:70); "We have certainly created man in the best of stature" (Quran 95:4); "It is Allah who made for you the earth a place of settlement and the sky a structure [i.e., ceiling] and formed you and perfected your forms and provided you with good things" (Quran 40:64). Hence, Islam was committed to the principles of human brotherhood, justice, equality, freedom, and respect for human beings regardless of their language, colour, degree of civilization, gender, and race. When Malik al-Ashtar was appointed over Egypt, Imam Ali bin Abi Talib advised him to be merciful, loving, and kind to his subjects, since they are "either your brethren in religion or your likes in creation."[89] Humans are humans regardless of their colour, language, gender, or race, which are considered as signs and evidence of God's power and greatness: "And of His signs is the creation of the heavens and the earth and the diversity of your languages and your colours. Indeed in that are signs for those of knowledge" (Quran 30:22). With this difference, acquaintance took place, and without it, there would be no need for making acquaintance among humans.

Thus, the difference of languages, colours, shapes, and races is a sign of the wisdom of the Creator and the perfection of His power, and hence they should not be a subject of boasting and differentiation, according to the Quranic perspective. Also, humankind is created from dust, a single origin, and they come back to the same origin: "From it [i.e., the earth] We created you, and into it We will return you, and from it We will extract you another time" (Quran 20:55). The Prophet says: "O people, your Lord is one and your father Adam is one. There is no favour of an Arab over a foreigner, nor a foreigner over an Arab, and neither white skin over black skin, nor black skin over white skin, except by righteousness. Have I not delivered the message?"[90]

The universality of the Islamic Mission is based on equality among humans, as the Prophet is a messenger for all human beings, and even though he was sent among the "illiterate" Arabs, his mission goes beyond Arabs to include all people, so he is the "Messenger of Allah to you all" (Quran 7:158), "And We have not sent you, [O Muhammad], except as a mercy to the worlds" (Quran 21:107). And the Messenger says: "I have been given five things which were not given to any one else before me ... Every Prophet used to be sent to his nation only but I have been sent to all mankind."[91] The Messenger is the Seal of the Prophets, which necessitates the comprehensiveness of his mission to all, and its openness to the previous Abrahamic religions on the Other: "Muhammad is not the father of [any] one of your men, but [he is] the Messenger of Allah and seal [i.e., last] of the prophets. And ever is Allah, of all things, Knowing" (Quran 33:40). "Say, [O believers], We have believed in Allah and what has been revealed to us and what has been revealed to Abraham and Ishmael and Isaac and Jacob and the Descendants [al-Asbat] and what was given to Moses and Jesus and what was given to the prophets from their Lord. We make no distinction between any of them, and we are Muslims [in submission] to Him" (Quran 2:136). "He has sent down upon you, [O Muhammad], the Book in truth, confirming what was before it. And He revealed the Torah and the Gospel" (Quran 3:3). Thus, Islam was able to embrace human beings no matter how different they were, even the infidels and the polytheists of Quraish, as misguided human beings in need of guidance. As for Jews and Christians, Islam welcomed them since they all meet in the Abrahamic belief.

However, this unity in humanity and belief was not able to prevent the clash between Muslims on the one hand, and polytheists and Jews on the other. The Quraish in Mecca considered Islam a threat to their local, pagan religion, and the Jews in Medina considered Islam a threat to their religion with which they distinguished themselves as "the children of Allah and His beloved!" (Quran 5:18). Islam had no choice but to confront them by either armed war or debate. Islam must spread and when there is a force standing in the way of its spread, then there is no choice but confrontation. "It is He who has sent His Messenger with guidance and the religion of truth to manifest it over all religion, although they who associate others with Allah dislike it" (Quran 9:33).

In the context of these confrontations, the Quran was rearranging the relationships between those groups in Mecca and Medina. At that time, negative images of the opposing groups began to appear. The infidels and polytheists are unclean or impure: "the polytheists are unclean" (Quran 9:28). And they are misguided, their error more severe than the error of cattle, and they live in complete and primitive ignorance. Jahiliya here refers to the situation in which people were ignorant of Islam as the true religion, but it may also mean savagery and primitivism. As for the words "al-Yahood" (the Jews) and al-Nasara (the Christians), they were used during the Medina period. However, the "People of the Book" was used for the first time in the last Meccan period, after the infidels and polytheists of Quraish were the Other, and the most prominent opponent to Islamic existence. When Islam entered into an armed conflict with the Jewish groups in Medina (Bani Qaynuqa', Banu al-Nadir, Banu Quraydhah), the term "People of the Book" began to fall out of use in favour of "Yahood" and "Nasara," with clear vilification of the Jews and praise of the Christians: "You will surely find the most intense of the people in animosity towards the believers [to be] the Jews and those who associate others with Allah; and you will find the nearest of them in affection to the believers those who say, We are Christians. That is because among them are priests and monks and because they are not arrogant" (Quran 5:82).

While Christians are praised in the Quran, Jews are negatively described with pejorative characteristics such as greediness, treachery, betrayal, dishonesty, arrogance, cowardice, foolishness, conspiracy, corruption, etc. The reason for that is perhaps because of the Jews' threat and hostility towards the Islamic Mission in Medina. However, this is not the only reason for the conflict between Muslims and Jews. In Ibn Kathir's *Al-Sira al-Nabawiyya (The Life of the Prophet)*, Ibn Ishaq states that

> Asim b. Amr b. Qatada related to him, from some of his tribe, as follows: "One of the things that brought us into Islam – along with the mercy of God Almighty and His guidance – was what we heard from a Jew. We were at that time polytheists and worshipped idols, while they, the Jews, were people with Scriptures who had knowledge we did not. There was always enmity between us and them, and if ever we bested them in some way they disliked they would tell us, 'The time is near for a

prophet; he will now he sent, and with him we will kill you just as Ad and Iram were killed.'"[92]

The narration indicates that the hostility in principle was not between Muslims and Jews, but between Arabs (the polytheists) and Jews, between the "illiterates" in Mecca who do not have a book, and the Jews in Medina, the "People of the Book." It is an old enmity that goes back to the pre-prophetic mission, when there were disputes and mutual aggressions between both sides.

Nevertheless, the Quran affirms the unity of human beings in creation and formation, and the unity of Muslims, Jews, and Christians in the Abrahamic belief, as well as the legitimacy of human differences in language, colour, race, gender, and others. Yet, these differences do not necessitate differentiation and bragging, but rather interaction or "acquaintance" according to the Quran: "O mankind, indeed We have created you from male and female and made you peoples and tribes that you may know one another. Indeed, the most noble of you in the sight of Allah is the most righteous of you. Indeed, Allah is Knowing and Aware" (Quran 49:13). Thus, blacks are not depicted negatively in the Quran. A black person is a human being like a white person. Both are created from dust, and from the same father and mother (Adam and Eve), who both are servants of God.

BLACKS: BETWEEN THE ISLAMIC MISSION INCLUSIVENESS AND THE CULTURAL LIES AND METAPHORS

According to Islam, human beings are created equally, and the Messenger was sent to all people regardless of their colour, race, ethnicity, etc. Yet, some scholars[93] believe that Islam deals with humans and Others differently, based on certain considerations. In Islam, dealing with the Other from a moral and faith point of view is different from dealing with them within the perspective of Sharia, enactment of laws, and practical policies. Although equality, brotherhood, and human solidarity are principles rooted in the moral vision of Islam, Sharia had to face a reality "in which blacks constitute the basis for the interests and stability of those merchants who have become venerable Companions or new elites."[94] With the expansion of the Islamic conquests, it became possible to own huge numbers of male and female slaves. A member of the Muslim elite (Sahabi) could own a thousand slaves after the conquests, and even a soldier could own servants, starting from one servant and up to ten. When al-Zubair, the husband of Aisha's sister, died in 656, he left behind a thousand male and female slaves.[95]

Facing such a reality, Sharia had to perform a dual but contradictory function: preserving the humane moral vision prescribed in the Quran and the Sunnah of the Prophet while maintaining the social and economic stability of society, where slavery is the most important stability factor at the time.

Muslims agree that slavery contradicts the humane principles of Islam. However, unlike drinking alcohol, which was gradually forbidden, Islam does not prohibit slavery. Islam closed the sources of slavery, limiting them to one source, which is *Ahl al-Harb* ("People of War"), excluding those Jews, Christians, and Magi who follow the conditions of *Dhimis* ("People of the Covenant"). If they breach those conditions, they would be included in *Ahl al-Harb*. Islam also dealt with this phenomenon in a way that would be gradually eliminated. If sources of slavery are narrowed and doors of slaves' manumission and emancipation are opened, this phenomenon would gradually end. However, the opposite happened because the Muslims "did not gradually practice emancipation due to the increase of slavery and the need for slaves."[96]

This system (masters and slaves) imposed its own structure on Muslims' lives, even the private and intimate aspects of it such as marriage. The Quran, for example, allows marriage to believing male and female slaves, and even prefers this type of marriage over marriage to free polytheists: "And do not marry polytheistic women until they believe. And a believing slave woman is better than a polytheist, even though she might please you." (Quran 2:221) The Prophet says, "A believing black female slave is better than a beautiful woman with no religion."[97]

However, the reality of the situation has made Islamic scholars and Fuqaha[98] speak about "necessities of marriage" to slaves and about the wisdom of avoiding marriage to female slaves without necessity. "A free man who has a dowry for a free woman cannot marry a female slave."[99] Hence, marriage to slaves is not only unacceptable and uncommon but also forbidden and only permitted by necessity, such as if one fears fornication, for necessity permits exemptions to prohibitions. Some scholars and Fuqaha went even further by prohibiting interracial marriage between whites and blacks regardless of their status (free/slave) and considered this type of marriage a deviation from God's creation and nature: "Tawus did not attend a marriage between a black woman and a white man, or a white woman to a black man, since he says, 'This is from the word of God, and alters Allah's creation.'"[100] Also, it was narrated by Ibn Abbas, "In the Almighty's saying, 'This is the natural colour of Allah. And who is better than Allah's colour?' he said: 'Whiteness,'"[101] meaning that God's colour is white, while black is the colour of Satan!

As for the metaphors of blackness, expressions such as "sawad al-Wajh" (the blackness of the face), "aswad al-Wajah" (black face), "sawad Allah Wajhak" (May Allah blacken your face), etc. have their counterparts, metaphors of whiteness," such as "bayadh al-Wajh" (whiteness of the face), "abyadh al-Wajh" (a white face), and "bayadh Allah Wajhak" (May Allah whiten your face). These expressions reveal the extent to which racism can sink deep into what we might call the "bottom of language," the substrate of linguistic ancient usage.

Metaphors of blackness are mentioned in the Quran in four places, the first of which is in Surat Ali'Imran, where God describes the condition of those who have recanted their belief: "On the Day [some] faces will turn white and [some] faces will turn black. As for those whose faces turn black, [to them it will be said], 'Did you disbelieve [i.e., reject faith] after your belief? Then taste the punishment for what you used to reject'" (Quran 3:106). The second place is in Surat Az-Zumar where God describes the condition of the unbelievers who lied about Him, so they are like apostates on the Day of Resurrection: "And on the Day of Resurrection you will see those who lied about Allah [with] their faces blackened. Is there not in Hell a residence for the arrogant?" (Quran 39:60) The third example is from Surat Al-Nahl where God describes the ignorant as full of shame, grief, distress, and anger upon hearing the news of having a female baby: "And when one of them is informed of [the birth of] a female, his face becomes dark, and he suppresses grief" (Quran 16:58). The fourth place is where the same ignorant person mentioned above does not shy away from attributing females to God Almighty: "And when one of them is given good tidings of that which he attributes to the Most Merciful in comparison [i.e., a daughter], his face becomes dark, and he suppresses grief" (Quran 43:17).

The blackness of the face, in these examples, implies infidelity, immorality, apostasy, ignorance, and lying about God. On the other hand, the whiteness of the face means faith and obedience. The relationship between the blackness of the face and the negative meanings does not exist in the language itself, but rather, it is a kind of metaphor or a metonymy, a deviation from the word's original meaning, as most Arab rhetoricians assume. The blackness of the face, they maintain, implies sadness, grief, fear, shame, distress, and anger, while the whiteness of the face symbolizes the radiance of the face, happiness, and rejoicing. However, this does not answer the question as to why God associates negative meanings with blackness and positive qualities with whiteness. Why not other colours? Saying blackness in the Quran is a just metaphor, or a metonymy for the aforementioned implications, still retains the relationship between blackness and its associated pejorative connotations.

Nevertheless, several Mufassirin (Quran exegetists) have not ruled out that the "blackness and whiteness of the face" is actual and not a metaphor, a reality in life and afterlife. For those Mufassirin, this interpretation does not carry any religious or moral prohibitions.[102] In this world, "too much anxiety makes the blood attack the face turning it into black and dark."[103] As for the Hereafter, on the Day of Resurrection, the person's *Zahir* (the evident/external) will match their *Batin* (the hidden, internal); it is the day of the appearance and revelation of the concealed. On that day, the face colour becomes the colour of the heart (intentions) and deeds. As the radiance and whiteness of the good will appear, so will the blackness of the evil and bad. That is why the believing black slave is promised to have a white face in Paradise. The Prophet says: "By Him in Whose Hand is my soul, the whiteness and brightness of blacks in Paradise is seen from a thousand-year distance."[104]

Blackness is perceived as an ugly colour and is always associated with negative meanings and derogatory values. So, whoever is black, it becomes their destiny and status, and whoever changes colour to black, it is because of their sins and evil deeds. When interpreting "the criminals will be known by their marks, and they will be seized by the forelocks and the feet" (Quran 55:41), a number of Mufassirin like al-Qurtubi and al-Tusi assert that the signs of criminals on that day are the blackness of the face and the blueness of the eyes.[105] Hence, it has become common in Arab culture that the blackness/darkness of the face, used realistically or metaphorically, is a form of punishment for committing sins, for disbelief, and for denial:

> Abu Hurairah narrated that regarding the saying of Allah, Most High: "The Day when We shall call together all human beings with their (respective) Imam," the Prophet (PBUH) said:

"One of you will be called out to be given his record in his right hand, he will be grown in his body to sixty forearm-lengths, his face will be whitened, and a crown of sparkling pearls will be placed upon his head. So he will go to his companions, who can see him from afar, and they will say: 'O Allah! Bring this one to us, and let us be blessed by him.' Until he reaches them, and says to them: 'Receive the good news! For each man among you shall be the likes of this.'" [He (PBUH) said:] "As for the disbeliever, then his face shall be blackened, he will be grown in his body to sixty forearm-lengths in the image of Adam, he will be given a crown, and his companions will see him and say: 'We seek refuge in Allah from the evil of this one. O Allah! Do not bring this one to us.'" He said: "So when he reaches them, they say: 'O Allah! Take him away' so they will be told: 'May Allah cast you away! Indeed for each man among you is the likes of this.'"[106]

Moreover, it is narrated of Umar bin al-Khattab that he said in false witness: "His face will become blackened, that is, it will turn black."[107] And of Imam Muhammad al-Baqir (d.117 AH) that he says: "The wine drinker on the Day of Judgment will be brought with his face all black, his tongue hanging down, and his saliva flowing on his chest."[108] In the interpretation of Ibn Sirin (110 AH), whoever dreams that "his face is black and his clothes are dirty, his dream implies that he is lying about God."[109] One of the consequences of fornication is that "it causes poverty, shortens life, and turns the face black."[110] "Whoever abandons prayer his face is turned into black."[111]

On the other hand, blackness is not only a consequence of committing the greater sins but also the origin and source of those sins. It has been decided since the beginning of creation that every black is in Hell, and every white is in Heaven, i.e., Heaven was created for the whites and Hell was created for the blacks:

> God drove Adam out of Paradise but did not cast him down from heaven. Then He rubbed the right side of Adam's back and somehow brought forth from it progeny in the shape of tiny ants, white like pearls. He said to them: Enter Paradise by means of My mercy! Then He rubbed the left side of Adam's back and brought forth from it something in the shape of tiny black ants. He said to them: Enter the Fire! I do not care. This is meant where God speaks of "companions of the right" and

"companions of the left." Then He took the covenant and said: "Am I not your Lord?" They said: "Yes." And (God) gave (Adam) a willing group and an unwilling group pretending piety.[112]

Arab culture has fostered and promoted negative values about blacks, to the extent that even the blacks themselves pray God to whiten their faces on the Day of Judgment. This negative representation of blackness was not a product of language, nor was it natural. It was a result of cultural and societal patterns, practices, and policies that control people's manners, perceptions, and communications. This was not a product of the Quran or Sunnah; rather, it was before the Quran and Sunnah. The Quran did not create *sawad al-wajh* (blackness of the face), nor was it the first to compare it to negative and derogatory connotations. Such a metaphor was used before Islam in Jahili poetry, for instance, by Imru' al-Qais and Antarah bin Shaddad.

If Islam was decisive in breaking with the pre-Islamic belief system, it was not so decisive in breaking with its metaphorical legacy. According to al-Jurjani, the Quran did not alter the language from its original usages, nor did it take the words out of their connotations; it did not require the people to change their habits, practices, and ways, nor did it prevent them from recognizing and using those similes, analogies, elisions, and extensions.[113]

SYMBOLISM OF BLACKNESS: DREAMS, CLOTHES, ANIMALS

It does not solve the problem to say that metaphors of blackness are a remnant of the ancient Arab heritage that has infiltrated Islamic culture. The questions here are: where did this inferior and detractive view of blackness in Arab culture originally come from? Why was Islam not decisive with those derogatory metaphors? Is this due to the symbolic and emotive power of colours, and of black and white in particular? Do colours affect human emotions and reactions so that their connotations become inherent? Or do colours acquire their symbolic connotations from their association with cosmic phenomena such as day and night, or with pessimistic events and beings such as the crow?

The association between the black colour and the negative connotations may entail that black is by nature a negative colour, and that this negativity is universal and common to modern and primitive psyche, according to Gilbert Durand.[114] Therefore, the black colour naturally and inherently represents sin, pessimism, doom, gloom, anxiety, etc., which may have been acquired from its association with darkness and the crow, along with their negative connotations.

In Arab culture, the hour of dusk often puts a person in a state of fear and gloominess. During the dusk, evil animals and the demons of Hell possess bodies and souls. Also, Satan is always considered black, and the Ghoul (demon-like creature) has black fur or a dark beard. Sin and evil are black, while good and virtue are white. Hell is black and its people are black, as stated in the interpretation of "*Al-Muhal*" in "And if they call for relief, they will be relieved with water like (al-Muhl) murky oil, which scalds [their] faces" (Quran, 18:29). For Al-Dahhak, *al-Muhl* is black water because Hell is black and so are its water, trees, and people.[115]

Pre-Islamic Arab culture was not unique in these negative metaphorical connotations of blackness and whiteness. The Christian symbolism of whiteness and blackness carries the same connotations, to the extent that Kevin Reilly and others have stated that this Christian symbolism of whiteness and blackness was created to "encourage a racist attitude toward Black people. This was the Christian symbolism of whiteness and Blackness. Christians thought of sin as the Blackening of a white soul. They thought of God, virtue, purity, and redemption, in terms of radiating light or whiteness."[116] In Judaism, blackness is associated with curse and servitude, since Noah called on his son Ham (Canaan): "Cursed be Canaan! The lowest of slaves will he be to his brothers" (Genesis 9:25).

These symbolic connotations are also present in various ancient cultures and religions such as the Neolithic Age, Zoroastrianism, and Manichaeism, and the belief in the existence of a perpetual battle between the evil forces of darkness and the good forces of light. Even more surprisingly, the negative symbolic connotations of blackness infiltrated some black African cultures. According to the Bambara people, the god of good and transcendence belongs to whiteness, while the gods of evil that have polluted the world belong to blackness. The "greater god of good," Faro, has a white woman's head, while the evil Musukoroni symbolizes darkness and magic.[117]

Another example of the infiltration of these negative connotations of blackness into African cultures can be found in the story of Creation in Kono/Guinea, and how Alatangana asked Sa for permission to marry his daughter. It was not granted, so, Alatangana eloped with the daughter, and they got married and had many children. However, the children – seven boys and seven girls – were different in colour and spoke different languages: four of the boys and girls were white, and the rest were black. When Alatangana asked Sa for advice, the latter admitted that it was he who punished the couple for their disobedience and made them unable to understand what their children said:

> I will give your white children intelligence and the ability to write so that they can write down what they want to say. I will give your black children tools so that they may feed and shelter themselves. But the black children must marry only blacks and the white children only whites.[118]

Undoubtedly, the night does not frighten us because it is black, but because its darkness may cause vision problems, leaving us to face the unknown. The crow is not inherently an ominous bird, since some societies consider it as a good omen. This means that its negative and ominous connotations, similar to its positive connotations, are human products. All the negative connotations of blackness have been nothing but a justifying act to legitimize blacks' enslavement and their pejorative representations.

The symbolism of blackness in Arab culture acquires its meaning from the context of Arab society and its negative representations of blacks. Symbolic representations and imaginaries reproduce, preserve, and maintain social conditions; "symbolism is not an effect of society, rather society is the effect of symbolism."[119] Symbolic images, illusions, and imaginations have historical effectiveness in shaping social reality. Thus, the symbolism of blackness (in dreams, clothing, animals, language, and skin colour) played a prominent role in reproducing the difficult social conditions of blacks in Arab/Islamic society.

Freud explains the nature of dreams,[120] emphasizing that "not all dreams are alien to the dreamer, incomprehensible and confused."[121] The dreamer sees things they know, but their features have been changed and disguised. Although a dream is an imaginary world, it is not entirely alien to the dreamer. Dreams are formed by the dreamer's own culture, and this is what makes dreams meaningful and significant for the dreamer:

> ... many dream elements are drawn from cognitive schemata in the culture to which the dreamer has been enculturated. They are structured by the categories, rules, roles, assumptions, beliefs, and values in terms of which the individual's waking world is constituted. The dreams of an individual from any given society will have many similarities to the dreams of other persons from that society, and these patterns will contrast markedly with those in dreams of people socialized in other cultural traditions.[122]

Even if the dream is exotic and fantastical, it acquires its significance only within the cultural patterns represented by the dreamer, and from the experience of the dreamer's social imaginary.[123]

During the expansion of slavery, negative interpretations of blackness and positive interpretations of whiteness in dreams, clothing, and animals proliferated and became very popular. Here are some examples:

1. The Prophet said, "I saw (in a dream) a black woman with unkempt hair going out of Medina and settling at Mahai'a, i.e., Al-Juhfa. I interpreted that as a symbol of epidemic of Medina being transferred to that place (Al-Juhfa)."[124] Although the image of the black woman here is neutral, it is the interpretation/interpreter that gives the image negative connotations to be a symbol of the epidemic.
2. A man came to Saeed bin Al-Musayyib and said: "I saw a white dove on the balcony of the mosque, and I was amazed by its beauty, but a falcon came and grabbed it." Al-Musayyib said: "If your vision comes true, al-Hajjaj will marry Abdullah bin Jafaar's daughter." Then that is what happened. Later, Al-Musayyib was asked how he deduced that interpretation? He said: The dove is a woman, and the white refers to her pure lineage. So, I have not seen any woman purer in lineage than the daughter of Abdullah bin Ja'far, and I looked at the falcon, and it was an Arab bird, not a foreign bird, and I have not seen among Arabs a better falconer than Al-Hajjaj bin Yusuf.[125]
3. The Prophet told Khadija that he dreamed of her cousin Waraqah bin Nawfal: "I saw him in a dream, and he was wearing white garments, and if he were from the people of Hell, he would have been wearing other than that."[126]

4. "The Messenger of Allah said: 'Wear white, for indeed it is very pure and cleaner, and shroud your dead in it.'"[127]
5. The faithful angel Jibril was dressed in white. The Prophet also emphasized his preference for white clothes and even chose white raiment for himself. Even for the dead he chose the white shroud.[128]
6. "The Messenger of Allah, O Allah, grant compensation to Muhammad and his family worthy of their services to Your cause, has said, 'It is detestable to wear black except three items such as slippers, turbans, and gowns.'"[129]
7. Once I was with abu 'Abd Allah, 'Alayhi al-Salam, in al-Hirah (a city in Iraq) when the messenger of abu Ja'far al-Mansur, the caliph, came to call him. He (the Imam) asked for a raincoat, one side black and the other side white, and abu 'Abd Allah, 'Alayhi al-Salam, said: "I wear it but I know that it is the dress of the people of fire." (Black was the emblem of Abbasid rulers. The Imam wore it due to Taqiyah (caution because of fear).[130])

In these narrations and hadiths, the negative implications of blackness are not intrinsic but extrinsic. The negativity of this colour comes from various reasons such as being the dress of Pharaoh, the people of Hell, and the enemies of God and His Messenger. The prohibition against or disapproval of wearing black occurs to avoid following those people. Perhaps there is a political reason behind the disapproval of wearing black clothes, such as the conflict between the Umayyads (with their red banner) and the Abbasids (with their black banner).

Muslim theologians assign special jurisprudence provisions not only for the black dress but also for black and non-black slaves in terms of value and price. A white or red slave is more valuable and has a better status than a black slave, and the reason, al-Shafi'i (Imam al-Fiqh al-Shafi'i, one of the four Sunni Imams) says, is because of "their weak brains."[131]

As for animals, negative and pessimistic connotations are always associated with black animals such as the crow (*al-ghurab*), which usually symbolizes death, separation, alienation, and bad luck. That is why Arabs "derived *ghurba/ightirab* (alienation) from its name."[132] Another example is the black cat, which is perceived as scary because it was a genie in origin. According to Al-Jahiz, Al-Damiri, and Al-Qazwini, "whoever eats a black cat, magic does not hurt them."[133] As for black donkeys, it was narrated from the Prophet: "Short black donkeys are the evilest."[134] Regarding black dogs, they are genies and devils and must be killed: "The black dog is a Shaitan."[135] "Abdullah bin Mughaffal narrated that the Messenger of Allah said: 'If it were not that dogs were part of a nation among the nations, then I would order that all of them be killed. So kill every one of them that is all black.'"[136]

The proximity between the symbolism of blackness in dreams, clothing, and animals, and the symbolism of blackness in humans can be seen in the representation and perception of the black person as a genie, a devil, evil, and a bad omen. For Muslims, dogs in dreams are slaves, and *"aghrabat al-Arab"* (Arab crows) are black poets of the pre-Islamic era. Sometimes, the negative connotation of blackness in dreams, clothes, and animals is derived from the reference to blacks, so that black animals have these negative connotations because of their resemblance to blacks.

While investigating the symbolic meanings of black dogs, al-Jahiz notices that if any part in the animal becomes black it would be good for the body's strength but not for its intelligence/knowledge, and if it turns completely black ("burned"), the animal "becomes like the zinji who is very ruthless and of little knowledge."[137] In this simple simile, the black animal (tenor) is compared to the zinji (vehicle) using the word *mithl* (like). The *tertium comparationis* is that both are black, ruthless, and of little knowledge and understanding. However, rhetorically speaking, as a vehicle, the zinji is darker, more ruthless, and more ignorant than the black dog (tenor). Thus, the zinji represents the source from which the black animal acquires these negative qualities. When discussing the crow, al-Jahiz says that the crow is "the blackest and most burned, just like the colour of al-Zanj who are the evilest people, and the worst creation in formation and temperament."[138]

In addition to the collective memory of wars and conflict with the Abyssinian blacks, such pejorative images have formed a fertile imaginary source about blacks in Arab culture. This imaginary has portrayed blacks as the extreme Other, who are different in colour, race, body, culture, religion, and language, and who are described as exhibiting ignorance, stupidity, brutality, and inability to speak or represent themselves. This has made blacks a malleable material for comical conversations, wondrous tales, sarcastic conversations, and constant journeys across lands and seas.

2

The Absolute Other and the Power of Representation

BLACKS AS THE ABSOLUTE OTHER

For Hegel, the black African represents the "absolute Other" because they are just an object or an animal with all its barbarism and lawlessness, and in order to understand them, we need to be stripped of all moral respect or sympathy towards them. In *Philosophy of History*, Hegel approaches the black African as the ultimate Other, the human animal who is barbaric and deviant from human morality and order. For him, "al-Zanj" do not view tyranny as "unjust," nor do they see cannibalism as abnormal. Although slavery is terrible, in their case it becomes a positive thing, because it is their only way out of the state of absolute slavery and of being a valueless object:

> The Negro, as already observed, exhibits the natural man in his completely wild and untamed state. We must lay aside all thought of reverence and morality – all that we call feeling – if we would rightly comprehend him; there is nothing harmonious with humanity to be found in this type of character ... Another characteristic fact in reference to the Negroes is Slavery ... BAD as this may be, their lot in their own land is even worse, since there a slavery quite as absolute exists; for it is the essential principle of slavery, that man has not yet attained a consciousness of his freedom, and consequently sinks down to a mere Thing – an object of no value. Among the Negroes moral sentiments are quite weak, more strictly speaking, non-existent. Parents sell their children, and conversely

children their parents, as either has the opportunity. Through the pervading influence of slavery all those bonds of moral regard which we cherish towards each other disappear, and it does not occur to the Negro mind to expect from others what we are enabled to claim.[1]

Let us compare this racist and colonial text par excellence, with another text in a book titled *Nukhbat al-Dahr fi Aja'ib al-Bar wa al-Bahr* (The elite of time in the wonders of land and sea), written by Shams al-Din al-Dimashqi, an Arab-Muslim writer from the fourteenth century, nearly five centuries before Hegel. He postulates that the equator is inhabited by blacks who are among the beasts and cattle. He describes them as follows:

Their colours and hair are the blackest black. Their morals and physiques are deviant. They are ignorant, with the darkest (burnt) hair. They are an arrogant, stinking race with a perverted temperament. Their manners are similar to beasts and cattle. The minds of those blacks are preposterous; their ideas are immature; and their mentality is rigid. They do not have dualisms such as honesty vs. dishonesty, loyalty vs. betrayal. There have no laws and no prophets, because they are unable to have dualism, and Sharia is a matter of command and prohibition, and reward and punishment.[2]

Al-Dimashqi's image is based on the animalization of blacks, which has formed the source and mother image from which all the negative stereotypes of blacks were born. Blacks, according to Dimashqi, are among the animals (beasts), and the natural ugliness, mood perversion, mental weakness, moral impotence, and lack of religion apply to them because animals do not need religion by virtue of being incapable of understanding dualisms such as good vs evil.

These demeaning features have created what I call here a "multi-faceted difference" between Arabs and blacks, meaning that it is not a simple difference, as is the case between Arabs and Persians, or Arabs and Indians, or Arabs and Chinese, or Arabs and Turks, and even between Arabs and what were considered Romans. It is a complex difference of several layers, in which Arabs cannot find any commonalities or ties that connect them with blacks, the absolute Other.

The Arab imaginary needed this multi-layered difference to justify the continuity of slavery, servitude, and cruel treatment of blacks, as commodities and objects. Moreover, this difference was beneficial to the Muslim Arabs because it would relieve them of guilt and remorse towards blacks since they are animals/beasts and not humans.

BLACKS AND THE NEED FOR REPRESENTATION

The black (zinji) was not the only Other that Arab culture knew, but it was almost the only Other with whom this culture did not find common ties or kinship, real or imagined, which might mitigate the intensity and violence of difference. Hence, this "black" remains the example of the absolute Other. Soon after the emergence of Islam, a massive archive of images, symbols, perceptions, repeated descriptions, and phrases formed around blacks to emphasize their marginality, decadence, and animality, and to highlight them as distant, marginalized, silent, strange, exotic, and lustful beings.

When Arab culture established itself in its own imaginary as the centre of the universe, it granted itself the right and privilege to represent and write about Others. And why wouldn't it do that? Aren't blacks incapable of representing themselves? Blacks lack the most important and yet dangerous tool to represent themselves and Others: language. All they have is nothing but animal "rumbling and humming," and expressions that do not rise above the animals' status.[3] Saying so indicates a strong desire to silence blacks, allowing them to hear only and not to respond or write about themselves.

The idea of the blacks' inability to represent themselves has persisted into the modern era, when Rifa'a al-Tahtawi postulates that blacks do not know how to write or read, for "they are always like roaming beasts, they do not distinguish between Halal and Haram. They do not read or write, and they do not know anything of the things that make it easier for them in this world or the afterworld."[4] As for Haji Khalifa and al-Qanouji, they mention that the Zanj and the Abyssinians – but only a few of them – had a writing system and that it resembles the Himyarite writing, which means that they either took it from the Arabs of the south, or were influenced by it.

Since blacks are unable to represent themselves, another culture needs to represent them and thus give them the opportunity to identify themselves and introduce themselves to others. They have no choice but to believe in the truth of this representation that describes them with ignorance, backwardness, stupidity, ugliness, animalism, sensuality, and distortion in creation and morality, and these are the most prominent stereotypes formulated and stored in the Arab imaginary.

AFRICANISM DISCOURSE AND THE FORMATION OF STEREOTYPICAL IMAGES

Arab culture has presented multiple representations of different cultures, but what distinguishes the representations of blacks in this culture is that they are characterized by frequency, consistency, and overabundance. The Arab imaginary has preserved different images of the Chinese, Indians, Persians, Romans, Franks (al-Franj),[5] Slavs, Bulgarians, and others, but none of these representations reached the scale of the representations of blacks.

Because this representation is well-established and deeply rooted in the Arab imaginary, one does not find a distinct and significant difference between what was written by a writer in the third century AH and what was written by another in the fifth, sixth, seventh, or eighth century, all the way to Tahtawi and Salama Musa, in the modern era. This representation has become a tradition imposed on everyone who wants to talk about or write about blacks, and this tradition has its own language and distinctive metaphors.

Thus, whoever steers away from this collectively accepted discourse would be faced with rejection, confrontation, and ridicule, as in the case of Abu al-Abbas al-Nashi' al-Akbar (d.293 AH) and Abu al-Abbas Muhammad bin Khalaf bin al-Marzuban (d.309 AH). When al-Marzuban wrote *al-Sudan wa Fadhlihim 'ala al-Bidhan* (On blacks and their virtue over whites), he was received with mockery and sarcasm. Regarding this book, Jalal al-Din al-Suuty says: "I do not find this surprising from this writer, because he wrote another book called *Tafdheel al-Kilab 'ala Katheer mimen Labasa al-Thiyab* (Superiority of dogs over many who wear clothes [humans]) where he expresses a preference for dogs over humans."[6] As for Abu al-Abbas al-Nashi', he composed *Risala fi Tafdhil al-Sood 'ala al-beedh* (Treatise on the virtue of blacks over whites), and the outcome was that he was accused of insanity and mania, as al-Suuty described this superiority as "making a comparison between gold and glass."[7]

This traditional representation of blacks is what I call here *al-Istifraq al-Arabi* (Arab Africanism), which refers to the discourse of perceiving, imagining, and writing about blacks as a subject of study. Africanism is a form of adherence to the rules of producing, preserving, representing, and promulgating Arab discourse on blacks in the Arab-Islamic culture.

In terms of its discursive formation, there are two types of Africanism: "latent Africanism" and "overt Africanism." As for the latter, it is a field that may change from one individual to another, from one field to another, and from one era to another, based on the way of representing blacks/"al-Zanj." "Latent Africanism," on the other hand, is a field of unanimous character; it is a well-established tradition that retains a set of unalterable and stable stereotypes of blacks.

Writers like Shams al-Din al-Dimashqi, Abu Zayd al-Sirafi, Sulayman al-Tajer, al-Tabari, Ibn Rastah, al-Masudi, Ibn Hawqal, al-Maqdisi, Ibn Jubayr, Zakaria al-Qazwini, Ibn Khaldun, Ibn Battuta, Ibn al-Muqaffa, al-Jahiz, Ibn al-Nadim, Abu Hayyan al-Tawhidi, al-Bayhaqi, al-Nuwayri, al-Ibshihi, al-Qalqhandi, etc., may differ in style and field of specialization, but they share the same view of blacks. None of these writers criticized the view of blacks as inferior, nor did they refrain from writing about it. None of them objected to describing blacks as animals, savages, debauched, bestial, backward, stupid, immoral, and deformed.

It is difficult to determine when exactly these derogatory images and representations appeared, but it is evident that these stereotypes are deeply rooted in the Arab imaginary during the Middle Ages since many of these images were circulated long ago, before and after the Islamic era. On the authority of Ibn Abbas, the Messenger said: "Beware of the Zanj, for they are the shortest in age and the least in provision. And be with the companion, he means the Romans, for they are the longest-lived people and the most abundant, so enjoy their long lives and share with them their provision."[8]

In interpreting the people mentioned in the Quranic verse "Until, when he came to the rising of the sun [i.e., the east], he found it rising on a people for whom We had not made against it any shield" (Quran 18:90), Qatada says: "They are called the Zanj, they are Taris, Haweel and Mensek, barefoot, naked, and blind to the truth. They have intercourse publicly like dogs and donkeys."[9] Hassan Bin Thabit (d. 54 AH) describes their smell and shape: "When they pass by other people, their smell is like the smell of dogs wet by the rain, You won't find human resemblance to Ham's children, only male goats with fur on their shoulders."[10] And, for Ibn al-Muqaffa, the Zanj are "roaming animals,"[11] and for Ibn Tauus, they are "mutilated servant[s] of God."[12]

But the most dangerous words are those attributed to the Prophet that contradict Islam's call for tolerance and respect for human dignity and creation. Those forged hadiths are false, as they contain an explicit vilification of blacks and al-Zanj, such as "Beware of the Zanj, for they are a deformed creation"[13]; "Blacks are beholden only to their stomach and genitals"[14]; "Evil people are as black as tar"[15]; "The black, when he is hungry, he steals and when he is sated, he fornicates."[16] Telling lies about the Messenger expresses the desire of this culture to utilize everything available in order to support its positions and beliefs.

Pejorative representations of blacks were circulated in the pre-Islamic era and in the first and second centuries AH. However, they increased, deepened, and reached their peak in the third century AH onwards. They were strongly formed during the predominance of Arab culture, starting with the conquests and trade expansions, to the journeys in various waters, lands, and kingdoms to discover new peoples, lands, and wonders.

In order to add validity and credibility to those representations, a new network of multiple fields of knowledge was utilized to interpret, maintain, and support them. Before, they were in people's imaginary such as poetry, daily conversations, stories, hadiths, etc., but after the third century AH, they were gradually ingrained in all fields of knowledge including language, literature, theology, geography, history, astronomy, philosophy, etc.

BLACKS' ANIMALITY: THE MOTHER-IMAGE AND ITS REPRODUCTIONS

The stereotypical image of blacks as roaming/wild beasts is the most solid and powerful image, and it is the image that generates all other images of blacks in the Arab imaginary. This image represents the womb from which all other images are procreated and reproduced. In the Arab imaginary, blacks are beings who possess excessive sexual energy with a natural tendency to immorality and decadence. They are depicted as naked, dangerous, and terrifying beings with a tendency to *"tarab,"*[17] joy and pleasure or pettiness and recklessness. They are fond of dancing to every rhythm, and are fools everywhere they go. All these proliferating images acquire their legitimacy from the mother-image.

They possess such an unruly and excessive sexual energy because they do not follow a religion or Sharia that would inhibit or normalize this sexual energy. They are like uncontrollable animals who fulfill their desires in all ways. Their danger lies in the fact that they lack a religion that disciplines their nature and a law that regulates their relationships. They are like wild beasts who kill hysterically, and that is why blacks find no problem with cannibalism, as they may eat each other alive or dead. As for their pettiness, recklessness, and joyfulness, Ibn Khaldun explains it as the "animal spirit," while al-Masudi attributes it to their weak brains. Also, the association between blacks and charcoal, ravens, and snakes is at the heart of the cultural connotation in the Arabic language.

BLACKS (AL-ZANJ) AND TARAB

Theories of Ptolemy (seven climes), Galen and Hippocrates (medicine), and Aristotle ("natural subordination") have constituted what we might call the basic references for the "scientific" interpretation of blacks in Arab culture. Ibn Nadeem mentioned tens of books translated into Arabic, among them Galen's writings such as *On the Usefulness of the Parts of the Body*, *On the Natural Faculties*, *On Temperaments*, etc. Those books were the main sources for Medieval Arab scholars in writing about blacks, such as the example below where Galen describes blacks with the following features:

> Galen mentions ten qualities found only in blacks and in no other group: frizzy hair, thin eyebrows, spacious nostrils, thick lips, jagged teeth, body odour, black irises, cracked hands and legs, a long penis, and much merriment. Galen adds: "Merriment dominates the black person because of his corrupt brain so his reason is weakened."[18]

Galen's narration is mentioned in many books and with slightly different words and with the focus on the number 10 in counting these qualities.[19] This kind of information allowed Arab scholars to interpret psychological and moral characteristics with physical terms and vice versa. Each of these traits is ascribed to a moral, social, and psychological significance, all of which ultimately form the mother-image/stereotype of blacks as animals or beasts. The sharp teeth indicate their savagery and capability to eat one another,[20] the long penis indicates the bestial sexual desire, the wide/flat nostrils is another evidence of this excessive sexual desire, and thickness of the lips indicates foolishness. As for the black skin colour, it indicates a physical disease caused by a weak spleen and the dominance of black bile, and it is also "evidence of deformation."[21]

In the Arab imaginary, blacks are associated with ecstatic engagement, amusement, disobedience, and debauchery. They are the ones who invented tarab, music, dance, and diversion: "Kanaan, Ham's son, was the first of Noah's sons who came back to the work of Cain's sons, so he worked in amusements and singing, using flutes, drums, lyres, and cymbals, so he obeyed Satan in play and falsehood."[22]

On the day that the Messenger arrived in Medina, blacks and Abyssinians played with their spears and shields in the mosque. Also, the first singers in Arab culture were blacks, for example, Ma'bid bin Wahab and Ibn Misjah. The latter, one of the best, brought singing from Persians to Arabs.[23]

As for black women, they are an essential element in singing and amusement: Ibrahim bin Hani demonstrates that "it is the perfection of mizmar (musical reed instrument) to be played by a black woman,"[24] and Ibn Butlan points out that "female zanj know no worries, as dance and drums are in their intuition and nature, and because of their incomprehensible pronunciation, they are assigned to play mizmar and dance."[25] Furthermore, al-Dimishqi postulates that tarab consists of ten parts, nine in blacks and one in the rest of the people.[26] As for al-Nuwayri, he states that "among the characteristics of blacks is tarab and that's why sadness is not known in al-Zanj."[27]

Recognizing tarab in blacks puts al-Masudi and other scholars in a critical position. Although those scholars insist on the animality and primitiveness of blacks, tarab, singing, and dance are innovative human arts; rather, they can be seen as spiritual arts that connect humans to spiritual happiness. When Abu Hayyan al-Tawhidi discusses the subject of singing, tarab, and playing music, he quotes Socrates stating that "singing is a fine art and a means to remove the veils of the soul so that it can see the honourable self and its spiritual happiness."[28] How, then is it possible to combine the animality of blacks with those culturally and spiritually refined human arts? Al-Masudi, al-Qazwini, al-Dimishqi, Ibn Khaldun, and others were aware of this contradiction, so they had to search for a plea to reinstate tarab to an animal and physical origin, a faulty brain, and weak mind. Some scholars find a connection between mirth, joy, pleasure, a carefree and weak mind, ignorance, and stupidity. For example, while al-Jahiz compares stupidity with animals' leisure and carefree mindedness, al-Qazwini attributes it to the moderation of blood in the heart. The other reason is a cosmic reason, represented in the effect of the planets on humans. The rising of the Canopus star on them every night is the reason behind their love for tarab and for not having grief and worry. When listing the benefits of looking at Canopus and the South Pole, al-Qazwini explains that "it brings joy and happiness to humans, and for this reason, a group of Zanj is characterized with more tarab because they are close to the orbit of the pole and Canopus."[29]

To prove blacks' animality, al-Masudi, al-Qazwini, Ibn Khaldun, and others, while underscoring either a natural internal cause (biological determinism) or an external cause (astronomical determinism), ignore the cultural and social factors of this phenomenon, or the cultural determinism that governed blacks' lives in Arab culture. The interest of blacks and al-Zanj in tarab, singing, and dancing is not due to an internal biological cause or an external astronomical cause. Rather, it may be due to an external cause, of a cultural or social nature: the effect of the conditions and culture of slavery on those blacks. Why did not Arab scholars notice this factor? Why isn't blacks' fondness for tarab a result of the harsh conditions caused by slavery and servitude? Isn't the biological and astrological determinism simply a justification for the cruel treatment of blacks? Did not Ibn Khaldun associate blacks' slavery with their animalism when he says: "al-Zanj nations are, as a rule, submissive to slavery, because they have little (that is essentially) human and have attributes that are quite similar to those of dumb animals."[30]

For Ellis Cashmore, the need to please the master and avoid punishment is another reason for blacks' fondness for tarab, singing, music, and dance. Some black slaves used to pretend their affection for tarab, not for an internal biological or an external astronomical reason, but in order to attain, for instance, the approval of their masters. Meanwhile, they hide their real feelings in fear of punishment. As advised by Ibn Butlan, "if the slave remains without work for an hour, their mind does not lead them to good," and some of them "perform only with a stick and threat, and they have no virtue other than enduring hardship and heavy work."[31] Another piece of advice from al-Mutanabbi says: "Never buy a slave without a stick to go with him, for slaves are truly filthy and ill-fated."[32]

THE CURSE OF BLACKNESS
AND THE CULINARY TRIAD

The explanations for blackness in Arab culture stem from two sources: the Biblical story of Ham and the Ptolemaic geographical theory. The first relies on the Biblical myth that infiltrated Arab culture through what is called *al-Isra'iliyyat* (the Israelites),[33] where blackness is seen as a divine curse that befell the offspring of Ham, following Noah's curse upon his son to be black and enslaved. As for the second explanation, it depends on the Ptolemaic geographical theory of the seven climes. The first region begins in the south where blacks and the al-Zanj are, and the seventh ends in the north, where Gog, Magog, and the northern primitives live. If the first explanation is based on a Biblical myth, the other is based, to utilize Levi Strauss's metaphor, on the "cooking triad," where the "undercooked/raw" is culturally transitioned to "cooked" or naturally to "rotten." As such, the Earth is depicted as food and the sun as a burning fire. Food varies depending on the proximity to the massive solar stove (the sun): some are not sufficiently touched by the fire (raw/undercooked); some are exposed to intense heat and come out burned (overcooked); and some are exposed to moderate heat (well-cooked).

BLACKNESS AND SLAVERY: THE BIBLICAL
ORIGIN AND THE ARABIC INTERPRETATION

The first interpretation of blackness and slavery goes back to a Biblical origin that was accepted in Arab culture but questioned by Ibn Khaldun and others. According to this theory, all humans go back to one origin, which is Adam, the father of humans, and from him human generations continued to Noah. After the Flood, only three of Noah's sons survived. Those were Shem, Ham, and Japheth. From these three, people were created and divided across the Earth. Ham dwelt in the south, Japheth dwelt in the north, and Shem chose the middle of the Earth in which to live. According to the Torah narration, this coincides with the event of the destruction of the "Tower of Babel." When the Lord destroyed the Tower of Babel, the people's tongues differed, and then they dispersed throughout the vast land.

In fact, the story of the Flood and the destruction of the Tower of Babel do not mention any explanation or reason, either historical or divine, for blackness. To fill this gap in the narration, Arabs had to reformulate or *re-emplot* this story to raise the status of Shem's sons, including themselves (Arabs), and in compensation to lower the status of Ham's sons, including blacks and "al-Zanj." According to Arabic narrations, the destruction of the Tower of Babel occurred in the days of Nimrod (son of Canaan/Kush, Ham's son). Nimrod is the one who was described in the Torah "Like Nimrod, a mighty hunter before the LORD" (Genesis 10:9), and according to the narration, he was the first mighty man on Earth. He was "black, with red eyes, deformed, with a horn on his forehead, and he was the first black to be seen after the Flood."[34] He is the king who lived during Prophet Abraham's time, and argued with him about his religion, and ordered his burning, but God made the fire cool and peaceful for him: "They said, 'Burn him and support your gods – if you are to act.' Allah said, 'O fire, be coolness and safety upon Abraham'" (Quran, 21:69).

If the destruction of Babel took place during the time of the first black king after the Flood (Ham's grandson) because of his oppression and his tyranny, then he bears responsibility for humans' dispersal and language confusion, and also the consequences of Noah's curse on Ham. Other narrations suggest that the first black person seen after the Flood was Canaan (or Kush), Ham's son. According to this narration, Ham avoided his wife, fearing that his father's curse would be fulfilled. When his father died, he had intercourse with his wife, and she became pregnant with Kush, son of Ham, and his sister. When Ham saw them, he was terrified of them, and he went to his brothers and told them that he asked his wife: "Did a demon or someone else other than me approach you? His brothers said: This is your father's curse. So, he was saddened by that and left his wife for a long time."[35] And this narration indicates that Ham was terrified because his children were black, and that is what made him flee to the south or to an unknown destination. When he returned to his wife, he "copulated with her and she gave birth to Qut and his twin. When he saw that, he fled and disappeared, and no one knew where he went."[36]

However, there are other narrations that attribute the reason for the division of the three sons of Noah to Noah himself when he divided the land among them. After the Flood, Noah "divided the earth among his sons, assigning to each a particular part."[37] In another version, Noah's three sons were the ones who divided the land among themselves: "the sons of Noah divided the land, so the sons of Shem dwelt in the navel [midst] of the earth, and among them were the brown and the white; the sons of Japheth dwelt in the north and Saba, and among them were the red and the blonde; and the sons of Ham dwelt in the south and Daboor, so their colours changed."[38] In the two narratives, the preference is always given to Shem and his offspring, as he is the one who dwells in the middle of the Earth, and it is God who gave him and his sons "the leadership, the revealed books and the prophets."[39] As for Japheth and Ham, they have the extremities of the Earth (the north and the south). This division and distribution will agree with the geographical explanation for the deviation of blacks and the moderation of the Shemites who lived in the moderate central regions.

All these narrations imply criticism of Ham's offspring, yet the most evident and common is the one that is in the Torah:

> Noah, a man of the soil, proceeded to plant a vineyard. When he drank some of its wine, he became drunk and lay uncovered inside his tent. Ham, the father of Canaan, saw his father naked and told his two brothers outside. But Shem and Japheth took a garment and laid it across their shoulders; then they walked in backward and covered their father's naked body. Their faces were turned the other way so that they would not see their father naked.
> When Noah awoke from his wine and found out what his youngest son had done to him, he said,
> "Cursed be Canaan!
> The lowest of slaves
> will he be to his brothers."
> He also said,
> "Praise be to the Lord, the God of Shem!
> May Canaan be the slave of Shem.
> May God extend Japheth's territory;
> may Japheth live in the tents of Shem,
> and may Canaan be the slave of Japheth" (Genesis 9:20–27).

The Arab imaginary has preserved this explicit criticism of Ham and his offspring in the Torah to serve the perception of the blacks of Ham's descendants. While al-Ya'qubi narrates this story as is, al-Masudi adds to it: "Nuh cursed his son Ham because of a well known quarrel between them, saying: 'Cursed be Ham, a slave of slaves shall he be to his brothers.' Nuh also said: 'Blessed is Sam. May God multiply Yafith, and may Yafith settle in the habitations of Sam.'"[40] Both narrations (the nakedness and the intercourse at Noah's Ark) have fed into the perception of blacks in the Arab imaginary, where blacks are portrayed as naked animals who have no shame and no human morals.

As for Ibn Khaldun, he rejects Ham's narration, partly because of the weakness in the validity and authenticity of the narration, and partly because of the disregard of the country's nature and climate. Therefore, he describes the narration as a frail and false tale, and as one of the narrators' myths and genealogists' illusions:

> Genealogists who had no knowledge of the true nature of things imagined that Negroes are the children of Ham, the son of Noah, and that they were singled out to be black as the result of Noah's curse, which produced Ham's colour and the slavery God inflicted upon his descendants. It is mentioned in the Torah that Noah cursed his son Ham. No reference is made there to blackness. The curse included no more than that Ham's descendants should be the slaves of his brothers' descendants. To attribute the blackness of al-Zanj to Ham, reveals disregard of the true nature of heat and cold and of the influence they exercise upon the air (climate) and upon the creatures that come into being in it. The black colour (of skin) common to the inhabitants of the first and second zones is the result of the composition of the air in which they live, and which comes about under the influence of the greatly increased heat in the south. The sun is at the zenith there twice a year at short intervals. In (almost) all seasons, the sun is in culmination for a long time. The light of the sun, therefore, is plentiful. People there have (to undergo) a very severe summer, and their skins turn black because of the excessive heat. Something similar happens in the two corresponding zones to the north, the seventh and sixth zones. There, a white colour (of skin) is common among the inhabitants, likewise the result of the composition of the air in which they live, and which comes about under the influence of the excessive cold in the north.[41]

The two main interpretations of blackness (Biblical and geographical) populate the Arab imaginary. Sometimes, both are found together in one place, regardless of their contradiction, because the purpose behind these interpretations is the same: to justify blacks' slavery and lessen the guilt among slave owners and masters in Arab culture.

THE SEVEN CLIMES THEORY

If the Biblical interpretation has been subjected to skepticism and criticism by Ibn Khaldun, al-Dimashqi, and others, then the geographical and environmental interpretation has had approval by almost the majority in Arab culture, including doctors, theologians, geographers, astrologers, navigators, writers, and historians as well as traders, rulers, commoners, and others, to the extent that Ali bin Razin al-Katib instructs that the king's confidant must know the names, features, and peoples' moods of the seven climes.[42]

Coming from Greece, this geographical theory infiltrated the Arab imaginary during a wide and active translation movement in the ninth century CE. The translation from Greek and Syriac into Arabic was part of a pioneering attempt to translate Greek knowledge in medicine, philosophy, logic, nature, metaphysics, cosmology, geography, astrology, geometry, ethics, rhetoric, and others. In this context, "the Caliph al-Ma'mun founded the Baghdad School in the year 217 AH/832 CE on the model of the Nestorian and Zoroastrian schools and called it *Bayt al-Hikma* [the House of Wisdom]."[43] At first, the Syriac Christian translators took on the task of translation. Many of the Greek works, interpretations, and summaries of Plato, Aristotle, Euclid, Galen, Hippocrates, Archimedes, and others made their way into Arab culture through translations of Yahya bin Masawaih, Hunayn bin Ishaq, his son Ishaq bin Hunayn, Matta bin Yunus, Yahya bin Adi, and others. Through this extensive movement of translation and knowledge transfer from Greek and Syriac into Arabic, the theory of the seven climes was presented to the Arab imaginary.

In *The Invention of Racism in Classical Antiquity*, Benjman Isaac argues that the primary proto-racism was invented in Greco-Roman antiquity in the fifth century BCE. This proto-racism had a powerful impact on justifying racism in the Middle Ages and in nineteenth-century Europe. But what is the basis of the racism of the ancient Greco-Roman world? For Isaac, it is based on extensive knowledge and interpretation of geographical, climatological, astrological, and genetic institutions (including the role of systems, laws, and institutions). However, "the first major topic to be considered is the environmental theory, in other words, the assumption that the physical environment influences or even determines group characteristics."[44] It is the theory that Herodotus, Plato, Aristotle, and others employed in an attempt to emphasize that "the Greeks are the ideal group in the middle"[45] between the coldness of Europe and the heat of Asia and Africa. However, the extreme form of this environmental and climatic determinism lies in Ptolemy's geographical and astronomical theory, which left no room for humans to improve or change, since the climate and the proximity to the sun and the stars have already determined everything, including human bodies, their humours, and temperament.

Inherited from the Greek tradition, and Ptolemy in particular, the seven climes theory refers to the divisions of the inhabited portion of the spherical Earth by geographic latitude. The theory first appeared in the field of geography, but it quickly spread to various fields of knowledge as a tangible scientific fact in which there was no room for debate. It was also employed in applied sciences such as medicine where Ibn Sina demonstrates the effect of the sun on moderating or deviating the peoples' moods, or as in the need for cupping and bloodletting of those who live in hot countries. People in hot countries such as al-Zanj and Abyssinians change their mood very often:

> … the mood heats up, and dries up then burns the surface of the body. That is why their bodies turned black, their hair turned nappy, the bottoms of their bodies were shrivelled, their faces sagged, and the mood of their brains deviated from moderation, so the actions of the speaking soul appear in them in terms of joy, mirth, and silence, and most of them are dull due to the corruption of their brains.[46]

This theory was also used in navigation, where well-known navigators like Ahmed bin Majid (the prince of the sea) attributes the blackness of blacks to their proximity to the sun and the equator, which burns them.[47] This interpretation was preserved until the Ottoman era, despite its contradiction with the navigational knowledge at the time. Such an explanation of blackness is based on the division of the Earth into sections: inhabited and uninhabited, prosperous and wasteland. Al-Masudi attributes this division to the sages who divided the land into four directions:

> … east, west, north, and south. They further divided it into two parts, inhabited and uninhabited, prosperous and wasteland. They also mention that the Earth is spherical and its location is

in the middle of the heavens with air surrounding it on all sides, and that with respect to the constellations it is as tiny as a dot.[48]

As the water surrounds it from all sides, half of the Earth is "covered by the sea, the greatest ocean, and the other half is exposed, like an egg submerged, half of which is in the water and the other half protruding from the water, and it is the exposed half."[49] This exposed half of the Earth is divided into the prosperous/inhabited and wasteland/uninhabited. And if the centre of the Earth is the centre of the heavenly spheres, then the centre of the inhabited and populous section would be the centre of the Earth and its navel, so it is neither in the south nor in the north nor in the east nor in the west, it is in the middle of the Earth and in its heart. Thus, the edges of the Earth are nothing but desolate uninhabitable places due to the climate. The moderate centre is precisely the middle of the third, fourth, and fifth regions. In those regions, people have moderate temperaments; they have the intellectual and practical crafts, and among them are the masters of wisdom, arts, and sciences, and also the prophets and the righteous and virtuous persons.[50]

Moreover, according to this theory, the colours of people range in these regions from black to brown to white to blond. While people in the first region are black, people of the second region are between brown and black. Most people of the third region are brown, while the fourth region, which includes most of the Islamic kingdoms and Arab countries, people are between brown and white. People in the fifth region are mostly white, whereas people in the sixth region are between white and blond.[51] As for the last seventh region, people are blond. Parallel to the gradation in colour, there is a gradation in human size from large and tall to moderate to short in stature: the blacks of the south are huge and tall, as in Andaman Islands where people not only eat others alive but also have "long legs, and their feet as long as arms."[52] Ibn Battuta mentions that "one person of Mogadishu usually eats as much as a group of us eats, and their bodies are very huge and big."[53] Whereas people in the temperate regions (the third, fourth, and fifth) are cultivated and well-proportioned. They are neither tall, nor short, nor dwarfs. Rather, they have fine faces and moderate statures, and among all humans, they are the finest in physiques and colours. As for the people of the seventh region, they are short and of a small stature. When Dhul-Qarnayn asked about the characteristics of Gog and Magog, he was told: "short ribs, wide faces, their length is half the stature of a squatty man."[54]

The gradation analogy in human bodies and colours is also applied to animals and plants, as in the elephant and giraffe, which are considered among the animals of blacks. Ibn al-Faqih states that the animals of blacks are bigger than the rest of the animals, while those of the seventh region are small.[55] In blacks' region, trees are bigger than usual as Amr al-Sirafi saw "huge trees in the land of the Sudan. In the land called *Kanam he saw two trees that shaded 30,000 horses ..." and in that country, "the cotton plant becomes a tree that a man can climb. Their bodies are in proportion to their trees."[56]

Furthermore, based on this theory, blacks of hot regions, contrary to the north regions, have a lot of sexual intercourse and children. For example, people of Zaghawa have "the most debauchery and sexual intercourse and plenty of children, and it is rare to see a woman walking without being followed by four or five children."[57] Also, people of southern countries, such as Abyssinia and al-Zanj, "have short lives, and their stomachs are weak due to indigestion."[58] It was narrated that the Messenger said: "Beware of the Zanj, for they are the shortest in age and the least in provision. And be with the companion, he means the Romans, for they are the longest-lived people and the most abundant, so enjoy their long lives and share with them their provision."[59]

This gradation is caused by the proximity to or distance from the huge solar stove (the sun): those who are close to the sun are burnt and thus black; those who are far from the sun are undercooked and thus white; and those who are exposed to it to a moderate degree are cooked moderately. Accordingly, human beings are of three types: burnt (black) humans, moderately cooked humans, and undercooked humans:

> The apparent reason for people's different colours, morals, and humours is in their connection to the different conditions of the sun, and that is in three categories. First, those who inhabit close to the equator along the Cancer's head, and they are called by the general name *al-Sudan* [blacks]. The reason for this is that the sun passes their heads once or twice a year, burning them, blackening their bodies, crinkling their hair, making their faces barren and their morals wild, and they are the Zanj and Abyssinians ... Second, those who dwell on the tip of Cancer's

head, along Ursa Major, and they are called by the common name of the whites; because the sun is not close on their heads nor very far from them, they are not exposed to extreme heat or extreme cold, and that's why their colours become moderate and their morals are virtuous, like the people of China, the Turks, Khorasan, Iraq, Persia, Egypt, and the Levant. Third are those who live along Ursa Minor, who are the Slavs and the Russians, and because they are far from the constellations and the hot sun, cold and humidity dominates them. Therefore, their colours have turned white, their bodies have become soft, their natures have turned to be cold, and their morals are savage and brutal.[60]

Since the southern and northern regions are the opposites in terms of heat and cold, blackness and whiteness, the middle region must be the moderate region, and it is the place that is specific to the most perfect human species in creation and manners:

> The inhabitants of the middle zones are temperate in their physique and character and in their ways of life. They have all the natural conditions necessary for a civilized life, such as ways of making a living, dwellings, crafts, sciences, political leadership, and royal authority. They thus have had [various manifestations of] prophecy, religious groups, dynasties, religious laws, sciences, countries, cities, buildings, horticulture, splendid crafts, and everything else that is temperate.[61]

The heart of these regions is the fourth region, and the heart of the fourth region is Babylon (Persia and Iraq), and the heart of Babylon is Iraq, and the heart of Iraq is Baghdad, for it is the heart of the world, the navel and best part of the Earth. Thus, people in Baghdad are temperate in colours and physique. They are saved from "the Romans' and Slavs' blondness, the Abyssinians and blacks' dumbness, the Turks' coarseness, the mountains and Khorasan peoples' coolness, and from the ugliness of the Chinese and the like." They were given "acumen, and adherence to knowledge and high moral standards."[62]

Nevertheless, this geographical distribution of regions, according to the theory of the seven climes, raises several issues that required the following solutions. First, it was necessary to exclude the Arab countries in the first and second regions from such features as blackness, savagery, animality, and deformation. Second, it was also necessary to exclude the countries that Muslim Arabs have proven to be civilized peoples who, like Arabs, have religions, sciences, and crafts, and those are the people of China, India, and Sindh. Regarding the first matter, Arab scholars resort to the same theory that they used in the past, which is that temperaments and humours are affected by the nature of the air and climate of the place, such as cold, heat, humidity, and aridity. Ibn Khaldun rejects any objection that may arise as a result of the presence of those Arab countries in the first and second regions:

> The (foregoing statement) is not contradicted by the existence of the Yemen, the Hadramawt, al-Ahqaf, the Hijaz, the Yamimah, and adjacent regions of the Arabian Peninsula in the first and second zones. As we have mentioned, the Arabian Peninsula is surrounded by the sea on three sides. The humidity of (the sea) influences the humidity in the air of (the Arabian Peninsula). This diminishes the dryness and intemperance that (otherwise) the heat would cause. Because of the humidity from the sea, the Arabian Peninsula is to some degree temperate.[63]

However, Ibn Khaldun did not realize that there are very hot and arid places in the Arabian Peninsula that are far from water. That is why it was not saved from blackness and burning by the heat. Harrah Banu Sulaym, for example, is located near Taiba, where everything is black: "stones are black, its people are black, their horses are black, their cows are black, their animals are black, their sheep are black, their donkeys are black, and their dogs are black, even if a Slavic ass lives there, it will turn black in a short time."[64] Ibn Khaldun also did not realize that parts of the blacks' lands and islands are surrounded by water, so he misinterpreted the climatic effects on the people of those parts.

As for India, even though it is one of the nations in the first and second regions, and even though its people are black, they are people of knowledge, manners, religion, and craftmanship. Hence, "in their rationality, politics, wisdom, bodily health, and clarity of colour the Indians differ from all other black races such as the Zanj, the Damadim, and so forth."[65] Other theories were used to exclude the people of India from the negative qualities of the first and second regions, such as the positive influence of the planet Mercury on their minds, so they became people with sound opinions and solid knowledge in numbers, geometry, medicine, astrology, natural sciences, and theology. Some of them are Brahmins (...), and among them are Sabians (...), and they have compositions in arithmetic, morality, and music.[66]

The people of China and India are equal to Muslim Arabs in terms of civilization, sciences, religions, and crafts, and they may even exceed them in some of that. In terms of science and crafts, nations are of two types: "Those who were concerned with knowledge, so various kinds of knowledge emerged from them, they are God's chosen among His creations, and those nations who were not concerned with knowledge ... The first includes the Egyptians, Romans, Indians, Persians, Chaldeans, Greeks, Arabs, and Hebrews, and the second are the rest of the nations, but the most important of them are people of China and the Turks."[67] In terms of religions, sects, and creeds, "the four great nations are Arabs, the Persians, the Romans, and the Indians." Arabs and Indian people are close to each other, since Indian people have the tendency to determine the properties of things by essences and facts and the appeal to spiritual factors. On the other hand, the Persians and the Romans have the tendency to determine the nature of things by the states and quantities and the appeal to physical factors.[68]

The Arab imaginary resorted to the Biblical story to explain the connection between the blackness of al-Zanj and the blacks and Ham's curse. When the Arab imaginary found this story mentioning the curse of slavery only, the curse of blackness was added. Then, the imaginary used the theory of the seven climes and the influence of the sun on these regions in order to explain the blackness phenomenon. It represented some nations with burning and deviation, and others with moderation and perfection. It also excluded some nations from the rule of burning and deviation, and included those nations in the moderate regions. There were many exceptions and contradictions, to the extent that the division of the regions became applicable only to the barbaric and savage nations. As for the peoples who were determined by Arab culture to be civilized and enlightened – the Persians, the Romans, China, India, and Sindh – they are not subject to the rule of nature, or the rule of the seven regions, because they are the origin and others are the subdivisions; they are the rule and others are the exception; they are perfect humans, while others are among the beasts and animals; they are "the best nation produced [as an example] for mankind" (Quran 3:110), and others are the worst and most evil of all creation.

AL-JAHIZ AND BLACKS: THE RHETORIC OF REPRESENTATION AND THE PROBLEMATIC OF PRAISE AND BLAME

Al-Jahiz is considered one of the most prominent writers in Arab culture, the most prolific author in the Middle Ages, and the most attentive to the issues of society. He is the most important author writing about others within that historical period, where cultural fanaticism, eulogies, satires, and debates erupted between different cultures at the time. Al-Jahiz engaged in those debates, authoring several books and treatises in this regard, such as *Fakhr al-Sudan 'ala Bidhan* (The pride of blacks over whites), *Manaqib al-Turk* (Virtues of the Turks), *al-Arab wal Ajam* (Arabs and non-Arabs), *al-Suraha wal Hujana* (Purebred and half-breed), *al-Radd 'ala al-Nasara* (Refutation of the Christians), *al-Qahtaniyya wal Adnaniyya* (Qahtanites and Adnanites), and *Shu'ubiyya*.[69] Indeed, Al-Jahiz himself is considered a prominent example of the blending of other cultures in the Arab-Islamic civilization. Al-Jahiz's relative, Yamut bin al-Muzarra says: "al-Jahiz is my mother's uncle, and al-Jahiz's grandfather was black and called Fazara, and he was a cameleer for Amr bin Qal' Al-Kinani."[70]

This information about al-Jahiz is important in this context. It is mentioned by many writers, including al-Dhahabi in *Siyyar A'lam al-Nubala*, al-Khatib al-Baghdadi in *Tarikh Baghdad*, Yaqout al-Hamawi in *Mu'jam al-Udaba*, and Abu al-Barakat al-Anbari in *Nuzhat al-Alibba fi Tabaqat al-Udaba*. In all these books, Yamut bin al-Muzarra is the one who speaks of al-Jahiz. The issue here is to find the lineage of al-Jahiz, as all those who translated his work mentioned that he is an Arab in loyalty, but his relative refers to al-Jahiz's origin, since his grandfather was a black cameleer. This means that al-Jahiz has a close individual memory of his origin as a grandson of a black cameleer in Basra. However, al-Jahiz also has a bigger collective memory, as an Arab Muslim living within Arab civilization. Therefore, al-Jahiz was in an internal conflict between the two consciousnesses, without resolving or settling in favour of one. On the one hand, al-Jahiz does not seem proud of his lineage to blacks, whom he satirizes severely in his books, except for *Fakhr al-Sudan*, which will be discussed later. His black origin brings him shame or belittlement, so that he wants to ignore, forget, or deny it. It is narrated that he said: "I forgot my teknonym for three days until my family told me about it."[71] In another narration, he used to say: "I forgot my teknonym for three days, so I came to my family and said: What was my name? They said: Abu Othman."[72] Forgetting one's name is a psychological mechanism to which the self resorts to overcome or deny its status. Since the name retains the memory of the individual, when this individual wishes to forget this memory, they must forget their name or erase it first, otherwise the name remains in their memory and will keep reminding them of their roots.

If erasing or forgetting one's own name is difficult to attain, then erasing the body and its features is virtually impossible. Al-Jahiz tried to forget his name, yet his family reminded him of it and brought him back to a consciousness of his origin. But what would happen if they also pretended to be forgetful and ignorant of his name? Who would recognize him? How would he be recognized? There remains something greater than his name and people's knowledge of it: the body, which is the undeniable companion attached to the self in this life. Al-Jahiz's individual memory – connections to black roots – was imprinted and etched its clearly defined tattoos on his body to eliminate his chances of renewing or forgetting his own self. Among the characteristics of the blacks and al-Zanj, who deviate from temperance in the far south, are distorted faces and bulging eyes. These two characteristics are inextricably engraved in al-Jahiz. He had an ugly face, protruding eyes, and a disfigured character,[73] to the extent that one poet of his time satirizes al-Jahiz saying: if the pig was to be deformed again, it would not be uglier than al-Jahiz.[74]

Al-Jahiz's relationship to his black roots and Arab culture and civilization was ambiguous, tense, problematic, and sometimes contradictory. In his books, he camouflages himself from his readers by subtly incorporating his opinion into others' multiple opinions, to the extent that it is difficult to identify what belongs to al-Jahiz and what belongs to others. Because of this vagueness, al-Masudi speaks about al-Jahiz's deviation. Al-Masudi also includes al-Jahiz with those who write for *Shu'ubiyya* like Dirar bin Amro and Thumama bin al-Ashras who claim "the Nabateans are better than the Arabs."[75] As for his position on Islam, al-Jahiz was accused by many, such as Ibn Qutayba, of inconsistency, lying, and ridiculing Hadith.[76] Al-Jahiz's contradictions and inconsistencies are caused by the two opposing identities: one related to the marginalized black minority and the other related to the dominant Muslim Arab majority. Many scholars have noticed this contradiction or ambivalence in most of al-Jahiz's books. He writes about the virtues of a nation, but soon satirizes them and lists their flaws.

This contradiction is what governs al-Jahiz's conception of blacks and al-Zanj in most of his writings. He praises their virtues while satirizing them, and he satirizes them while praising their virtues. For al-Jahiz, blacks and al-Zanj are associated not only with black animals but also with animals in general; and they are not associated with some objects, but with objects in general. In *Kitab al-Haywan* (Book of animals), al-Jahiz speaks of well-known or unknown water springs, but when he mentions "Hawara" spring, he attributes the following opinion to others: "they claim that Hawara releases something like al-Zanj,"[77] i.e., it releases black water like al-Zanj's colour, as if the Zanj is the origin of blackness. For him, al-Zanj are not only the origin of blackness but also the origin of all ugly and reprehensible traits, or even a good one, provided that it is found in an animal. The odour of goats represents the ultimate example and source of stench, but this can be exceeded by the al-Zanj's sweat, which is stronger than the goat's odour. While describing the goats and their stinking skin, he compares them to al-Zanj armpits: "The skins of goats, and the skins of the Zanj armpits are fetid with sweat."[78] Also, al-Jahiz reports that people of knowledge claim that "al-Zanj are like donkeys in everything, even in al-Hulaq.[79] For there is no zinji on the Earth who is not Huliqi. But they made a mistake, there is no zinji on the earth who does not want to be sexually penetrated."[80] Al-Jahiz mentions that there are those who claim that the Zanj resemble donkeys in everything, even in diseases specific to donkeys, such as al-Hullaq, where the penis becomes red or peels due to excessive sexual intercourse. There is no medicine for the donkey, no cure except castration, from which it may die or survive and be excluded as a stallion. Castration of donkeys and al-Zanj with al-Hullaq disease would cast them out from among the stallions to among the eunuchs and females, both of whom desire stallions.

These diseases, flaws, and black colours are not all that al-Jahiz's imagination has fabricated to associate the zinji with the animal. Al-Jahiz indicates that the primary and essential similarity between the zinji and the animal lies in the lack of language, elegance of expression, and clarity of exposition. For al-Jahiz, these represent the essence of a human being, without which they are merely animals. For al-Jahiz, the zinji is not the only one who lacks these features, but also women, who are regarded among animals. He attributes inarticulateness and foreignness to women's language. Whenever he talks about animals, the course of the conversation takes him directly to talking about the woman and the zinji. By including the zinji in the female gender, along with their poor linguistic capacity and lack of elegance, al-Jahiz tries to strip the zinji of *"al-Fuhula."*[81] The only example that combines blackness, *Fuhula*, eloquence, and wisdom is Luqman the Wise. He was a black person from Nubia, but Arabs praise and honour him for these qualities, as al-Jahiz indicates. Al-Jahiz narrates that "Luqman's sister said to Luqman's wife: I am a woman who bears foolish children and Luqman is a strong procreative man. I have my period tonight; would you sleep in my bed tonight? So she stayed at Luqman's house, and Luqman slept with her so she gave birth to Luqaim."[82] As long as Luqman is wise and eloquent, he must be a prolific stallion, but since he was a black Nubian, *al-Fuhula* had to be eliminated along with its praise and honour. This is because Luqman violated incest taboo and got his sister pregnant. Hence, it was not surprising that al-Jahiz questioned the identity of this Luqman: it is not conceivable that this black Luqman who commits incest is the same Luqman the Wise who is mentioned in the Quran.

Al-Jahiz believes that the civilized nations are four: Arabs, the Persians, the Romans, and the Indians, because they are the only nations that have "morals, manners, judgment, and knowledge."[83] Therefore, "the minds of blacks and their like are lower in class to those of the brown people."[84] By brown people, al-Jahiz means Arabs, the Persians, or the people of the Babylon region in general. Due to temperance, "the minds and the beauty of the people of Babylon and its territory are superior to others."[85]

Furthermore, al-Jahiz is no different from any Medieval Arab scholar who wrote about blacks, using the culinary lexicon: well-cooked/ripe, overcooked/burnt, undercooked/raw. Based on their proximity to the stove fire (the sun), blond Slavs, Gog, and Magog are undercooked in their womb, and black Zanj are overcooked and burnt in their womb (clime/zone).[86] In his view of blacks and al-Zanj, al-Jahiz was no different than his contemporaries or those who came after him. Blacks and al-Zanj are roaming beasts or wild animals; they are stinking, naked, and foolish people who do not understand a word, just like animals.

Despite his pejorative and demeaning depiction of blacks, al-Jahiz is the first author to praise blacks and their superior qualities over whites in his treatise *Fakhr al-Sudan 'ala al-Bidhan* (The pride of blacks over whites). Strangely, al-Jahiz did not receive the criticism or accusations that targeted other authors who praise blacks (e.g., al-Nashi', al-Marzuban). But why did al-Jahiz write this treatise? Was he trying to prove his superior linguistic skills, magic of eloquence, and dialectical style and argumentation? Or was the treatise a sophist argument? There is nothing in the treatise to prove this assumption, nor is there anything to explicitly deny it. In *Manaqib al-Turk*, al-Jahiz mentions that "the most useful praise for the praiser and most effective praise for the praised is when the praise is sincere and honest."[87] However, the praise in *Fakher al-Sudan 'ala al-Bidhan* is characterized by humour, ridicule, and sarcasm.

Al-Jahiz's three most famous treatises are *al-Radd 'ala al-Nasara* (Refutation of the Christians), *Manaqib al-Turk* (Virtues of the Turks), and *Fakhr al-Sudan 'ala al-Bidhan* (The pride of blacks over whites). Al-Jahiz often supports the political system of his time by reinforcing the same "opinion that the authority holds about the Other, an opinion charged with sectarian and political ideologies that reflect, to a large extent, the degree of tension and power struggle that characterized the eras of the Abbasid Caliphate."[88] As for *al-Radd 'ala al-Nasara*, several scholars indicate that it reflects and supports al-Moutawakel's oppressive policy towards Christians who announced disapproval for the Abbasid State.[89] As for *Manaqib al-Turk*, its political nature is clear and explicit. It was written during the reign of al-Mutasim, who was born of a Turkish mother and who recruited a large number of Turkish Mamluks in his army and state. Some scholars argue that al-Jahiz's *Manaqib al-Turk* was a trick by al-Jahiz, who was a Mutazilite, to get out of the ordeal that the Mutazilites were subjected to during the reign of al-Moutawakel. He did so by praising the Turks, and by his connection to al-Fath bin Khaqan. Hence, due to their political context and significance, such treatises (*Manaqib al-Turk* and *al-Radd 'ala al-Nasara*) are presented with sincerity and honesty. On the other hand, al-Jahiz's *Fakhr al-Sudan 'ala al-Bidhan* was not subject to any political influence nor was it written under any precautions. In its opening, al-Jahiz mentions that the reason behind writing the treatise is because of a request made by an unknown person, who is high in rank and position. This person read al-Jahiz's *al-Suraha wal Hujana* and did not find any reference to blacks, so he asked al-Jahiz to write about the virtues of blacks.

Al-Jahiz excels in listing every praiseworthy black thing, including humans and non-humans. For example, among the virtues of blacks is that among them are such noble and great people as Luqman al-Hakim, Bilal (the Prophet's muezzin), Saeed bin Jubayr, Mihja', al-Miqdad bin al-Aswad, Wahshi, Makhoul al-Faqih, al-Hayqutan, Julaybib, Faraj al-Hajam, Sunaih bin Rabah, 'Ukaim al-Habashi, and others. Also, black dates are the sweetest; the best palm trees are those with black trunks; the best greens are the dark ones; the best and most expensive wood is ebony; the hair of the people in Paradise is black; the noblest human part is their black eye pupils; the most beneficial human part is their black liver; the dearest human part is the bottom of the heart, which is black; the best kissable lips of a woman are black; the best and coolest shade is the black one; the night is black for rest and calmness; the most gracious perfumes are black musk and amber; the blackest stones and trees are the strongest; the most honourable stone is the black Stone ... etc. Moreover, al-Jahiz goes back to his previous criticism of blacks and rectifies it using his distinctive power of argumentation and manipulation of the evidence. For example, al-Jahiz mentions that blacks are good and generous people, and this trait is evidence of their weak minds, lack of deliberation, and ignorance of the consequences of matters.[90] Further, after severely criticizing their language, al-Jahiz comes back to say that blacks and al-Zanj are the most articulate people, who speak with no stutter, stammer, pauses, or inarticulacy. There is no language on Earth that is lighter on the tongue than theirs, nor people with more expressive tongues than theirs.[91] Also, al-Jahiz rejects the religious determinism of Biblical origin, which holds that the blackness was a divine curse. Instead, he believes in the natural determinism where blackness is caused by the proximity to the sun. However, al-Jahiz refutes the concepts of distortion and temperance and their associated value judgments:

> God almighty did not make us black to distort our creation, but the country environment did that to us ... blackness and whiteness are caused by the nature of the country, its water and soil, its distance or nearness to the sun, and not because of a deformation, a punishment, a distortion, nor a shortcoming.[92]

PART TWO

The Imaginary and the Literary Representation

BLACKS AND THEIR REPRESENTATION IN LITERATURE

Arabic literary representation of blacks is not different from the pejorative images in the Arab cultural representation. While reinforcing them, literary representation employs those images to create its own paradoxes, ironies, and satires. In this part, I will explore the representation of blacks in the following:

1. Major narrative works of unknown authors such as the folk biographies (*siyyar*): *Sirat bani Hilal, Sirat al-Amirah Dhat al-Himma, Sirat Antarah bin Shaddad, Sirat Saif bin Dhi Yazan,* and *Alf Layla wa Layla (One Thousand and One Nights)*.
2. The poetry of poets who clashed collectively with blacks after the Zanj Revolution[1] and the destruction of Basra, such as Ibn al-Rumi, or clashed individually, such as al-Mutanabbi with Kafur al-Ikhshidi (Ikhshidid ruler, d.968 CE).
3. Poetry written by black poets as a counter-representation such as that of Antarah bin Shaddad, Suhaim Abdu Bani al-Hashas, al-Hayquta, 'Ukaim al-Habashi, etc.

3

Blacks in Narrative Representation

The representation of blacks explored in the previous chapters was produced by the "formal" or "high" Arab cultural discourse and recognized by the "intellectual" elites. Was this representation of blacks different in popular "low" discourse, specifically in the popular folk narrative spread among the common people? In fact, those popular narrations converge with those formal and elite narrations in their view of blacks and blackness. In this section, I will focus on narratives that have some commonalities, which is why they have been chosen as a representative sample. As for the aforementioned biographies (*siyyar*), they belong to what is called "folk biography," whereas *One Thousand and One Nights* belongs to the mythical or wonder and fantasy genre. Also, between these two narratives, there is a convergence and overlap that I will refer to later. Moreover, these narratives are popular folk narratives in terms of language, composition, and circulation. They are of oral origin (with some local dialects) whose documentation happened at a later stage by some chanters, storytellers, and scribes. And because of their oral and folk nature, those narratives have gone through several alterations, and were severely criticized by the "culture guardians" and elites, charging those biographies with deceit, obscenity, slander, confusion, ignorance, and stupidity. In addition, the authors are unknown, which has made the narratives a fertile breeding ground for the interference of the collective cultural imagination. The collective authorship or the absence of the author is a ploy used by the Arab cultural imaginary to infuse derogatory representations of Others.

The last common feature among these biographies, which concerns us most here, is the prominent presence of the Other, and blacks in particular. The Other is abundantly present in most popular biographies, as a sworn enemy, friend, or ally. Among all the Others, the presence of the black Other remains at the heart of these narratives, and it is strange that the hero in three of the most important Arab popular biographies is black, as in the case of Antarah bin Shaddad, Prince Abd al-Wahhab bin al-Amira of al-Himma, and Prince Barakat (Abu Zaid al-Hilali). It is true that the black Other is present in most popular biographies. Blacks as slaves, for example, are present in *The Biography of al-Zahir Baibars, al-Zir Salem, Hamza al-Arab or al-Bahlwan* and other works. However, in the following selected biographies, the black, as an external or internal Other, is present as a central issue and a subject of cultural significance, a crucial component in building the narrative and directing its events.

THE BLACK INFANT AND THE TRAUMA OF BIRTH

The birth of a hero is one of the recurring events in popular biographies, and perhaps it is one of the "most important phenomena that we encounter in the whole world of folk literature."[1] The heroes are usually born strange and rejected, and they are often separated from their parents immediately after birth or shortly thereafter. This is what makes them live in "birth trauma," a concept in Freudian psychology, in which birth is seen as the first experience of anxiety and therefore is the source and basis of anxiety. Otto Rank claims that "birth is the ultimate biological basis of life and that the physical experience of passing from a state of contentedness and union with the mother in the womb to an environment of harsh separation creates a trauma that causes lasting anxiety."[2] For the child, the mother's womb is like a paradise in which they live in absolute happiness and universal bliss, but they feel, when separated from this womb, as if they were expelled from paradise.

How is the birth trauma relevant to those popular biographies? Abu Zaid Al-Hilali's biography has a close relationship with the concept of "birth trauma," which is here a double "birth trauma": the one who is shocked in the first place is not the newborn, but rather the cultural imaginary of the family and the tribe. The tribe is the one who faces the "shock of birth" and the one who goes through this initial anxiety that obliterates the state of joy while waiting for the newborn. The newborn does not survive the trauma of birth.

He faces this shock, not only because he is separated from the mother's warm and safe womb but also because at the moment of his birth he faces an existential dilemma resulting from the trauma of the family and the tribe.

The first predicament that the hero confronts is the dilemma of affiliation and not recognizing his sonship.[3] Barakat (Abu Zaid al-Hilali) and Prince Abd al-Wahhab face this dilemma, despite their noble lineage on the side of the father and mother. Barakat's father is Prince Rizq bin Nael bin Thabet bin Tamer bin Jaber bin al-Mundhir bin Hilal bin Amer bin Abi Laila al-Muhalhal. And his mother, al-Khadra, the daughter of Prince Qurdab al-Sharif bin Hashim, is a descendant of Banu Hilal, the ruler of Mecca. As for Prince Abd al-Wahhab, from the father's side, he is the son of al-Harith bin Zalim bin al-Sahsah bin Jandaba bin al-Harith, the king of the kings of Banu Kilab, who is of noble ancestry and lineage. On the mother's side, he is the son of Princess Dhat al-Himma, Fatima bint Mazloum bin al-Sahsah bin Jandaba bin al-Harith. However, this honourable lineage does not save the two from facing the dilemma of affiliation and sonship. Although the newborn is shocked, he does not wish that he was not born, but rather he remains close to his mother, and her tenderness, kindness, and care for him. We will begin by analyzing the birth of Barakat and the circumstances surrounding it, and then the birth of Prince Abd al-Wahhab. Because the analysis will focus on the event of birth, I find it necessary to summarize this part using phrases from the biography.

Sirat Bani Hilal: The Hero's Blackness as a Transient Dilemma

The narrator of the Bani Hilal biography mentions that Prince Rizq and al-Khadra had a daughter after a year of marriage, and that she was named Shihah or Shiha. Prince Rizq asked God to grant him a son who would make him happy, bear his name, and be his successor. After that, his wife became pregnant, and she asked God to give her a son. One day, they went out to an orchard, and she saw a black crow chasing the crows out, conquering and killing them. She said: "My God, give me a son, even if he is black, so that he may grow up to conquer and defeat the knights just like this crow." When she finished her prayer, she returned home, and later she gave birth to a dark-skinned boy.[4]

The narrator mentions that the messenger went to Prince Rizq and gave him good tidings of the newborn boy, so the prince rejoiced and slaughtered the sacrifices, and the people came to congratulate him. When asked about the child's name, Rizq said: Barakat, and handed him over to the daughter of Asjam to nurse him. After seven days, Prince Hazem, his son Sarhan, and the rest of the princes of Bani Hilal came to Prince Rizq. Barakat was brought out to them, but when Sarhan saw him, he bit his fingers in disappointment and said to Rizq: "This boy is as black as a slave." He lamented Prince Rizq's misfortune, for perhaps this black boy's father was a black slave. Upon hearing Sarhan's words, Prince Rizq became angry and divorced al-Khadra, and he ordered that she be sent to her family with her son, Barakat.

Al-Khadra was satisfied, or at least not shocked, by the blackness of her son. What about Prince Rizq? Was he not shocked by the blackness of his son? The narrator mentions that the prince rejoiced at the boy's arrival and slaughtered the sacrifices for him, but did the prince see his son before he expressed his joy and slaughtered the sacrifices? The narrator does not mention anything in this regard, leaving it vague for the reader who may assume that the prince saw his son, because it is not conceivable that Prince Rizq waited seven days to see his son. If this assumption is correct, it means that Prince Rizq was also satisfied and not shocked by the blackness of his son. But he was shocked when he heard Sarhan's words, accusing Khadra of adultery with a black slave, which is something that Prince Rizq could not tolerate, so he divorced his wife.

Such an incident, where the parents are white and the son is black is a frequent phenomenon in Arab history. Ibn Hazm al-Andalusi tells a story that is somewhat similar to the story of Barakat. A black infant from white parents was brought to al-Qafa (an expert who can identify the father of the newborn by looking at their physical features). Al-Qafa could not identify the father, so he went to the place where the parents had intercourse. There he saw a portrayal of a black person located in parallel with the wife's eyes. So he said to the father that because of this picture he had a black son.[5] Many similar stories are narrated that occurred in the era of the Prophet, in chapters on "marriage," "divorce," "oath of condemnation,"[6] and "slander of fornication," and this part of the biography deals with accusations of adultery and divorce.

A similar incident happened during the Prophet's time:

It was narrated from Ibn Omar that a man from the desert people came to the Prophet (PBUH) and said: "O Messenger of Allah, my wife has given birth on my bed to a black boy, and there are no blacks among my family." He said: "Do you have camels?" He said: "Yes." He said: "What colour are they?" He said: "Red." He said: "Are there any black ones among them?" He said: "No." He said: "Are there any grey ones among them?" He said: "Yes." He said: "How is that?" He said: "Perhaps it's heredity." He said: "Perhaps (the colour of) the son of yours is also heredity."[7]

Although these cases are similar to the incident of Barakat's birth, the difference is that all those who came to the Prophet with shock, came not to inquire, but to seek divorce, oath of condemnation, or accusation of adultery, or to disown the newborn. However, the trauma of Barakat's birth continues to affect Barakat himself (Abu Zaid al-Hilali) later in his life. This trauma later affected the princes of Bani Hilal, and Sarhan in particular, whose fear of the possibility of such an incident happening created anxiety in his life. Upon seeing Barakat, Sarhan felt shocked then disappointed and said:

O Prince Rizq, this is not your successor ... His father is a black slave. You named him Barakat[8] and the bliss is gone ... Joy has left us, and misery has come, O Rizq, you have lost your lineage with the Prophet ... Happiness has died, and your jinx will live.[9]

Prince Rizq became angry because his newborn was neither good-looking nor his hoped-for successor. However, what angered him most was Sarhan's attitude and his mockery, the winking of the Bani Hilal princes at each other, and the laughter of his cousins in his presence. Later, Barakat (Abu Zaid al-Hilali) blamed his father, indicating that his behaviour was a violation of and objection to the word of God and His wisdom in His creation:

If you are given a dark-skinned child ... This is His creation, Creator of the signs. Look at the creatures, all of them ... You will see their images are always different. Some are white like a full moon in the sky ... Some are charred black.[10]

Here, Barakat (Abu Zaid al-Hilali) appears to be objecting to the axioms of the Arab imaginary regarding blacks, as he refers to the concept of justice intended in the Quranic verse: "And of His signs is the creation of the heavens and the earth and the diversity of your languages and your colours. Indeed in that are signs for those of knowledge" (Quran 30:22). Thus, colours are not the will of humans, nor are they subject to their desires and choices. Rather, they are created by "the Creator of signs." Therefore, objecting to these colours is an objection to God and a violation of His wisdom.

Making Barakat the hero of the biography does not show a real desire to raise the issue of colour and discuss it extensively, or to undermine the stereotypical perceptions stored in the Arab imaginary. It is nothing more than a passing dilemma imposed by the adherence to the narrative structure in the folk biography, where the hero must face a dilemma at the beginning of his life. Accordingly, the black colour of Barakat was nothing but a reason for the hero to face the dilemma of affiliation, and then follow the narrative structure, where he proves his heroism and conquers a country and then receives the recognition of the father and the tribe.

Sirat al-Amirah Dhat al-Himma: The Black's Successor and Otherness

Al-Amirah Dhat al-Himma (Princess of high resolve) tells the story of al-Harith bin Zalim who wanted to marry his cousin, al-Amirah (Fatima), but she did not want to marry him. Al-Harith asked the Caliph al-Mansur to mediate between them, so he did and offered her to marry al-Harith, but she refused. Nevertheless, Uqba al-Sulaymi (the treacherous judge) asked the court judge to expedite the marriage contract despite her refusal. Although they were married, Fatima did not allow al-Harith to approach, or even see, her. Al-Harith went to Uqba seeking his advice. Following Uqba's scheme, al-Harith bribed Marzouq, a black slave and Fatima's milk brother, to put a sleeping drug in Fatima's drink. After drinking it, Fatima fell asleep and al-Harith came and had intercourse with her. When the princess woke up, she knew what had happened to her, so she got angry and decided to kill both Marzouq and al-Harith. Time passed and she gave birth to a boy whose colour was like a murky night, with muscly arms, black eyes, and dark eyebrows.[11]

Despite having white parents, prince Abd al-Wahhab's colour was the darkest black "as if he was a child from the Nubia." As in *Sirat Bani Hilal*, those who were shocked at the beginning were not the newborn or his mother, but the family, relatives, and the tribe, who thought, like Sarhan in *Sirat Bani Hilal*, that this black newborn was the result of the princess's adultery with a black slave. The women who attended the birth, upon seeing the black baby, were shocked and saddened, then asked the princess: "we only know you are faithful, honest, and innocent ... tell us your story." The story those women wanted to know was the story of her infidelity with this black slave: Who is he? Why? When? And how? Just as al-Khadra tried to defend herself, the princess also tried to explain to the women that she was innocent and faithful, and that the blackness of the baby was not evidence of betrayal with a black slave. Rather, it is God's creation who brings forth the living from the dead and the dead from the living, and who brings forth the white from the black, and the black from the white. The princess's defence was not successful, so some women asked her to hide or kill the baby. The princess did not submit to these pressures, but she was convinced of the need to hide the baby in a nursery, and it was rumoured that the princess had given birth to a son from al-Harith, but the baby had died. This plan worked for some time, but it was revealed by one of the princess's maidservants who was in love with one of al-Harith's servants. She told him that "the princess gave birth to a black child, and he is from a slave, and she hid the baby from people so that they would not accuse her of adultery with Marzouq."[12] The news reached al-Harith, so he went with his father and a group of notables to verify this news. When the princess presented Abd al-Wahhab (the baby), they were all astonished by the blackness of his colour, in spite of the parents' whiteness. As for his grandfather, Zalim, he laughed until he lay on his back, and when he finished his laughter, he declared war on the princess and her son.

Unlike *Sirat Bani Hilal*, the blackness of the child was the reason for the outbreak of war between cousins, and later between Arabs and Romans. When Prince Abdullah (Prince of Bani Sulaym) was unable to resolve the conflict, he asked them to go to al-Qafa (pl. Qa'if) in Mecca to determine the kinship of Abd al-Wahhab. They went to Mecca and al-Qafa declared that Abd al-Wahhab was al-Harith's son. Upon hearing the judgment, al-Harith cried out and rejected the judgment. Then they went to seek judgment from Imam

Ja'far bin Muhammad al-Sadiq, who also judged that the boy was al-Harith's son. Again, al-Harith rejected the verdict, and went to Baghdad where Caliph al-Mahdi reiterated the same judgment. When al-Harith and his father refused the verdict, the Caliph got angry and ordered the beating and imprisonment of al-Harith, his father, and his group.

The fire of war grew and expanded, and the reason was the blackness of Abd al-Wahhab. At first, the war was between Zalim's and Mazlum's groups, then it extended to their allies from Bani Sulaym. Then the conflict extended to a war between the princess's Muslim troops and the Roman troops. Thus, the blackness of Abd al-Wahhab was transferred from a personal, familial, or tribal dilemma to a major religious dilemma. Abd al-Wahhab's blackness was the spark that inflamed the conflict between the princess and her Muslim soldiers on the one hand, and the Romans and their "infidel" soldiers on the other. After the Caliph released al-Harith and his group, and on the way back to Malatya, Uqba said to al-Harith and his father: "There is nothing left after our persecution among those nations except John, Mary, and the Cross. We must drive Arabs from their lands and turn Hijaz to rubble with bloodshed this year."[13]

Indeed, they went to Constantinople and met with the Roman king:

> The priests and monks led them to pledge allegiance, and the king gave them money and asked them to take off their clothes to be baptized. They renounced Muhammad (the best of creatures). Then they wore the Cross around their necks, prostrated themselves to the images on the walls, and tightened the sashes at their waists. And they spoke the word of debauchery and perjury, and then they returned to the hands of the reprehensible king, after which they were expelled from the gate of the Self-subsisting [God].[14]

They joined the Roman army and promised the king to conquer the Islamic countries. Several battles took place between the two armies (Romans and Muslims). In one of the clashes, Prince Abd al-Wahhab stabbed and killed his father, al-Harith, and his grandfather.

Both Barakat and Abd al-Wahhab were born black of white parents and caused a crisis within the tribe because of this blackness, which was interpreted in the two biographies as evidence of adultery with a black slave. However, the difference lies in the fact that the blackness of Abd al-Wahhab was not an incidental element that the narrator resorted to in order to put the hero in the dilemma of affiliation, as was the case in al-Hilali's biography. The blackness of Barakat has no role in directing or developing the events except in a limited part of the biography that does not exceed fifteen per cent of its size. As for Abd al-Wahhab's blackness, it is the hidden drive of the Otherness, which expands gradually from a fight between Princess Dhat al-Himma and al-Harith to one between the princess's father and his allies and al-Harith's father and his allies, and then to one between the Arab Muslims and the Roman Christians.

On the other hand, it can be noted that the blacks were present from the beginning to the end of the biography as allies to the Princess of al-Himma and her son, Prince Abd al-Wahhab, and his son, Prince Zalim, in their wars against the Romans. The intimate relationship between Prince Abd al-Wahhab and his black allies is an exceptional relationship that does not exist in any other Arab biography. When Prince Abd al-Wahhab was captured, "blacks said: What do we do with life without our Lord [Abd al-Wahhab]?"[15] Prince Abd al-Wahhab did not treat his blacks as slaves. Even the narrator did not describe them as slaves. When mentioned, they are described with positive and praiseworthy words such as "nobles," "leaders," "heroes," "venerable," etc. Their description as such indicates the prince's desire to make them equal to the people of Kelab, since both groups sacrificed themselves for the victory of Islam. Thus, while the criterion for virtuousness in the *Sirat Bani Hilal* is nationalistic/tribal (being a true Arab, and a courageous Hilali knight), the criterion for virtuousness in *Sirat al-Amirah Dhat al-Himma* is religious (being a true Muslim who defends Islam and Muslim lands). Perhaps the recognition of this criterion in the *Sirat al-Amirah Dhat al-Himma* is the reason behind the adoption of the Islamic religious vision of the essence of humankind, a vision that does not recognize any privilege (colour, language, race, etc.) but the religion of Islam because "indeed, the religion in the sight of Allah is Islam" (Quran 3:19).

There is a real desire in *Sirat al-Amirah Dhat al-Himma* to spread Islamic values of tolerance, based mainly on the principle mentioned by the narrator at the end of the seventh part of the biography, which included the event of the prince's birth. This principle is that the Prophet of Islam was sent "for the white and the black, and he is the master of Arabs and non-Arabs."[16] This requires the denial of the inferior view of blacks and the rejection of the derogatory representations stored in the Arab imaginary. Such a rejection is based on several Islamic and theological arguments, chief among the argument that Sharif al-Murtadha (a prominent Shia scholar) presents: God does not do evil and does not emanate defect nor shortcomings. Since blackness is God's creation, it is good, and it is not permissible for it to be described as evil, a defect, or a distortion.

Moreover, the narrator in *Sirat Bani Hilal* does not explain the reason for the blackness of Abu Zayd al-Hilali, and instead refers to al-Khadra's vision of the black crow in the orchard. However, in *Sirat al-Amirah Dhat al-Himma*, the narrator explains the blackness of Prince Abd al-Wahhab as a result of al-Harith's intercourse with the princess while she was menstruating and unconscious. The use of a sleeping drug to have intercourse with "white" women and the involvement of a black slave is common in similar stories, such as the tale of King Umar al-Nu'man in *Alf Layla wa Layla*, and the story of Rabab, the wife of al-Harith al-Kalabi, the great-grandfather of Princess Dhat al-Himma. As for the reference to menstruation, it is forbidden in Islam: "And they ask you about menstruation. Say, 'It is harm, so keep away from wives during menstruation. And do not approach them until they are pure'" (Quran 2:222). There is no reference in the Prophet's narrations that states that whoever has intercourse with his wife while menstruating, their child would be black. However, the Shiite narrations refer to a severe physical consequence – in addition to sinning – awaiting those who violate the Quranic prohibition in this regard. According to those narrations, the newborn comes with deformation or leprosy or albinism.[17] Strangely, most of these narrations are quoted from Imam Ja'far al-Sadiq,[18] who was chosen by the narrator of the biography to judge in the case of Prince Abd al-Wahhab's blackness. But why did the narrator choose "blackness" and not the other outcomes explicated by the Prophet (genetics/heredity) or by al-Sadiq (leprosy, albinism, deformation)? Perhaps using the Prophet's explanation with camels as the example would be incomprehensible to the urban audience of the biography, who were not familiar with camels and nomadic life, let alone that the Prophet's rationalization does not incriminate anyone.

The narrator made a clever choice (blackness) to achieve several goals. First, the issue of blacks and their offspring (Prince Abd al-Wahhab) was presented in a serious and intentional way, perhaps with the aim of dispelling the stereotypical perceptions of blacks stored in the Arab imaginary. Second, an attempt is made to convince urban audiences and to address them with what they are familiar with. Third, it incriminates al-Harith for having intercourse with the princess while she is menstruating, despite the Islamic prohibition of this act, which necessitates punishment (twenty-five lashes).

Sirat Antarah bin Shaddad: The Diversity of Otherness

The *Life of Antarah bin Shaddad* is rich with various Otherness, as diverse as Antarah's wars and movements between various peoples in the east, west, south, and north. Therefore, before identifying the types of Otherness in this biography, I will identify those Others within the course of Antarah's journey, movements, wars, and agreements, from his first war through his death, and to his sons' revenge on Bani Nabhan at the end of the biography.

The Familiar Other and the Strange Other

Antarah was born black, from a Habashi mother owned by Shaddad bin Qurad, one of the nobles of the Bani Abs tribe, who were the first Other to be shocked by Antarah. In their view, he was a despicable slave without an honourable lineage and status. When he managed to wrest and win the lineage and prestige with his sword, another tribal Other appeared in his surroundings, the southern Banu Qahtan. Since the Abs tribe belonged to the Adnanite Arabs of the north, their opposite were the Arabs of the south from the Bani Qahtan; therefore, the first tribal Other for Antarah was the southern Banu Qahtan. Antarah fought his first war against Banu Qahtan, before his father recognized his filiation to him and to the Abs lineage – that is, before he settled the conflict with his personal Other.

After his tribal Other, Antarah faces many tribes where Otherness is determined on a national or a religious basis or both. The most prominent of those Others are the Manazira in Iraq, the Ghassanids in the Levant; the Persians in Persia; the Romans in Constantinople; the Christians in Andalusia, Cyrenaica, Tunisia, Kairouan, Alexandria, Egypt, Nubia, Beja, Sudan, and the Habashis; the Indians and the Jews of Khaybar; and others.

Antarah's personal Other does not disappear with the father's recognition of his sonship and lineage inclusion with the Abs. Throughout the biography, there are those who reproach him with servitude, and with being an illegitimate child with a faulty lineage. This rebuke comes from various people, including Umara bin Ziyad and his brother al-Rabee' bin Ziyad; people of Yemen; the writers of the Mu'allaqat such as Tarafa bin al-Abd, Imru' al-Qays, and Labid; and also the King of the Banu Abs, Qais bin Zuhair.

There are two types of Otherness in this biography. The first is the historical Other, that is, the Other who had a historical presence in the context of Arab consciousness in the pre-Islamic era, which is the historical time of the hero of the biography, Antarah bin Shaddad. The second one is the narrative Other, which does not necessarily have a historical presence at that time but, rather, derives its Otherness from books and notations of late first and second centuries AH in Arab culture. The narrator of this biography draws on numerous narrations and works in literature, news, history, geography, the biography of the Prophet, etc.

Moreover, scholars of the *Biography of Antarah bin Shaddad* often claim that the biography embodies the struggle against racial discrimination in Arab culture. In fact, this is a misplaced exaggeration, because Antarah is torn between his ethnic, colour, and class identities. He is a slave, an Arab, and a black of Abyssinian origin. Thus, the main question is: how does Antarah rid himself of this crisis within these troubled identities? Identities (master/slave) and (Arab/black Abyssinian) cannot be resolved except by either violence or renouncing one of them. Hence, Antarah resolves this crisis by asserting himself as an Arab master only. Faced with rejection as the son of a black bondmaid, he tries to extract his identity recognition with his courage and the power of his sword on one hand, and by approaching an Arab woman and reciting poetry on the other hand. But before he approaches his lover "Abla" and competes with the great poets, he must prove his lineage. Antarah works hard to resolve the dilemma of affiliation for his beloved, who demands that he hang his poem on the walls of the sacred house (al-Kaaba): to do so requires an accurate and honourable lineage. When Antarah decides to prove his Arab heroism by hanging his poem on the Kaaba, he faces the problem of black slave lineage. So, Arabs say: "There is no honour for that poor-natured slave, who is of despicable origin and offspring."[19] As for the authors of the Mu'allaqat, they are unanimously agreed that Antarah meets all conditions of the Arab gallantry in terms of courage, eloquence, and quality in composing and reciting poetry, but their only objection is Antarah's problematic lineage. For example, Tarafa bin al-Abd addresses Antarah:

> Woe to you, O black! What eloquence and chivalry you show! By God, if your mother was an Arab, you would be proud of all Arabs. But the name of slavery is a bad status, and if it were not for that, we would have allowed you to hang the poem.[20]

When these people finally acknowledge Antarah's eloquence and courage, and are satisfied with his poem being hung on the Kaaba, he addresses them: "I want each of you to be an initiator of obedience, and for this Mr. Abdul Muttalib, the masters of Mecca and its leaders, and all Arabs, to bear witness that you have included me in your eloquence, and in your esteem and noble lineage."[21] These are the ambitions that are driving the development of events in the biography: affiliation, woman (beloved), poetry, bravery. Those aspects serve as conditions for completing the requirements of Arab chivalry and heroism.

Furthermore, the biography is full of derogatory references to blacks: they are as big as buffaloes, with wide lips and large noses[22]; they are nude as if they were from the people of Thamud and Aad, with spears and shields in their hands,[23] and tyrants like Pharaohs,[24] with stinky armpits,[25] strange creatures with long legs[26]; and they resemble demons of jinn.[27] In fact, Antarah himself describes blacks as beasts, and the offspring of monkeys.[28] In the Arab imaginary, "black women have no desirable qualities except for the purity of their mouths and the warmth of their vaginas, and their reprehensible qualities are predominantly cracked skin and lips, bad bodies, small vaginas, stinky sweat, and vicious morals."[29] On the other hand, the narrator describes Zabiba (Antarah's mother), the black Abyssinian, as a "beautiful woman who as tender skin, soft curves, good colour and shape, coquettish eyes, charm of the eyelids, attractive physique, beautiful cheeks, large-heartedness, the sweetness of articulation, and the balance of stature."[30]

The most terrifying and racist words in the biography are said by Antarah when he arrives at the country of Sudan: "as if I would not spare anyone from the Sudan, I would kill all their knights, and I would not let anyone rule it except the whites."[31] It is as if Antarah, despite his kinship to Sudan, repeats what Wahriz said and did when he conquered Yemen.

Sirat Seif bin Dhi Yazan: Rally of Prophecies and a Terrifying Lie

Sirat Seif bin Dhi Yazan (Biography of Seif bin Dhi Yazan) is based on the Biblical story of Noah and his three children and the rebirth of humanity after the Flood. It is one of the oldest stories where blacks are criminalized. Between the time of Adam and Noah, people were equal in colour and status, but the situation changed after Noah's curse to make the offspring of Ham slaves and blacks. The reference to Noah's curse is mentioned by Yathrib, the vizier of Dhi Yazan. This vizier found, in the ancient books and great epics, that a king of the Tubba' dynasty will fulfil Noah's prayer/curse. At the hands of this awaited king, "the religion of Islam will prevail, and people will be commanded to worship the All-Knowing King, and all Abyssinians and blacks will be slaves and servants to the children of Shem bin Noah (PBUH)."[32] The story is mentioned again by the wise Saqrdis, the vizier of Seif Arad, King of Abyssinia, when the latter thinks of fighting King Dhi Yazan and Arabs. The vizier advises the king not to fight, fearing Noah's curse would happen to the Abyssinians and the blacks. When Seif Arad asks about the origin of this curse, Saqrdis tells him the Biblical story of Noah's curse.

What is striking in the story above is that Saqrdis does not mention Japheth in the story, while Biblical and Arab narrations mention that Japheth was there when Shem covered Noah's naked body. Some narrations mention that Japheth helped Shem cover their father and was thus included in Shem's bliss; others narrate that Japheth stood up and did not help cover Noah's body, and thus was included in the curse that Japheth's offspring would be the slaves of Shem's children and be the evilest among people.[33] By deleting him from the story, the narrator does not want to involve Japheth in the war between evil (represented by Ham's offspring) and good (represented by Shem's offspring). Noah's curse consists of two parts: blackness and servitude. Since the first one has already happened (the blackness of Abyssinian people), the second part of the curse is going to happen soon. Many characters in the biography tell their prophecies about Noah's curse and the upcoming enslavement of blacks at the hands of Shem's offspring, which create fear and anxiety among the Abyssinians. The narrator wants to mislead us – after deceiving the characters of the biography – that the climax of the plot in this biography is the enforcement of Noah's curse in the descendants of Ham. However, the events of the biography reveal that the prophecy (curse) was nothing more than a scary lie, or a prophecy whose purpose was misinterpreted by the narrator and those prognosticators. At the end of the biography, blacks did not become slaves to Shem's offspring. Seif bin Dhi Yazan did not want to enslave them but to spread Islam among them, and that was what happened at the end of the biography where many of blacks and Abyssinians became Muslims. King Seif gave the blacks two choices: convert from fire and Saturn worship to Islam or face death. Thus, Otherness here is based on religion not on race; the Other is *al-kafir*, the fire worshipper, not the black/Abyssinian.

ONE THOUSAND AND ONE NIGHTS: BLACKS' EXCESSIVE SEXUAL LUST

Negative stereotypes of blacks have permeated the aforementioned biographies, but they reach their peak in *One Thousand and One Nights*. It is perhaps problematic to explore *One Thousand and One Nights* as part of the Arab imaginary and its manifestations since it was circulated across several cultures and transported between the Indians and the Persians until it settled with Arabs. The problem of the authorship and origin of this work is still unresolved. However, what makes this work part of the Arab imaginary is that Arab culture received, embraced, and spread it, as if it agreed with its mood and fulfilled its desires. Also, "the circulation of what is foreign in the midst of an Arab-Islamic cultural structure for such a long period, strips it of its characteristics and gives it new characteristics."[34] The origin of *One Thousand and One Nights* did not remain foreign when it entered Arab culture. It was submerged and redistributed in Arab culture, to the extent that its foreign origin was forgotten, deleted, while some of its tales were rewritten till it became a new work that belongs more to its destiny than its origin.

Before *One Thousand and One Nights*, negative representations of blacks were common in Arab culture, but *One Thousand and One Nights* collected every negative representation that was scattered here and there and put them in one book. So, it is a collection of recurring tales of lustful black slaves (savage cannibals) debauching the women of their masters. They are tales with a similar narrative plot: it begins with seduction, then sexual intercourse between a woman and a black slave, and ends with the punishment of both. Those tales use humour, amusement, or conviviality as a disguise to pass on their derogatory representations of blacks (the external Other) and women (the internal Other).

The woman and the black slave represent the "axis of desire," which combines the woman who desires and seeks sexual gratification, and the desired object, which is here the black slave. The woman tries to fulfill her sexual desire in any way, even fraud, maliciousness, and lying. Each tale is an exploring journey by the woman to find the object of her desire, which is the black slave, and to achieve gratification and to satisfy her flaming sensuality. Often the woman attains her desire, but this desire does not reach an end nor full gratification, but remains an open desire. Thus, the tale continues as a journey in search of unachievable fulfillment, with a desire that often ends with restraint and punishment.

The events of the main framing story revolve around two brother kings, Shahryar and Shahzaman, who rule over separate lands. After living apart for a long time, Shahryar misses Shahzaman and asks to see him. Shahzaman agrees to meet with his brother. While on his way to Shahryar, Shahzaman forgets something he needs and returns to his palace to pick it up. When he enters his bedroom, he finds his wife lying in bed with a black slave. Enraged, Shahzaman kills both with his sword. Upset and sad, he leaves to see his brother. When Shahryar sees his brother in this condition and thinking to comfort him, he asks Shahzaman to accompany him on a hunting trip, but Shahzaman refuses. So Shahryar goes alone, and his brother remains in the palace. One day, Shahzaman sees twenty maidservants and twenty slaves leaving the palace, and his brother's wife (the Queen) walking among them. When they arrive at the orchard fountain, they take off their clothes, and then the Queen calls for a black slave named Masoud. He comes and embraces her, then they have sexual intercourse, and so do the rest of the slaves and concubines. Upon seeing that, Shahzaman is relieved from his agony. When his brother comes back, Shahzaman tells him about his wife and the black slave, and also about what he saw at his brother's palace. After seeing the scene again, the brothers lament their misfortunes and decide to leave the palace.

On their quest to find someone whose misfortune is greater than theirs, they stop to rest near a tree by the sea. Suddenly, the sea rages and a black post comes out of the sea. Scared, the kings climb up the tree, watching what is going to happen. A tall and wide jinni carries a glass chest over his head. The jinni sits next to the tree and opens the chest, and a beautiful woman comes out. She had been kidnapped by the jinni on her wedding day. When the jinni falls asleep, she has intercourse with both kings. After sleeping with the brothers, she asks for their rings to add to her collection of 570 rings, the total of those whom she has slept with since being trapped in the jinni's chest. The two kings realize their hopelessness in the face of women's plots and tricks, and that when a woman wants something, nothing can stop her, neither a jinni nor a king. They return to their kingdoms. Shahryar orders his queen killed along with the maidservants and slaves. Then he starts to take a new bride every day, deflower her, and then kill her the next day. He continues doing this for three years until no virgin women are left except for his vizier's daughter, Shahrazad. Shahrazad and her younger sister, Dinarzad, devise a scheme whereby Dinarzad will be called to the palace on the day of the wedding, and will request her sister to recount a tale before dawn. Their strategy works. Following the marriage's completion, Shahryar permits Dinarzad to pay Shahrazad a visit. Dinarzad then requests that she tell the king a story to pass the time. With the king's approval, Shahrazad starts a story but purposefully ends it before dawn. Shahryar chooses to hold off on killing his bride in order to see how the story turns out. Shahrazad tells the stories over the course of many nights, starting a new one as soon as the previous one is finished, and always stopping before dawn to add an extra day to her life. After a thousand and one nights of this, Shahrazad informs Shahryar that she has given birth to three of his children, demonstrating her unwavering loyalty. Shahryar, who has grown to love and trust Shahrazad, spares her life at her request, and keeps her as his consort and queen.[35]

The tale emphasizes the hypersexuality of both blacks and women. Women are characterized by malice and deceit, used to satisfy their unbridled sexual desire, as in the woman in the jinni's box. She was kidnapped by the jinni on her wedding night, put in a box within a chest, locked with seven locks, and thrown into the bottom of the sea; yet she managed to deceive the jinni and sleep with 572 men. The woman's unquenchable sexual desire and her malice and treachery are the focus in these tales. Therefore, Shahryar decides to kill every woman he marries, but not every black slave. Nevertheless, the killing of excessively sensual black slaves could be carried out symbolically, through castration or the amputation of the penis. If a woman's disgrace is purified by killing her, then a black slave's defilement is purified by killing him or by castration and cutting his penis, that is, by removing the causes of impurity, as in the story of the three eunuch slaves in "Ghanim bin Ayyub" tale. Adultery is initiated sometimes by the slave but usually by the woman. The tale ends with the killing of the woman and the slave, or the killing of the woman and the castration of the slave.

In the tale of "Ghanim bin Ayyub," three slaves are castrated. The first slave is castrated because he has sex with his master's daughter. The second slave does not have sex with any woman. He is a liar, who lies to his master telling him that his wife and children died, and then telling his master's wife that her husband died. Because of his lie, his master gets paraplegia, so he castrates him and then sells him. When he wakes up after castration, his master tells him: "Just because you've burned my heart for the dearest thing I have, I burned your heart for the dearest thing you have."[36] The third slave represents excessive and unlimited sexual power, which cannot be restrained or tamed. He is a slave who has been castrated but, by his own admission, deserved more than that because he had sexual intercourse with both his lady and her son together.[37]

In such tales, sex is depicted as the dearest wish of the black slave, and thus the penis is the dearest thing to his heart. Hence sensuality is one of his essential characteristics, without which he ceases to exist, just like women. The excessive sensuality of women in *A Thousand and One Nights* is based on a common idea in the Arab imaginary, that of the insatiable urge for sex:

> "Amir al-Mu'minin, 'Alayhi al-Salam, has said, 'Allah created desire of ten parts, of which nine parts are placed in women and only one part in men. If He did not place shyness in women of a similar (nine out of ten) amount in women like desire, nine women would attach themselves to one man.'" ... "Abu 'Abd Allah, 'Alayhi al-Salam, has said, 'Allah has placed in women a degree of patience which is ten times greater than the patience of men. If excited she has a force of desire which is equal to ten men.'"[38]

The conclusion is that "the lust of women is stronger than the lust of men," as the narrator in *One Thousand and One Nights* says.[39] This strong desire is not satisfied by ordinary "white" men like Shahzaman or Shahryar. It is satisfied by the black slave with his extraordinary bestial desire: those blacks have bigger penises, fast and lasting erections.[40] The sex between the queen or master's wife and the black slave reverses the societal roles between the two: the black slave becomes the master, and the queen, who grovels to him submissively, becomes his slave. The common characteristic of both the woman and the black slave is excessive lust and bestiality.[41] The black slave, when he becomes the lover and the master of the lady, insults the dignity of the real master, and thus threatens the sovereign and patriarchal norms of society. Therefore, it is necessary to separate the world of women and the world of black slaves, because any meeting between these two worlds may undermine the system.

4

Representation of Blacks in Poetry

Most cultures practice different means of excluding and dominating the Other through what Althusser calls the "repressive state apparatus" and "ideological state apparatus," or through what Pierre Bourdieu calls "symbolic" power. Arab culture has used both means in dealing with the Other black or zinji. The enslavement of blacks was not without physical violence such as beating and whipping, which were used extensively with black slaves. However, there is another type of violence that the Arab culture practised on the black Other, which is ideological/symbolic violence, by invoking the black in poetry as an element of the poetic metaphor, or as a subject of direct and explicit satire.

The direct poetic violence, through satire and outright contempt, was marked by intensity and the refusal to accept the black Other. Rather, it was one of the most powerful tools for excluding and humiliating them. There are those who argue that it was this kind of poetry that successively bequeathed this hostility and violence to other forms of expression.[1] Such violence and hostility will be discussed when examining the position of Ibn al-Rumi and al-Mutanabbi on al-Zanj. As for the indirect poetic violence, it appears in transforming blacks into a poetic subject evoked by analogies and similes, like camels, cows, zebras, tusks, wine, orchards, deserts, and other topics. In this way, the Arab poetic discourse tries to annihilate, subjugate, and dominate the black Other. The black is subject to contempt, mockery, and ridicule. The black is also invoked in comparison to animals, plants, planets, etc. For example, Abu Nawas compares aged wine to a daughter of nappy-hair man, whereas Di'bil al-Khuza'i describes a bunch of dense grapevines as a zinji's hair. Also, Abu al-'Ala al-Ma'arri compares his sins to the zinji and Nubia phalanxes, and Ibn al-Mu'taz describes the darkness of the night as "Habashi."[2]

In Classical and Medieval Arabic poetry, there is a gendered difference between representations of a black man or a black human, and representations of a black woman. The black man is a topic for expulsion, exclusion, contempt, satire, and humiliation, while the black woman is a topic for sexual objectification. Black women in poetry are the object of men's lust and desire because of their "unique" beauty, powerful lust, hot vaginas, and pure mouths. Thus, "the zinji woman, with her desirable sexual qualities, regains the lost value of the zinji man. In the battle between abstract cultural and religious values and repressed desired fantasies, desire prevails."[3] Here are a few examples of the representation of black women:

1. Al-Farazdaq: Perhaps, some beautiful tender zinji girls ... carry an oven[4] of blazing fire.[5]
2. Ibn al-Rumi:
   A black woman, intact of the blondes' freckles, sunspots, and vitiligo
   And having no rigid hands nor cracked lips, nor stinky sweat
   Rather, from the soft daughters of kings,
   Entice even those with dead lust.[6]
3. Love of black women is from the pleasure of living, the life of the heart.[7]
4. If you go mad about her, it is not heresy that the origin of madness is her blackness.[8]
5. O Lord, a black woman enchanted me, love gets better with her like the night, where sinning becomes easy, and the forbidden becomes sweet.[9]
6. I love her so much that I love all blacks and even black dogs.[10]

Literary texts are full of such tales and poems by well-known poets who flirt with their black female slaves, such as al-Farazdaq, Bashar, Ibn al-Rumi, Ali Bin al-Jahm, al-Sharif al-Radi, al-Sabi, al-Abbas Bin al-Ahnaf, Ibn Sukkara, Ibn Khafajah, Ibn Rashiq, Abu Ali al-Basir, Ibn al-Khayat, Ibn al-Wardi, Abu Hayyan al-Andalusi, Abi al-Shis, and others. The strange thing is that some of those poets satirize blacks yet fall in love and flirt with black women. For example, al-Farazdaq was in love with his black maidservant, yet this love did not stop him from attacking blacks in his poetry. When al-Farazdaq was defeated in a poetry competition by Nussaib bin Rabah (a black poet) in the presence of Suleiman bin Abdul-Malik who applauded Nussaib and gave him a prize, al-Farazdaq left saying: "The best poetry is of the honourable men, and the worst poetry is by the slaves."[11]

Another example is Bashar bin Burd, who flirts with a black woman saying: "And a black ghada[12] as bright as water, in sweetness and softness, as if it was created, for those lucky, from amber mixed with musk."[13] Then, the same poet describes blacks thusly:

> If the zinji's stomach is full, he insults his god
> And against me, he arouses al-Zanj and Nubians
> He steals whatever comes in his way,
> He is too tarub,[14] do you know a non-tarub zinji?![15]

Whether Arab poets praise the black woman's beauty or denigrate the black man's ugliness, both (black man and woman) are nothing more than an object of domination and subjugation. Al-Farazdaq, Bashar, Ibn al-Rumi, and others are not contradicting themselves when they blame/satirize the black man and approve the black woman. Both (black man and woman) represent objects of blame from a moral perspective; from an intellectual perspective, blacks' culture is preposterous and invalid; and in terms of taste, their colour is ugly and hideous. However, looking at blacks pragmatically, in terms of benefiting from them, makes them desirable and attractive topics. It is this utilitarian interest that has created competition between the masters over the possession of slaves and made them inspect slaves like animals or objects. It is the same reason/interest for owning a black woman: service benefit (maid-servant) and pleasure (sexual) benefit (concubinage).

Arab culture was able to create and maintain its own representations of blacks while suppressing the voice of blacks, robbing them of the available representation tools and depriving them of the most effective one: writing. It is not an accident that freedom is a condition of the official writer in this culture. According to al-Qalqashandi, the required qualities of a writer are ten, the third of which is freedom. In this way the discourse of the dominant culture monopolized the right of official representation of Others and protected its culture from being the object of any other representation. However, writing is not the only representational tool. Speech is as effective as writing in the Medieval Arab society. If it is easy to control writing as the official means of representation, it is difficult to do the same with speech, which is available to everyone who can speak and articulate. Writing is not available to everyone since it requires such materials as tools, stationery, and pens, and also requires scribes who help with publication and distribution. On other hand, speech, unlike writing, is an inexpensive effort and does not require materials or scribes. Hence, some blacks were able to transcend their harsh conditions through their talent of eloquence and poetry. Among them are Antarah bin Shaddad, al-Sulayk bin Salaka, Khufaf bin Nudbah, Suhaim Abd Bani al-Hashas, Nussaib bin Rabah, Abu Dulamah, al-Hayqutan, 'Ukaim al-Habashi, and Sunaih bin Rabah. Those poets tried to create a new image of blacks, different from that formed by the Arab imaginary.

IMAGINARY SHOCK AND MEMORY PROVOCATION

Hegemonic cultures often produce derogatory representations of dominated cultures in order to protect and maintain existing power relations. However, conflicts in the real world may undermine power relations, and reverse the roles between the dominant and the dominated, as in the case of al-Mutanabbi with Abu al-Misk Kafur. This undermining could be shocking when characterized by surprise and an explosion of the oppressed, as in "Thawra al-Zanj" (the Zanj Revolution). Such destabilizations of existing power relations take two different conflict forms: (1) individual – between the black Nubian Kafur and al-Mutanabbi, the Arab fahl poet; (2) collective – between the Zanj and black slaves, on the one hand, and the Abbasids' authority and society, on the other. The defence mechanism used in both forms was mainly based on stimulating the Arab memory regarding the perception of blacks historically, religiously, and culturally. This mechanism was used as part of a mobilization process aimed at provoking the Arab imaginary against blacks to quell their revolution, and also to topple Kafur at the hands of Egyptian people.

The Zanj Revolution shocked the collective Arab imaginary and rendered the event intolerable. How could those blacks feel entitled to revolt?! Who gave them the right to ask for their own human rights?! How dare they deviate and disobey their masters?! How could one accept the role reversal where the slave becomes a master, and the master becomes a slave?! Ibn al-Rumi – representing the collective Arab imaginary – not only rejected but also was unable to comprehend a situation in which the Zanj were the masters while Arab women were slaves sold in the slave market. It was the same reason that caused al-Mutanabbi's shock, resentment, and anger when he entered Egypt to see Kafur (a black slave) as ruler and commander, who was obeyed and prayed for in the Hijaz, the Egyptian lands, and the Levant.

Ibn al-Rumi and al-Mutanabbi are influential Arab poets whose weapon of poetry was used to galvanize Arabs to fight the Zanj and to kill Kafur. Both poets were aware that this weapon would not be as sharp as a sword unless attached to pejorative images of blacks in the Arab collective imaginary. Thus, al-Mutanabbi invoked those images and attributed them to Kafur. Similarly, the historical and poetic Arab discourse of the "Zanj Revolution" conjured up all those negative images too. Ibn al-Rumi's famous poem comes at the forefront of this poetic discourse. It was recited after the destruction of Basra in 257 AH, expressing the official political position on the Zanj Revolution. It tried to conceal the political and social dimensions of the conflict, and instead highlighted it as if it were a religious and ethnic conflict. Hence, the rebellious blacks were depicted as cursed infidels, malicious traitors, and violators of Islam's sacred principles and prohibitions. This representation was used to mobilize and legitimize a holy war in the name of Islam between the soldiers of Arab masters and Ham's slave soldiers.

Ibn al-Rumi and the Rhetoric of Incitement to Racism

Abu al-Hasan Ali bin al-Abbas, known as Ibn al-Rumi (836–896 CE), was not different from other Arab poets of that era, since poetry was a means to make a living and to get closer to caliphs, governors, and dignitaries. Like his fellow poets, Ibn al-Rumi threw himself at the feet of dignitaries and notables, asking them for aid and favours.[16] If Ibn al-Rumi was unsuccessful in connecting with the caliphs directly, like al-Buhturi for instance, he succeeded in connecting with the senior officials of the Abbasid state, including ministers, judges, and prestigious and influential writers. Hence, his poetry supported the state and its official discourse in times of prosperity and distress. The state needs a discourse that defends it, proves its legitimacy, and justifies its transgressions. However, the need for this discourse intensifies in times of distress and crisis, especially when the authority faces a serious revolutionary threat such as the Zanj Revolution, which lasted fifteen years. Historians mention that it was a disaster and a catastrophe in the nation. People in Basra, Wasit, Ahwaz, and al-Abila were displaced;

life stopped in most of the neighbouring Iraqi cities; and the Caliph was perplexed. The country was devastated, and so many people died that historians were unsure about "the number of the dead among the sultan's companions and other men, women and youths who were killed by the sword, burning, drowning and starvation."[17]

The revolution was led by a man called Ali bin Muhammad, who claimed lineage to Ali bin Abi Talib (the Prophet's son-in-law and cousin). He was "a virtuous, eloquent, articulate, and intelligent man, who won over the hearts of slaves from the Zanj in Basra and its surroundings; so many people gathered around him, so he became stronger and greater."[18] After ten years of war, Ali bin Muhammad was defeated by the Abbasid army in 270 AH. He was beheaded and his head was carried to Baghdad.

The violence committed by both the state and the revolution was reciprocal. However, the revolution began and ended with killing and destruction. Still, the state's violent discourse (writings, narrations, history, and poetry) exceeded the violence in the war field. The rhetoric of the state discourse propagated and emphasized the corruption of the revolution. Among the most famous authors who lived during the revolution were al-Tabari and al-Ya'qubi (history) and al-Buhturi and Ibn al-Rumi (poetry). They were writing for the state as part of its ideological apparatus. Ibn al-Rumi was one of the Diwan scribes, and al-Buhturi was closely connected to the Abbasid caliphs, known for praising them, their ministers, writers, and judges. As for al-Yaqubi, he held high positions such as the ruler of Armenia, Azerbaijan, and Egypt. Regarding al-Tabari, the minister al-Khaqani wanted to make him a judge.

The Abbasid regime did not have a problem with al-Buhturi or al-Yaqubi or Ibn al-Rumi who fell under its control and worked within its apparatus; rather, the problem was with writers who worked outside its control and grip, especially outlawed writers such as Muhammad bin al-Hassan bin Sahl. Unlike his uncle al-Fadl bin Sahl, Muhammad was against the Caliph al-Mu'tadhid, whom he plotted to kill, but he and his followers were captured. Al-Mu'tadhid released all of them except for Muhammad, who was burnt and "baked like a chicken," mutilated, then crucified.[19] So, the first book about the Zanj Revolution and its writer were eliminated. We may ask: was he killed because of his rebellion against the Caliph or because of his writings? Historians prefer the first reason, but an examination of this man's writings and his life circumstances leads to the belief that the second reason may also have a chance of validity. This man wrote a book entitled *Kitab Akhbar Sahib al-Zanj wa Waqa'i'hi* (Book of accounts of the lord of the Zanj and his battles) and *Kitab Rasayilihi* (The book of his letters). He witnessed and experienced the revolt, and as Ibn Nadeem states, he was with Sahib al-Zanj. He was the first author to write about the revolt; thus, his is considered the founding book of the revolt, and those who came after him relied on his book. This was the case with al-Tabari, who quoted from his book occasionally. Hence, the only solution for the Abbasid regime was to annihilate the book and burn its author, and to present the texts of al-Tabari, al-Ya'qubi, Ibn al-Rumi, al-Buhturi, and Ibn al-Mu'taz as the founding texts, whose example and approach should be followed by those coming after.

In a world governed by power relations, there is no innocent or neutral discourse. Every discourse has a purpose, and as the discourse itself is part of power relations, there comes a struggle to monopolize and supervise it by the people in power. In *The Archeology of Knowledge*, Foucault indicates that "the production of discourse is at once controlled, selected, organized, and redistributed according to a certain number of procedures, whose role is to avert its powers and its dangers, to cope with chance events, to evade its ponderous, awesome materiality."[20] Hence, Muhammad ibn al-Hassan's books were discarded, because he deviated from the terms of discourse-production and violated the rules imposed by the authority. The authority has several means of rejecting the discourse of the opposing Other; exterminating the book and burning its author is only one means. I will explain these means as they were manifested in Ibn al-Rumi's inflammatory text, which later infiltrated the historians' discourse.

Historians mention two decisive times regarding the revolt. The first, in 257 AH, was the year in which Basra was destroyed, and this incident was called "Fitna al-Zanj" (al-Zanj insurrection). The second decisive moment was in 270 AH, when al-Zanj were defeated, killed, and exterminated, their leader killed, and the whole revolution crushed. Both moments witnessed horrendous events, brutal killing, and the complete destruction of both cities, Basra and al-Mukhtara – the fortified city built by Ali bin Muhammad. However, the discourse of the authority prohibited talking or writing about the events of the second moment, which witnessed the killings in, and destruction of, al-Mukhtara. On the other hand, the authority incited its various apparatuses to exaggerate the destruction of Basra in the first moment, to the extent that al-Tabari dedicated more than two hundred pages of the Tarikh al-Rusul wa al-Muluk (Annals of the prophets and kings), to this event. That is why many poems and narrations were written describing the details of the first moment, the killings and destruction of Basra. However, silence prevailed about the second moment, when al-Muwaffaq's army was killing, annihilating, destroying markets, looting houses, and burning and drowning their owners. The strange thing is that none of the previous historians endorsed this revolution, nor did they refer to its humanitarian goals for social justice and liberation. Rather, most of them deliberately distorted the essence of the revolution as a political struggle (between the ruler and the ruled) or a social struggle (between masters and slaves), a religious conflict between Muslims and anti-Muslim outlaws, or a racial conflict between Arabs and Zanj. The caliphate of Banu Umayyad and Banu al-Abbas faced many revolutions and rebellions, but the discourse of power and culture together singled out the Zanj Revolution with a curse. Just as the reaction of the political authority was violent, the reaction of Arab culture was no less violent and cruel towards the Zanj Revolution.

Just as the rhetoric of the authority's discourse overstated the devastation in Basra, ignored the destruction of Mukhtara, and depicted the conflict as a religious or racial one, it utilized an "appellation" strategy in its propaganda with the aim of achieving symbolic or imagined victory over the rebels. Before the destruction of Basra, the authority's discourse portrayed Ali bin Muhammad as a rebellious revolutionary and called him "Sahib al-Zanj" (Lord of the Zanj). The defamation and disparagement in this appellation lies in associating this rebel with the Zanj who are pejoratively represented by the Arab imaginary. Most historians who chronicle the revolution refer to Muhammad first as Sahib al-Zanj, but when they reach the incident of the destruction of Basra, this label is replaced with a torrent of satanic labels such as the damned, the ugly, the immoral, the debauched, the traitor, the malicious head of al-Zanj, the tyrant of al-Zanj, the impostor of Basra, the seceder, the pretender, the liar ... etc.[21] On the other hand, after eliminating the revolution and destroying Sahib al-Zanj, al-Muwaffaq was called "al-Nasir Lidin Allah" (defender of God's religion).

As for Ibn al-Rumi, although he grew up in Baghdad and never visited Basra, his poem on the destruction of Basra is filled with anger and heartbreak, and it contains many references to minute details about the incident. Where did he get this knowledge of what happened in Basra? What is the reason behind his anger in the poem? Perhaps he wrote it under the circumstances of that moment when the authority was facing a real threat, and the people were grieving for what happened in Basra. Circumstances like those made al-Rumi address the people with comforting, consoling, and inciting words, while supporting the authority and calling for solidarity. This can only be done by using the maximum capabilities of figurative and rhetorical language to provoke and mobilize people.

The first part of the poem consciously incorporates the self into the scene of the devastation that befell Basra. The second part tries to bring the readers into the same scene to witness the destruction, and the third part incites revenge against the Zanj for what they did to Basra and its people. The poet opens his poem by expressing his own sadness for the horrible incidents that happened in Basra, which deprived him of the "delightful sleep" and filled him with "raging tears," declaring: "What sleep after the Zanj openly violated the prohibitions of Islam?" They entered Basra like the darkness of the night. Then the poet indulges the reader with horrific images of massacres, killings, rape, pillaging, destruction, and vandalism committed by the Zanj in Basra. This is to establish the argument against those who knew what happened there and did nothing, and thus would be accused of negligence and failure to help the people of Basra, which is, according to the poet, "the dome of Islam." The poet paves the way to the most important part where he incites the readers to revenge against al-Zanj ("Ham's family").

First, al-Rumi addresses the people through God's voice: "O My servants: Were you not angry for Allah's sake, Lord of Glory and Honour? Have you forsaken and shunned your brothers, woe unto you wicked people?"[22] Then he addresses them through the Prophet's voice: "My nation, where were you when a free noble woman called my name, She cried out: O Muhammadah! Would my righteous people help her?!"[23] Next, the poet calls the people to revenge against al-Zanj: "Go forth, dear ones, light and heavy, to those wicked slaves!"[24] The poet urges jihad and states that whoever does not fight will be banned from the eternal paradise that has been prepared for the believers who defend God and His religion. Perhaps the most dangerous of these images is when al-Rumi portrays revenge as a holy war and a legitimate duty on Muslims, portraying the revolutionaries as cursed tyrant slaves, traitors, apostates, and violators of God's prohibitions, while identifying Basra and its people with "God's honour" or "God's people," "His sanctities," "the nation of the Messenger," "the noblest nation," and "The Dome of Islam." These judgments are based on assumptions rooted in the poet's imagination and the imagination of the cultural group to which he belongs, and for which he writes. Al-Zanj are cursed, renegades, and naturally disposed to immorality and transgressing the sanctities of God and His Messenger. They are originally slaves owned by their masters, and they were destined to be so. Therefore, it is against the cultural and social norms to reverse the roles between masters and slaves, which is shocking and painful for the poet and his people.

Al-Kafuriyyat and the Arab Imaginary

If Ibn al-Rumi's poem is one of "'uyun al-Shi'r al-Arabi" (the best of Arabic poetry), then all of al-Mutanabbi's poetry is of 'uyun al-Shi'r al-Arabi. Al-Mutanabbi was the most famous Arabic poet of his time, and perhaps of all time. This poet, more than any other, played a prominent role in shaping the Arab imaginary by adding so many derogatory images of blacks that it became difficult to distinguish between what is his and what is others'. When satirizing Kafur, al-Mutanabbi brings up the huge stock of negative images that the Arab imaginary formed about blacks, but when praising Kafur, the poet turns the connotations of those images from negative to positive, to show Kafur in a unique light that transcends his own people.

When we speak of the relationship between the poetic text and the imaginary, we are speaking about an intertextual relationship between "two kinds of texts: literary on the one side, and cultural on the other."[25] The literary text (poetry) adds to the imaginary, and it acquires its signification from the imaginary, thus "the intertextuality of literary discourse is a sign not only of the necessary historicity of literature but, more importantly, of its fundamental entanglement with all discourses."[26] The intertextuality between the poetic text and the imaginary is based either on conformity, where the text matches the imaginary in its connotations and derives its images from it, or on deviation, where the text inverts the familiar connotations in the imaginary in order to invent new ones that contradict or transcend those of the imaginary. There is no one in Arabic literature who masters this aptitude as effectively as al-Mutanabbi who, in *al-Kafuriyyat* (Poems on Kafur), utilizes it to praise then satirize Kafur. When he satirizes Kafur, he conforms with the perceptions of blacks in the Arab imaginary, but when praising Kafur, he deviates from the Arab imaginary.

Kafur was the ruler of Egypt, the Levant, and the Hijaz, and also a black eunuch. Hence, when al-Mutanabbi praises him, he focuses on his uniqueness among kings in that he became a ruler, despite being a black eunuch. However, when he satirizes him, he evokes his servitude, blackness, ugliness, and all the derogatory stereotypes that the Arab imaginary has about blacks. Ibn Rashiq (390–465 AH), Arab poet and literary critic, states that poetry is of three types: praise, satire, and poetry that is neither praise nor satire, but a position between the two types.[27] The truth is that al-Mutanabbi's *Kafuriyyat* conforms to all three types. Al-Mutanabbi praises Kafur saying, "you are an honourable master," but when satirizing him, he says, "you are a despicable black slave." In the third type of poetry, al-Mutanabbi only negates Kafur's slavery and its derogatory attributes, for example, by emphasizing his nickname "abu al-Misk" (father of musk) to remove from Kafur the stereotype of blacks' offensive smell. As for his blackness, al-Mutanabbi creates many pictures to detach him from the ugliness and darkness of his blackness, for example, describing him as "a shining black sun."

Al-Mutanabbi was unwilling to communicate with Kafur, let alone praise him for being a black slave. When Kafur invited him to visit Egypt, he first refused then said, "I won't visit the slave, and if I enter Egypt, my intention is to visit his master."[28] If this is true, then al-Mutanabbi used to despise Kafur for his slavery and blackness, and when he praised him, it was dishonesty and hypocrisy. But who says that a panegyric poem must be honest and truthful? Was it not al-Mutanabbi who defined praise when he said, "Praise of people is truthful and false?" Even if the praise is false and motivated by lies and hypocrisy, it must be convincing in order to obtain its benefit and perform its assigned function. Hence, al-Mutanabbi praises Kafur in the first meeting. The mastery of praising a black ruler like Kafur could only be achieved by portraying him in the image of a ruler who surpasses other white rulers and masters. Therefore, al-Mutanabbi's panegyric *Kafuriyyat* (poems praising Kafur) is based on a comparison (between Kafur and white rulers/masters) and a preference for Kafur over those rulers and masters. In the first panegyric, al-Mutanabbi praises and raises Kafur above other rulers and masters, including Saif al-Daula, who is "treacherous" and "unfaithful":

I loved you, my heart, before you loved him, who is now distant[29];
He has been treacherous, so you be faithful.

The poet differentiates between Kafur (the sea) and Saif al-Daula (streamlet):

> Seeking Kafur, forsaking all others,
> For he who seeks the sea despises streamlets.[30]

Or through a comparison between the benefactors (Saif al-Daula) and those who are more benevolent than them (Kafur):

> On the steeds we abandon other benefactors and head
> For him whose benefits we see bestowed upon them[31]

The poet portrays Kafur (the black patron) as the one and only who has surpassed Saif al-Daula (the white patron) and all people:

> They have brought us to the pupil of the eye of his age
> And have left behind the whites and corners of the eye[32]

Al-Mutanabbi makes Kafur "the pupil of the eye of his age" and other people are white and "unnecessary, for the sight is in the blackness of the eye, and its surroundings have no meaning."[33] Ibn al-Shajari and al-Tha'alibi go on to say that "no black man has been better praised than in this" poetic line.[34] The poet goes on praising Kafur:

> His noble deeds rank high above the matronly;
> He performs no deeds but virgin ones.
> He destroys his coveters' enmity with kindness,
> And if their enmity is not destroyed, he destroys them.[35]

Both praise and satire are equal in the *Kafuriyyat*; what al-Mutanabbi affirms for Kafur, he takes away when satirizing him. So, "Father of Musk" and "Father of all fragrances" becomes "Father of stench"; the "noble man" or the "king" becomes a "black slave"; "Kafur" becomes "Kuwaifir"[36]; "Fahl" becomes "eunuch"; the "lion" becomes a "dog" or a "pig"; the generous becomes "stingy"; etc. And who knows, as Taha Hussein says, "perhaps if al-Mutanabbi had time for Kafur and had an organized life, he would have satirized him as much as he had praised him, and he would have reversed every panegyric poem with a satirical one, similar to it in weight and rhyme."[37] And he did that in some of the *Kafuriyyat*. After al-Mutanabbi had recited his first panegyric poem, Kafur smiled, got up and put on sandals. Al-Mutanabbi saw cracks in Kafur's feet, so he wrote his second *Kafuriyyat* poem, contradicting his first poem. Satire derives its strength in this poem – as in other satirical *Kafuriyyat* – from the intertextuality with the Arab imaginary and its stereotypical images of the black slave, which becomes the origin of Kafur's evils and his moral and physical defects. He describes Kafur as "dishonest, treacherous, mean, cowardly, and disgraceful."[38] While the panegyric *Kafuriyyat* poems are based on deviating from the collective Arab imaginary by portraying Kafur in the image of the noble master, in contrast to the negative images of blacks established in the Arab imaginary, the satirical *Kafuriyyat* poems are based on conformity with the Arab imaginary so that Kafur is nothing but a despicable black slave. In al-Mutanabbi's satirical poems (*al-Hija'iyat*), Kafur is depicted as a vile slave, liar, hypocrite, fool, mean, miser, pig, dog, rhinoceros, crow, and an animal with offensively smelling soul and body. The power of the imaginary reaches its climax in the last satirical poems after al-Mutanabbi has left Egypt in 350 AH, or when he resolves to flee from it. In those poems, there is a clear focus on the physically repulsive qualities of Kafur and of blacks in general, and they are the same ones mentioned by al-Masudi, al-Qazwini, and Shams al-Din al-Dimashqi prior to and after al-Mutanabbi's poetry:

> I never thought I'd live to see the day
> I'd be ill-treated by a slave and he'd be praised!
> Nor I did imagine that all mankind
> Would be lost (to me), and one like Abu'l-Baida[39] would be found!
> Nor that this puncture-lipped black slave
> Would be obeyed by these cowering lackeys!
> Who ever taught the black castrate a noble deed?
> His noble kin? His regal forebears?[40]

Satirizing Kafur's feet, al-Muanabbi says:

> Your feet in shoes evoke my admiration since I see you wearing shoes
> When [in fact] you go barefooted.
> You know not, in your ignorance, whether your colour is black or
> Whether it has turned pure white.
> The stitches in your heel remind me of the cracks that once were
> There and of your walking naked in a robe of oil.[41]

As for his offensive smell, al-Mutanabbi writes:

> The morality of a slave does not go beyond his stinking crotch or
> Or his molars.[42]
> Father of Stench, how often, did you shackle me with [false]
> Promises for fear of my heart-gripping verse![43]

Al-Mutanabbi blames Kafur in a way that goes against what has been established in the Arab imaginary, since he removes from Kafur the Fuhula and the excessive sexual prowess and unrestrainable lust associated with blacks:

> If only because white stallions are incapable of kindness.
> [This being so] what chance have eunuch niggers got?[44]

For al-Mutanabbi, Kafur is a black slave, but because of his despicableness and the distortion of his character, he is lower than even black slaves, for they surpass him in their masculinity, which he lacks by being a eunuch or androgyne:

> Of every loose sphinctered fat-flanked eunuch,
> Counted neither among men nor among women
> The eunuch there is now the runaways' imam,
> Till the freeman is enslaved, the slave revered.[45]

The paradox between the black and the eunuch evokes ridicule and mockery, but the paradox between the black slave and the ruler evokes anger and rage, especially for a poet like al-Mutanabbi, who says "the status of people is by their kings, so it doesn't work that Arabs are ruled by non-Arab kings" – so how about Arabs that are ruled by a non-Arab, black, and eunuch king at the same time?! It is an intolerable and incomprehensible paradox for al-Mutanabbi and his Arab culture. This is an abnormal and wrong situation, and therefore it is necessary to correct it by killing this black eunuch slave. The presence of this black slave at the helm of power provokes ridicule from his subjects and his soldiers, and renders their dignity and their "white" Fuhula questionable. How could the Arab masters and white stallions be ruled by this black eunuch slave?!

Those whom your hands control overstepped [the bounds of] their
[true] worth, and so, through you they were made to realize that
A dog is over them.
Nothing is more hideous than [the sight of] a stallion with a
Penis led by a slave-woman without a womb.
The leaders of every kind of race are from among themselves, but
The leaders of the Muslims are vile slaves.
Is it the ultimate goal of religion that you should shave off your
Moustaches, O community whose ignorance has become
   the laughingstock
Of all nations?
Is there no gallant lad who will plunge the Indian blade into his
Head in order that the doubts and misgivings of people may disappear?
For he is a proof whereby materialist, agnostic, and atheist alike
Torment men's hearts.[46]

Medieval Arabic poetry had no greater poet than al-Mutanabbi. His unique ability to represent blacks in an exemplary manner is incomparable to any other poet in the history of Arabic literature, even Bashar bin Burd or al-Farazdaq. Al-Mutanabbi's poetry on Kafur expresses the unbridled desire to completely eliminate and dominate the black Other. We are facing an "Arabist" and "nationalist" poet whose chauvinism, enmity, and rejection of the Other makes him indulge excessively in his subjectivity, his tyrannical ego, and his contempt for the Other.[47] According to al-Mutanabbi, ownership is only for honourable people, i.e., "white" Arabs. If slaves become slavers, the human condition will be inverted and thus disrupted. For him, the slave should be enslaved and the free should be revered. If these roles are reversed, a divine punishment befalls all of humanity!

If al-Mutanabbi regretted praising Kafur and thus atoned for his guilt by writing *Hija'iyyat* (Satirical poems on Kafur), his commentators (e.g., Ibn Jinni, al-Wahidii, and Ibn Husam) regretted the dissemination and publication of those panegyric poems and thus tried, through satirical commentaries and explanations, to turn the praise into satire, and the sincerity in those poems into humour and mockery. They questioned the sincerity and seriousness of this praise, and then asserted that it was a veiled satire.

Al-Mutanabbi himself admitted his insincerity towards Kafur:

> Many a poem I have written in praise of that rhinoceros,
> Fluctuating between poetry and incantation.
> That was not a eulogy to him, but rather a satire on mankind.
> And I began by praising him and thought it a pastime to say to
> The miserable fool, "O man of discernment."[48]

Ibn Jinni explains al-Mutanabbi's panegyric poems on Kafur as satirical poems, while highlighting the veiled satire: "This is his practice in most of his poetry because he inlays panegyrics with satire, owing to his skill in the art of poetry and his shrewdness and cunning in speech."[49] For example, when al-Mutanabbi addresses Kafur:

> My joy when I saw you was by no means a novelty; I had always hoped
> To see you and be filled with joy![50]

Commentators indicate that the verse above is like ridiculing Kafur, as if al-Mutanabbi says:

> I enjoyed seeing you like a human enjoying seeing a monkey
> that pleases him and makes him laugh. Ibn Jinni said: when I read
> this verse to Abi al-Tayyib [al-Mutanabbi], I said to him: "What,
> have you made a monkey of the man?" So he [al-Mutanabbi]
> laughed at that [remark].[51]

As for Ibn Husam, he postulates that al-Mutanabbi's panegyric poems work through ambiguity, concealment, and mystification, and by showing one thing and hiding another. For example, in interpreting the following,

> O lion in whose body lies the noble spirit of a lion! Yet how many
> Lions are there whose spirits are [as base as] dogs?[52]

Ibn Husam explains that there is a hidden meaning in these lines:

> He [the poet] is putting Kafur with dogs, because he first
> makes him a lion, and he makes the spirit in his body the spirit
> of a lion, then he says: "Yet how many lions are there whose
> spirits are [as base as] dogs?" as if he is saying: "And you are
> one of them."[53]

Taha Hussein attributes the assumption of the veiled satire, and turning praise into satire by al-Mutanabbi's commentators and readers of the time, to the fact that they knew about the poet's negative opinion of and anger with Kafur (the praised). Had they read the poetry without this knowledge of the poet and the praised, they would not have reached such an assumption.[54] The conversion of the *Kafuriyyat* from praise to satire was achieved by the collaboration of al-Mutanabbi with his commentators, as they all read and wrote under the domination of the Arab imaginary and its repository of pejorative images of blacks.

THE BLACK POET AND THE RESISTANCE OF REPRESENTATION

Every representation has a counter-representation, and "wherever there is power, there is resistance."[55] The stronger the power and its representation get, the stronger the resistance and its counter-representation become. If the Zanj Revolution is a social and armed counter-response to the hegemony of power, then the poetry of black poets is the counter-representation of the hegemony of the Arab culture over them. This counter-representation is the cultural resistance that confronts the power of the Arab representation of blacks and their culture. Blacks were the most prominent example of the silent and voiceless beings represented by Arab culture. But here they recover their voice, moved by a desire to speak, to represent themselves by themselves and to reveal a new history, a new reality, and a new representation, which collides with the representations of the host culture. However, this resistance is not united or strong enough – a feature that characterizes "minority literature" in general since "some members of minorities may wish to forget the past in order to join the majority; others may want to work in coalition with the majority, without renouncing minority ways and traditions."[56]

Whoever examines blacks' poetry in Arab culture will discover that there are two different voices/poets. First is a voice that represents the assimilated black within Arab culture. Such a voice seeks to integrate into Arab culture and thus forget their "Abyssinian, Nubian, or Zinji" past, and in turn surrender to their representation by Arab culture. The black poet writes or recites poetry under the cultural power whose representation assimilated him, to eventually become part of the host culture, thinking like its people, and then reproducing the imagery of blackness and whiteness in the same view formed in the Arab imaginary. Black poets such as Antarah, Nussaib, and Abu Dulamah were slaves and were hurt in their inner selves because of their blackness. Therefore, they tried to lighten the burden of their blackness by all means, and to cover up their blackness by apology and justification, or to make up for their blackness with the whiteness of their moral standards. Hence, their poetry has become an integral part of Arabic literature, and they are included among Arab poets.

As for the other voice, it represents an extreme case from black poets who are angry and repulsed by the representation of the host culture. They represent the rebellious voice against the attempts of containment, assimilation, or integration imposed by Arab culture. This group refuses to be represented by this culture, and instead confronts it with a counter-representation to take revenge on the cultural hegemony. They insist on representing themselves and their culture themselves. The most prominent of these poets are Suhaim Abd Bani al-Hashas, al-Hayqutan, Sunaih bin Rabah, and 'Ukaim al-Habashi.

Most of these poets did not possess the ultimate representational tool, which is writing, and those who knew how to write did not use it effectively. Thus, oral poetry remained their only tool to represent their cultural identities on the one hand, and the identity of Arab culture on the other. Some of this poetry found its way into writing by known or unknown scribes, but the strictness of cultural surveillance over the writing process prevented the completion of this process. So, the collections of some of these poets were mostly incomplete, with inaccurate attributions and fabrications, as in *Diwan Antarah bin Shaddad.* Many poems were lost and not a single complete poem was preserved, as in the case of Nussaib. From poets like Suhaim, al-Hayqutan, Sunaih, and 'Ukaim al-Habashi, only one poem by each was documented. Arab culture was dealing with discourses by Others with the utmost caution, censorship, and apprehension, which led to the obliteration of many counter-representation poems. Perhaps the culture distorted or trimmed those poems, or cut their harmful appendages (harmful from the perspective of the dominant culture) through selection and filtration, except for what was slipped into books by writers like al-Jahiz, who injected poems by al-Hayqutan, Sunaih, and 'Ukaim.

The Assimilated Black:
Dual Identity and the Concealment of Blackness

No black person was happy with their representation in Arab culture, but some of them fell into the traps of this representation and reproduced it, believing that they were opposing or resisting it. Even when they refused such a representation by Arab culture, they were under its dominance and sway. Rather, they gained their strength by submitting to it and responding to its dictates. If one of the postulates of this representation is that blackness is an indication of lack, ugliness, illness, and deformity, then the submissive black has no choice but to accept that. The submissive black does not refute this representation; rather, he accepts the ugliness of his blackness and the deformity of his body, which is evident in his desire to cover his blackness by all means.

A black poet such as Antarah, Nussaib, or Abu Dulamah had his own means of concealing his blackness. If *al-Furusiyya*[57] (knighthood) was the means of Antarah bin Shaddad, then cozying up to the caliphs and exaggerating their praise was Nussaib's means. The image of blacks formed by those assimilated black poets was not different from that shaped by the Arab imaginary. The desire to renounce their blackness and be proud of the whiteness of their character was evidence of feeling ashamed of their black colour. Those who were not embarrassed by their blackness, like Abu Dulamah, used to blame themselves and vilify their colour and ugliness, just like any Arab poet who satirized blacks for their ugliness. The cultural identity of those poets was in a state of conflict, torn between two selves or two identities: being a black and being an Arab. They were aware that they were black, but at the same time they sought to be Arab. Denying their blackness was an unattainable endeavour since blackness is a mark engraved in the body. There was nothing left for them but to adhere to the Arabism acquired by their upbringing and living in an Arab culture, as in the case of Abu Dulamah, or by affiliating with an Arab father, as in the case of Antarah and Nussaib. Accordingly, those poets sought to create an imagined situation that would allow them to be black (Abyssinian, Nubian, or Zinji) and Arab at the same time.

ANTARAH BIN SHADDAD: BLACK SKIN, WHITE CHARACTER[58]

Antarah bin Shaddad (525–608 CE) is perhaps the most famous black poet in Arab literature, and the one with the greatest desire to integrate into his Arab community. Perhaps his Arab community was not as interested in any black poet as it was in Antarah. It is narrated that the Messenger said: "I have heard about many Bedouins, but Antarah was the only one I loved to meet."[59] If the Prophet's love of Antarah stems from the latter's noble manners in his poetry, the audience's attraction to his popular biography is due to his courage, chivalry, and ability to transcend the conditions of slavery and colour in his society. However, Antarah is not spared from exclusion and ostracism, either in his poetry or in his life. Perhaps the naming of him, along with Khufaf bin Nudbah and Sulayk bin Salaka, as "Aghrabat al-Arab" (Arab crows) reveals this contradictory perception towards these poets. This appellation reveals a desire to assimilate these black poets but also reveals a desire to be distinguished from them by describing them as crows (black birds symbolizing pessimism in Arab culture). This hurts Antarah from within because it reminds him of his blackness and servitude. He does not find a way to get rid of this complex except by embracing the "white" qualities adopted by his Arab community. Since al-Furusiyya is the most prominent social characteristic in pre-Islamic Arabia, Antarah and the black poets of his time find in this characteristic their only chance to conceal their blackness and get rid of the inferiority complex they are living with because of their blackness. To be a true *faris* (knight), one must have several characteristics, chief among them strength, valour, poetry composition and recitation, and *al-Fasaha* (clarity, purity, eloquence of articulation).

Al-Fuhula and al-Furusiyya might be beneficial in eliminating slavery (lower status) in a society that appreciates poets and knights, but they are ineffective against the blackness of those poets. Slavery is a social status that can change, but blackness is a natural trait, or an "incurable disease" as Antarah describes it:

If I am black, musk is my colour
The blackness of my skin has no remedy[60]

Thus, if Antarah is able to get rid of his slave status through his furussiya and fuhula, getting rid of the blackness of the skin is impossible, as it is a natural characteristic of him; rather, it may act on his behalf when Arabs address him, not with his name but with his colour "Aswad" (black) or "Aswad Bani Abs" (the black of Bani Abs). Antarah makes others look at him as a poet and a knight who is not harmed by the colour of his skin:

> Enemies shame me for my black skin
> But the whiteness of my traits erases blackness.[61]

He also says:

> If my mother is a crow [black],
> From the children of Ham,
> As you have shamed me
> I am as elegant as white swords
> And as tanned as the spears when they fly at me.[62]

As for his fearlessness and valour on the battlefield, he says:

> I am death and the son of every death;
> The blackness of my skin is its dress and cover.[63]

Antarah's blackness arouses the curiosity of others and makes them taunt and ridicule him. He does not shy away from using his famous weapons (al-Furusiyya and poetry) to defend himself. With furusiyya, he is fighting to protect his lineage to his mother. If he is honourable in lineage to the father, then he will protect his other half, that is, his lineage to blacks, with his sword:

> I am from the best origin [father's side] in Abs people
> And I protect the other half [mother's side] with the sword.[64]

Hence, Antarah is using his sword and poetry to respond to insults and reproach others, that is, conceal his blackness from his enemies' eyes. However, when he fails in this endeavour, he resorts to apologizing for his blackness, and compensating for the blackness of his skin with the whiteness of his character, deeds, and moral qualities. For him, the colour of the skin has no value in itself, but the value is in what this skin conceals of qualities, morals, and actions:

> If they fault the blackness that I am covered with,
> The pearl is hidden under a robe of seashell.[65]

The colour of the skin is like a garment one wears. Just as it does not harm the pearl to be covered by a "robe of seashell," Antarah is not harmed by this black skin, if the skin is just a cover and what lies beneath are the hidden treasures. Therefore, if a person wants to

Representation of Blacks in Poetry

be proud, they should be proud of the whiteness of their moral principles and actions, not the whiteness of their skin:

> If I am black, musk is my colour.
> The blackness of my skin has no remedy.
> But evil is far from me,
> As far as the Earth is from the sky.[66]
> They shame me for my black colour
> Yet their deeds of malice are darker than my skin.[67]

A comprehensive look at Antarah's poetry reveals that it is based on the dialectic of concealment and revelation, or the dialectic of invisibility and manifestation. It expresses a strong desire for concealment and disguise at times, and disclosure and manifestation at other times. According to this poetry, a person has two sides: a hidden side, which includes virtuous morals, manners, and actions, and a visible side, which is the skin colour. But this black skin, which is a cover for the white virtues and deeds, needs covering and concealment, so the blackness of the cover (i.e., the skin) itself becomes concealed, like a robe for a pearl. Antarah covers up his blackness with his furusiyya and fuhula, while his black skin conceals his morals and deeds. If Antarah's furusiyya and fuhula cover the blackness of his skin, then this blackness – a shell of the pearl – exposes the morals, deeds, and qualities beneath it, so it is the hidden and the hiding part at the same time. It is the hiding part because it contains the pearl, and it is the hidden part because the pearl (virtuous morals, manners, and deeds) is a tool that Antarah uses to conceal his blackness. Hence, the pearl becomes a covering shell, and the shell (blackness) becomes a concealed pearl.

Figure 4.1 Dialectic of concealment and revelation

Whether Antarah succeeds or fails in concealing his blackness, it is clear that he is under the power of the Arab representation of blacks. Arab culture does not suppress his voice, but rather makes him speak what it wants, by making him express the ugliness of blackness, and the necessity of covering or removing it if possible. It is as if this poetry is the voice of the culture, not the voice of this black knight and poet. When we study Antarah's poetry, we may feel his specific voice that resists the hegemonic voice of culture, which is evidently present in the popular *Sirat Antarah bin Shaddad*.

Ibn Sallam al-Jumahi points out that Antarah has "a lot of poetry,"[68] but that most of this poetry is apocryphal. This is due to the mixing of the poetry of the Diwan (collection) with the poetry of the biography, that is, the mixing of Antarah's voice with the voice of Arab culture. Many of Antarah's poetry collectors and commentators are aware of this issue. For instance, Karam al-Bustani, who issued *Diwan Antarah* (Antarah's anthology) in 1958, divided the *Diwan* into two distinct sections: "authentic poetry" and "apocryphal poetry."[69] As for Khalil Sharaf al-Din, he was skeptical of attributing any poem to Antarah, except for Antarah's "Hanging Ode." As for *Diwan of Antarah*, which was explained by al-Khatib al-Tabrizi and verified by Majid Tarrad, it originally contained only forty poems: twenty-seven transmitted by al-A'lam al-Shantamari and thirteen transmitted by al-Batalyusi. The rest of the poems in the Diwan – which is to say, the majority – are taken from different books and sources, and most are from the poetry of the biography.

The forty poems are devoid of any reference to blackness or servitude. Blackness as an issue is in other poems, which raises the possibility that those poems are fabricated. But why are these forty poems devoid of reference to Antarah, the black slave who apologizes for the blackness of his skin colour and replaces it with pride of his white qualities and deeds? Some scholars think that Antarah rose above that and deliberately refused to refer to or deny the problem of his skin colour in his poetry, hoping that people would forget it.[70] However, his people did not forget. Rather, they made him express it, as if they wanted to condemn blacks through the voices of blacks themselves. It is as if this culture says to Antarah: you have no right to integrate into our culture unless you renounce the blackness of your skin.

NUSSAIB BIN RABAH: BLACK POETRY AND WHITE PRAISE

If Antarah is embarrassed by the blackness of his skin in a society that despises blackness and in a culture that makes him repudiate his blackness, the grandchildren of Antarah, the subsequent black poets in Arab culture, are not better than or different from him. It is this culture that makes another black poet, Nussaib bin Rabah (d.108 AH), feel ashamed of the blackness of his skin. It is the same culture that makes him recite the same verses that are attributed to Antarah, in which he apologizes for the blackness of his skin with the whiteness of his character:

> If I am black, musk is my colour
> The blackness of my skin has no remedy.
> My generosity is far from evil
> As far as the Earth is from the sky.[71]

However, the similarity between Antarah and Nussaib does not stop at these lines. Nussaib's upbringing is almost identical to that of Antarah. Both were born from black Abyssinian female slaves who had intercourse with their Arab masters. Both have tense relationships with their uncles (paternal side). Just as Antarah grew up herding camels, Nussaib was born to find himself tending the camels of his masters. Just as poetry is one of Antarah's means to rid himself of slave status and his black complex, poetry is the only way for Nussaib to escape slavery and his black complex. Or rather, poetry is the only means to free his family from the humiliation of slavery. When he praises Abd al-Aziz bin Marwan in Egypt and receives his prize, he comes back to Medina and pays money to free his mother, grandmother, and his cousin (maternal side).[72]

Antarah, the poet knight, was not a subject of ridicule. Not so, Nussaib. To lack al-Furusiyya and at the same time to be a poet and a black slave is a strange phenomenon, which evokes laughter and irony in a culture that associates poetry with white skin and high status. For this reason, Nussaib is often confronted with the words of objectors from the guardians of this culture, who say to him: "Oh, slave, what have you to do with poetry!"[73] Nussaib, aware of this situation, conceals his poetic talent. When he dares to recite poetry to his masters from Bani Dhamrah bin Bakr and Khuza'ah, he recites the poem and then attributes it to some of their poets, so they applaud him. And when he hears that from them, his pride in his poetry increases, so he decides to go to Abd al-Aziz bin Marwan, the crown prince of Abdul Malik bin Marwan in Egypt. When he shares his plan with his sister Amama, she pities him and says: "To God we belong and to Him is our return! O son of mother, have the two traits met in you: a black, and a laughingstock?"[74] Thus, the combination of poetry and blackness in a person is an anomaly, and if it happens, is a reason for ridicule and laughter.

When he goes to Egypt to meet Abd al-Aziz bin Marwan, he does not find anyone to welcome him; rather, he is removed from the council of the nobles and superiors, so he sits behind them. And when he has the opportunity to meet Abd al-Aziz bin Marwan, the latter is surprised and turns him into a subject for ridicule. How can poetry be recited by a black slave like Nussaib?! Abd al-Aziz bin Marwan looks up at Nussaib and points at him: "Then he said in amazement: Are you a poet? How dare you! I said: Yes, Prince. He said: recite for me, so I recited, and he liked my poetry."[75] At that time, Nussaib thinks that he has achieved his goal, but soon the prince returns to his nature and makes Nussaib a subject of mockery. When the prince's close poet Ayman bin Khuraim al-Asadi enters, the prince asks him: "How much do you see the price of this slave [Nussaib]?" And in another narration, the prince's attendant tells the prince that there is a black man at the door "asking permission to recite a panegyric that he has prepared for you," so Abd al-Aziz bin Marwan thinks that he is one of those who can be mocked and laughed at, so he says: tell him to come on the day we need him. Nussaib leaves and waits at the prince's gate for four months till the prince orders to see him and then makes fun of him in front of the people. It is as if this black poet is a toy for the prince and his companions, or a commodity offered for sale in a market that resembles a slave market.

Poetry in Arab culture is a manifestation of noble and lofty status, and this is only for the white Arab masters. As for the black slaves, poetry is not for them, and if it is, it will be like them, black and enslaved, since white poetry is the product of only a white master poet. Even if Nussaib is a poet, his poetry is black. This is what Ayman bin Khuraim said when he met Nussaib in the council of Abd al-Aziz bin Marwan. When the prince asked Ayman bin Khuraim to guess the price of Nussaib, he said: one hundred dinars, so the prince said: he is an eloquent poet. Ayman bin Khuraim was astonished and said: Who is this to recite poetry?! Does someone like this recite poetry or be good at it?! So, the prince asked Nussaib to recite some of his poetry, which he did, then "Abdul-Aziz said: what do you think, Ayman? He said: a poetry by a black (or a black's poetry), he is the best among the people of his skin."[76] As for linking Nussaib's poetry with slavery, it came from al-Farazdaq: "The best poetry is of the honourable men, and the worst poetry is said by the slaves."[77] Thus, in such a culture, there are two types of poetry: a praised white poetry composed by honourable white men, and a reprehensible black poetry composed by black slaves. Hence, Nussaib had to confront this cultural divide to prove that his poetry is as white as the poetry of the free white masters.

Nussaib tries to compensate for the blackness of his skin with the whiteness of his character and deeds, as his predecessor Antarah bin Shaddad did. It is narrated that one day when Nussaib passes by his cousin Suhaim (whom he freed from slavery) while he is dancing and blowing the pipe with blacks, he reprimands Suhaim for having both "disgraceful manners and black skin colour."[78] The black person is rejected and despised because of the blackness of their skin, which can be deepened by having bad manners. Combining blackness with bad manners represents the utmost flaw, lowliness, and inferiority. In order to alleviate baseness, blacks must be of good manners and deeds. This is what Nussaib realized and demonstrated in his poetry:

> Blackness is not my defect as long as I have
> This tongue [poetry] with a solid heart
> Whoever is raised by their origins,
> My poems are made my origins.[79]
>
> ----
>
> If my colour is dark,
> I have a sound mind[80]
>
> ---
>
> My black clothes have no harm,
> Underneath is a dress of sublimity, white in elegance.[81]

Similar to Antarah, who has to cover blackness with the whiteness of his deeds and manners, Nussaib has to face another dilemma, to cover the blackness of his poetry. Unlike Antarah whose furusiyya preserves and supports his poetry, Nussaib is not a knight. Therefore, he has to search for a way to preserve his poetry and make others recognize not only his poetic ability but also his poetry as white Arabic poetry. Nussaib is liberated from slavery, but he has to liberate his poetry from the charge of blackness and servitude, and he has no choice but to lean on the connection he created with caliphs, princes, and rulers. The praise of those people is the only guarantee that will elevate his black poetry to the status of white poetry. He has a strong insight regarding this matter. Since his poetic talent flourishes, he only seeks caliphs, princes, and rulers. He is famous for his praise, and he is "regarded by the kings, well-versed in their praise and elegies."[82] Nussaib does not leave a caliph or a prince unpraised. So he is connected with Abd al-Aziz bin Marwan, Abdul Malik bin Marwan, Suleiman bin Abdul Malik, Hisham bin Abdul Malik, Omar bin Abdul Aziz, al Waleed bin Abdul Malik, Yazid bin Abdul Malik, Abdul Allah bin Ja'far, Ibrahim bin Hisham (the governor of Medina), and others.

What is known about Nussaib is that he was a poet who excelled in *nasib*[83] (amatory poetry) and praise, but had no luck in satire. However, he quit nasib and devoted his poetry to praise (*al-madih*). It is narrated that Nussaib met with Umar bin Abdul Aziz and the latter said to Nussaib: "O black! You are the one who defames women in your nasib?!" Nussaib responded: "O Commander of the Faithful, I quit nasib and I promised God Almighty not to say it anymore."[84] Nussaib quit his nasib out of abstinence or out of fear of those who mocked his love and derided his whims. Once he declared his love, Abu Ubaidah and other people laughed at him; they could not imagine that a black Abyssinian could be in love. He did not express *hija* (satire), because someone like him who was black and ugly could not criticize others. He also did not express anything in *fakhr* (self-exaltation poetry), except for some verses in which he is proud of the whiteness of his character. This is not inability on his part, but he is fully aware that his poetry will not get rid of the accusation of blackness and slavery except by praising kings and princes. It is narrated that Nussaib praised Abdullah bin Ja'far and the latter rewarded him. "Someone said: O Abu Ja'far, how did you give this black slave all these gifts! He said: By God, if he is black, his praise is white, and his poetry is Arab, and he deserved for what he said more than he has been given."[85] This recognition of the whiteness of his praise and the Arabness of his poetry is what Nussaib was waiting to hear from the caliphs and princes.

Antarah sought to cover his blackness through his powerful poetry and furusiyya, and Nussaib through his praise of kings, caliphs, and princes. The poetry of the assimilated black poets expresses a strong desire to remove the burden of their black skin. However, it developed and advanced, to the extent that we see a black poet who is not embarrassed to reveal his blackness; rather, he is not embarrassed to criticize his blackness and blame himself and his relatives for that. He is Zand bin al-Jawn, known by his nickname Abu Dulamah (d.161 AH).

ABU DULAMAH: THE HUMOUROUS BLACK AND THE CANDOUR OF BLACKNESS

Antarah was famous for his poetic, chivalrous manners of help, generosity, and chastity, and Nussaib was also famous for being a virtuous and big-hearted poet, to the extent that "he never says Nasib except on his wife."[86] Perhaps this was a way to conceal their blackness, cover the ugliness felt by others, and repudiate the stereotyped images stored in the Arab imaginary such as immorality, hypersexuality, and animalism.

In contrast to the model represented by chivalric Antarah and virtuous Nussaib, Abu Dulamah presents a different model for the blacks assimilated into Arab culture. He does not refrain from confessing his immorality and corruption. It was known about him that "he was corrupt in religion, of bad faith, breaking God's prohibitions, not following Islamic obligations, openly."[87] When Musa bin Dawood al-Hashimi decided to go to Hajj, he asked Abu Dulamah to go with him, and promised to give the latter ten thousand dirhams. Abu Dulamah took the money, ran away, and used the money to get drunk. He was an alcoholic and did not like to do any of the five obligations, such as praying or fasting. He was imprisoned several times because of drunkenness. He did not feel the need to cover his blackness, as he was open about his blackness and ugliness, and did not refrain from satirizing his whole family as "hideous black with ugly names"[88] and himself as vile, a monkey, and a pig:

> Shall I tell you about Abu Dulamah?
> He is not of the honourable nor has honour.
> He is a monkey when wearing a turban,
> And a pig if he takes it off
> I have both ugliness and vileness
> Likewise, vileness is followed by ugliness.[89]

He did not refrain from satirizing his wife:

> At home, I have no companion to make my bed
> But a skinny old woman
> Her legs are like jerked meat
> Her face is uglier than
> A gooey fish in a mush.[90]

As for his daughter, he carried her on his shoulder one day and she urinated on him, so he threw her off his shoulder saying:

> You wet my dress, shame on you!
> Shall a cursed devil urinate on you!
> Neither Mary, the mother of Jesus, gave birth to you,
> Nor did Luqman the Wise, raise you
> But, you were born to a bad mother,
> Who is cared for by a vile husband.[91]

Even his female mule did not escape his satire:

> I was given a lazy female mule
> Her best quality is indolence.[92]

Despite the openness of his blackness, ugliness, and debauchery, the obsession with covering was not non-existent in Abu Dulamah. The cover that Abu Dulamah sought was not related to his blackness but to his bad actions and manners. He found his salvation in humour and witticism, for they prevented others from holding him accountable for his bad actions and decadence. When he escaped from the Hajj to get drunk, he was arrested and brought back to Musa bin Dawood, but he managed to escape his punishment by reciting a few witty lines. Sometimes he was released and rewarded for his humour. One day, he got drunk and was then arrested and imprisoned in a chicken coop:

> When he was brought to al-Mansur, the latter asked: Where have you been imprisoned, Abu Dulamah? He said: With the chickens. Al-Mansur asked: What were you doing there? He said: I was clucking with them until the morning. Al-Mansur laughed. He released Abu Dulamah, then rewarded him.[93]

Abu Dulamah was one of the most famous witty and humorous poets in Arab culture in that era, and because of his humour and whimsical anecdotes, the caliphs of Banu al-Abbas, such as al-Saffah, al-Mansur, and al-Mahdi, liked him and enjoyed his company. Such a phenomenon can be read as an indication of a change in the era and in the attitude of the political authority. During Nussaib's time, the Umayyad caliphs did not recognize humour and wit in the poet, and the era of Antarah did not appreciate the poets for their jokes or whimsical anecdotes. Both eras hardly witnessed a humorous and witty poet. The need for a humorous poet did not appear until the Abbasid era, and it is remarkable how Abu Dulamah, who witnessed the last days of the Umayyad caliphate, was not as famous then as he was during the Abbasid era.[94] Abu Dulamah found the conditions of the Abbasid era suitable for him. During that time, the political authority was in dire need of jesters and companions whose talent for poetry and humour made them laugh and feel happy.[95]

Despite his debauchery and corruption, Abu Dulamah's humour aided his assimilation into society. Unlike Abu Dulamah, Suhaim Abd Bani al-Hashas was the black poet who was not absorbed by the society and, instead, wanted to be burned and killed. His corruption went beyond the religious taboos to include the social taboos that could not be tolerated.

THE REBELLIOUS BLACK: THE RESISTANCE OF HEGEMONY AND THE REPRESENTATION OF THE SELF

In this section, we will see blacks of a different kind: blacks who are not subjected to representation by others. Rather, they are the creators of their own literature, history, and image, and critics of Arab culture and its representations of the Other. Such a phenomenon has led some scholars to consider these dissident blacks as the fathers of Shu'ubiyya because they were among the first to criticize this culture and confront its representations using the same tools.

The confrontation was violent in the case of Suhaim, who was the example of the vengeful black due to his enslavement and rejection by Arab culture and society. Suhaim's poetry, which stains the honour (women) of his masters from Bani Asad bin Khuzaimah, represents the climax of the confrontation with a culture that seeks to burn and kill such a black poet in retaliation for his poetry. The poetry of the black Wrath Trinity (al-Hayqutan, Sunaih, 'Ukaim) represents an extreme case of confrontation with the host culture. They composed their poems in a state of excitement and anger at the culture's denigrating view of them.

In both cases, culture has its means to take revenge on those who stand in its way or confront its symbols and postulates. Suhaim was killed and burned in a unique way that reflects deep hatred. As for the trio of poets, Arab culture deliberately destroyed and eliminated their poems. If al-Jahiz had not kept some poems of the three angry poets, we would not know anything about them and their poems. This is what led Abduh Badawi to say that there is a "conspiracy of silence that Arab writers have set"[96] against these angry black poets who rejected all attempts of assimilation and representation.

Suhaim Abd Bani al-Hashas: The Revenge of the Black Fahl (Stallion)

Suhaim (d. 41 AH) was not a brave knight like Antarah nor a eulogist like Nussaib nor humourous like Abu Dulamah, but he shared with them a black skin and a slave origin. And while Abu Dulamah's father was an emancipated slave, and Antarah's and Nussaib's fathers were Arab masters, Suhaim was a non-Arab black Nubian slave bought by Banu al-Hashas (group of Banu Asad), and he remained a slave until he was killed and burned in a trench. This is what distinguished Suhaim from those three who experienced the taste of freedom at the beginning or the end of their lives: Suhaim was born and remained a slave with no knowledge of his parents and lineage. He found himself a slave in a country that was not his country, and among a people who despised him, and every black slave such as him. Hence, we may understand the hidden motives behind Suhaim's desire to take revenge on his masters from Banu Asad, who persecuted him because of his colour, ugliness, and servitude.

As much as Suhaim had experienced humiliation from those people, he would take revenge on them in retaliation for his offended dignity not by fighting or satirizing them, but by violating their honour and ravishing their women to hurt them and destroy their pride. Therefore, Banu Asad decided to kill this black slave *fahl* (stallion). Before that decision, some of them bit him to make him stop sleeping with their women, but all in vain. So they took him to the sultan who imprisoned and whipped him eighty lashes, but he went out singing:

> Prison is nothing but a house shadow I've entered,
> A whip is nothing but a skin touching a skin.
> Aba Ma`bad, by God, her love was not unbound
> With eighty lashes, but rather increased my attachment.[97]

Even when being thrown into the fire, he satisfied his thirst for revenge by reminding them that he had wounded their masculine pride by leaving a *maisam* (a branding iron), a mark of stigma, on their honour. They killed him in order to save their pride and honour, but he reminded them that killing him would not erase their shame and disgrace for they had been branded with his name from which there was no escape.

Ugliness was not the reason for society's rejection of Suhaim. Rather, he was shunned among the tribe's men because he crossed the boundaries of slavery to compete with his masters in their most private property, which is the ownership of women. The woman in Arab society is a protected being, and violating her is a violation of men's honour, authority, and pride.

This black stallion had a strong desire to defeat his Arab masters not through a physical confrontation, but through his black virility, which was the weapon of his revenge. Unlike his white Arab masters, he was incapable of bragging about his origin, lineage, colour, and class, but he was able to turn their women and girls into whores, who sought out him, instead of their men, to satisfy their sexual desires.

All attempts to assimilate him by invitation and intimidation failed. Neither imprisoning and flogging him nor rewarding him with gifts dissuaded him from his opposition. On the contrary, all these attempts made him desperate to oppose the host culture and its representations of him. Suhaim did not praise anyone in his poetry, nor did he succumb to the temptation of the caliphs and princes. When Omar bin al-Khattab invited him to recite his "al-Ya'iyya" poem (A poem rhymed with "yaa"), he started with: "Grey hair [old age] and Islam are enough prohibitions." Omar said: "Continue this poem and I will reward you." But Suhaim went against the Caliph's desire by reciting nasib poetry instead:

Then we [the poet and his mistress] spent the night on two pillows,
Near a big tree and on sand swayed by the wind;
A cold north wind blew,
We had no cover, but our clothes
Touched by her robe,
The aroma on my robe
Lasted a year, until my robe wore out.
I swear by God, upon seeing her,
She embraced me with her 20 fingers.[98]
So, Omar said: woe unto you! You are dead![99]

Suhaim was a slave, but a vindicative and rebellious poet. The host culture was unable to silence or absorb him, as it did with Antarah, Nussaib, and Abu Dulamah. The problem was not solely his poetry – otherwise they would have cut out his tongue. It was his poetry and his immoral actions with their women. Therefore, the only way to deal with him was to kill him.

Al-Hayqutan, Sunaih, 'Ukaim:
The Black and the Re-emplotment of History

Suhaim represented a unique and disturbing phenomenon in the history of Arab culture, and thus was the first hope for the oppressed blacks to be liberated from the shackles of imagined cultural slavery. It was the first time that a black poet was proud to stand face to face with this culture. And if Suhaim's confrontation with society was characterized by sexual capacity and defilement of honour, other black poets' confrontation was characterized by historical and cultural resistance. Among those poets were al-Hayqutan, Sunaih bin Rabah, and 'Ukaim al-Habashi.

Unlike Suhaim, those three were not pariahs in society and in Arab culture, since some of them were recognized for their virtue and knowledge. 'Ukaim al-Habashi, according to al-Jahiz, was eloquent, "and Levantine scholars learned from him as Iraqi scholars learned from al-Muntaja' bin Nabhan."[100] As for al-Hayqutan, he was known for his sound opinions, intellect, and mentality. Those poets did not threaten the stability of society, nor did they violate its honour, as Suhaim did. They did not initiate aggression or confrontation, but they responded to the satire and ridicule of society, which stirred their resentment and anger against that society and against Arab culture and pride. The verbal assault against them was instigated by individual Arab poets such as Jarir and Hakim bin Ayyash al-Kalbi, yet the response of those angry black poets was always comprehensive and collective. This is because they were aware that the verses of Jarir and Hakim did not represent the poet's viewpoint only, but that of the whole culture, whose collection of derogatory representations was stored in the Arab imaginary.

Arab culture created its own history of the relationship between blacks (Abyssinians) and Arabs, utilizing a heroic plot that raised the status of Arabs and lowered that of blacks. Blacks, too, had the opportunity to *re-emplot* this history, by creating a satirical plot where blacks triumphed over Arabs, and satirized their history. And if this was not possible, then there was the opportunity to cast doubt on the superiority of Arab history. The obsession – with re-emploting or questioning the dominant Arab narrative of history – stirred the opposition of those three black poets and provoked their anger in the following situations.

The first situation was between Jarir and al-Hayqutan. Jarir saw al-Hayqutan on the day of Eid while he was wearing a white shirt. Jarir made a mockery of al-Hayqutan:

> It is as if, when he appears before the people,
> He is a donkey's penis wrapped in paper.[101]

When al-Hayqutan heard it, he responded with a flaming poem:

> If I have nappy hair and charred skin,
> I am of bright generosity and honour.
> The blackness of (my) skin does me no harm;
> I am boasting with the sword on the combat day.
> If you claim glory when there is none,
> The Negus people are more glorious than you.
> Al-Julanda people,[102] the son of Khosrau and Harith[103] refused,[104]
> So did Hawthah,[105] the Coptic, and the great Caesar.
> Yet he (Negus) delightfully won it[106] over other kings;
> So, his invincible and ensured realm remained.
> Among them (blacks) were Luqman (the Sage) and his son too,
> And Abrahah the King, whose might cannot be contested.
> Abu Yaksum (Abraha) invaded you in your very home,
> Though you were as plentiful as grains of sand or more.
> Like waterfowl when falling on dry land,

Their claws became twisted and muddy.
If it was not Allah who defended it,[107]
You would have learned the consequence from experienced people.
There would be no honour except you work for it.
Soon, your war-fire shall spark,
Then, your begrudging chief advances.
Sometimes we fight him, sometimes he turns his back.
As for your claim of prophethood,
You couldn't even protect the Covered Haram (Kaaba).
If you claimed *laqah*,[108] we don't pay tax.
Paying tax is nobler for you than fleeing (the fight).
If there was a crown's desire to conquer it (Mecca),
Homerite kings would have invaded it.
It has no Winter or Summer resort
And unlike Juatha,[109] whose water gushes forth,
It has no green parks, no hunting grounds;
It is only for trading, and traders are disdained.
Are you not *Kulaib*[110] and your mother is an ewe?
Fat sheep are both your shame and pride.[111]

The poem starts with an allusion to the idea that blacks' defence strategy has not changed: al-Hayqutan apologizes for the ugliness of his black colour and nappy hair and compensates for that with the whiteness of his morals (character), generosity, and honour, just like Antarah and Nussaib used to do. However, the third verse disrupts the expectation, as it goes beyond the apology to boasting (fakhr) about the civilization and history of blacks, on the one hand, and vilification of the Arab civilization and history, on the other hand, as well as satire of Jarir and his tribe.

The poem reveals the black poets' need to break free from the representations imposed by Arab culture, and from the dominant historical narrative of the relationship between Arabs and blacks. Submitting to these representations undermines blacks' pride, history, and civilization. The first thing this poem denies is that blacks are savage with no history, social, or political life to be proud of. The reference to the Negus and the Abyssinian victories over Arabs is not arbitrary, for al-Hayqutan is aware that, during that historical moment, Abyssinians were powerful and dominant, and Arabs were powerless. Such a historical moment provides evidence of Abyssinians' glorious history, compared with Arabs' disgraceful history, and that is when Abraha al-Habashi's (the Abyssinian) army invaded the southern gate of the Arabs (Yemen) and his elephants invaded Mecca, the sacred heart of the Arabian Peninsula. At that time, the black Abyssinian was the master, and the white Arab was submissive and unable to defend his sacred place and honour.

In his poem, al-Hayqutan tries to expose and undermine the Arab emplotment of history, as a prelude to stripping Arabs of all honour and pride. If Mecca, Arabs' honour, was ruined, then Arabs' glory was ruined too, and if Quraishi Arabs boast that they are honourable and thus do not pay tax to the victorious kings, then, al-Hayqutan reminds him, paying tax is better than fleeing and surrendering their home to the enemy despite their large number. Also, Mecca, regarded as the most honourable land for Arabs, is a barren land, which does not have summer or winter resorts, nor water springs. Moreover, it is devoid of parks, and hunting is forbidden there. Therefore, there is no incentive to conquer it, and even if there is a desire for it, it would have been invaded by Yemeni kings, but it lacks all the natural features that might tempt any king to invade it. Also, if Mecca is renowned for trade, then trade is a despised profession.

Al-Hayqutan strips Arabs of their last pride, prophethood, for the Prophet of Islam is a Quraishi Arab. The poet reminds Arabs that they have no pride in that, for prophethood is a revelation from heaven, and Arabs did not acquire it through special effort, work, or merit. When Islam came, the first to deny it were the Quraishites from Mecca, in addition to many Arabs of Jazeera, such as the two sons of al-Julanda, the Azdis (kings of Oman: Jaifer and Ayaz), as well as al-Harith bin Abi Shamir, Hawtha bin Ali al-Hanafi, Caesar (King of the Romans), Khosrau, and al-Muqawqis. In contrast to those who disbelieved in Islam, the only one who accepted and believed in *al-Dawah* (the Prophet's invitation of others to Islam) was the Negus (King of Abyssinians). If there is pride and honour, it is for the Negus and his people, who were the best neighbours for Muslims, receiving and welcoming them when they migrated from Mecca to Abyssinia to escape the persecution of the Quraishites. Al-Hayqutan does not forget to be proud of a number of blacks who did not witness Islam, yet are honourable as they set an example in wisdom and soundness of opinion like Luqman al-Hakim (Luqman the Sage).

While Jarir's satire is based on description and analogy, al-Hayqutan's satire, like Suhaim's, is based on reminding. He reminds Jarir that the latter is one of the Banu Kulaib who were infamous for having intercourse with sheep and ewes. Despite all this outrageous satire, Jarir did not stop satirizing blacks. Jarir enraged another black poet, Sunaih bin Rabah, when he criticized the people of al-Akhtal Bani Taghlib:

Don't seek Khu'ula[112] in Taghlib
For al-Zanj's Khu'ula is nobler than them.

Sunaih responded angrily:

What is the matter with Kulaib's dog[113] to insult us?
He [Jarir] is not equal to Hijab and Iqal.[114]
If someone makes Maragha[115] and her son [Jarir],
Equal to al-Farazdaq, he is unjust, and wrong.
And al-Zanj, when in the battlefield,
You see them as noble heroes
Ask Ibn Amr, when he faced their spears,
Did he not see the Zanj's spears to be long?
They killed Ziyad's son, then
They dismounted their horses to fight.
Their horses are tied up in their courtyards,
While sheep and lambs are tied around you.
Bin Nudbah,[116] among your warriors, was of our sons,
So was al-Khufaf, the burden bearer.
And the sons of Zabiba: Antarah and Harasa,
Their examples have none among you (your people).
Ask Ibn Jayfar, when he invaded our homeland,
How vicious were they [Zanj] in defending their land?
And Sulayk, the ferocious lion, when he attacks
And Abbas, the master, they all outshine you.
And Ibn Khazim ibn Ajla, are among them [al-Zanj];
He surpassed all tribes in courage and honesty.
They were all sons of noble women,
Like lions raising their lion cubs.
If our Khu'ula is nobler than Kulaib,
Then you are viler than them,
And the sons of al-Hubab are lancers and nourishers
In winter, when the wind of the North blows.[117]

The poem questions the Arab emplotment of history and reminds Jarir of the bravery of al-Zanj who killed Hafs bin Ziyad bin Amr al-Ataki and his companions, and decimated his army, when he was in charge of al-Hajjaj police. It also reminds him of the fate of Jayfar, al-Nu'man bin Jayfar bin al-Julandi, who invaded the country of al-Zanj but was killed and his army seized by al-Zanj. However, this reminder comes as a prelude to prove the right of al-Zanj to recover their stolen rights. The most important of those rights is of those noble heroes (from Zanj mothers) whom Arab culture has monopolized, severing their ties with their original lineage. Among those heroes are Antarah bin Shaddad and his brother Harasa, Khufaf bin Nudbah, al-Sulayk bin Salaka, Abbas bin Merdas, Abdullah bin Khazim al-Salmi, and Banu al-Hubab. Blacks' ownership of those heroes is undeniable, for their colours and lineage to their black mothers prove the legitimacy to reclaim them.

The third poem in this angry black trinity is the poem of 'Ukaim al-Habashi. It is like the poem of Sunaih in terms of occasion, but it is closer to the poem of al-Hayqutan in terms of self-exaltation and a satirical approach. When Hakim bin Ayyash al-Kalbi said:

> Do not be proud of a (maternal) uncle from Bani Asad,
> For the Zanj and the Nubians are more honourable than them.

'Ukaim al-Habashi responded:

> In Ghumdan battle,[118] we were like lions and
> On the day of Yathrib,[119] we were the stallions of Arabs.
> The Elephant's Day[120] struck fear in Arabs' hearts,
> So they all fled on their camels.
> Among us are The Negus, while Dhul Aqsayn[121] is your brother-in-law,
> And Abraha's grandfather, the Hami Abu Talabi.[122]
> Let me forgive the Adnanites for mocking us,
> But what do the Himyarites have to do with lineage?
> They are Hammarah,[123] collected from everywhere,
> Like fish caught in a fishnet in a stormy sea.[124]

'Ukaim is aware that satirizing al-Zanj is necessarily satirizing him, which is why he responds. He does not reclaim al-Zanj glory stolen by Arabs, but he opens his objection by directly reminding Hakim and re-emploting the history of the relationship between Arabs and the Abyssinians. During that history, the Abyssinians destroyed the fortress of Ghumdan Palace in Yemen, attacked Mecca and terrified its people, and violated the honour of the people of Yathrib in The Battle of Harra (63 AH).

The poem is a collective satire of both the Adnanite and the Qahtanite Arabs. As for the Adnanites, they are reminded of the Battle of the Elephant, when Abyssinians invaded Mecca, and the Battle of al-Harra when blacks invaded Medina. As for the Qahtanites, they are reminded of Abyssinia's destruction of Yemen as well as the lowliness and meanness of their origin. They do not have a pure lineage since they are a group of "Hammarah" (mixed), or different mixed fish caught in a fishnet in a tumultuous sea.

These three poems reveal a shift in the cultural discourse that shaped the relationship between the Arab masters and the black slaves, and determined who had the right and eligibility to represent the Other or be the subject of representation by the Other. These poems reverse the roles of representation and the re-emplotment of history. These poets boast about their lineage and heroism, and direct their satire towards Arabs and their history, accusing them of weakness, inferiority, and cowardice when facing the glorious Abyssinian invader.

The power of Arab representation of Others has been shaken by the recent colonialization, which has brought Arabs and blacks together in one destiny and fate. At the forefront of the modern scene, a new player from the West emerged and extended its dominance over vast territories in Asia, Africa, and Latin America. This has redistributed the hierarchy of cultures, the ranks of nations, the hierarchies of races, and the scale and degrees of progress. It has redistributed roles of representation, in which the Arab, like the black African, became the object of an active, superior, and exclusionary representation process.

The discovery of the Other involves a tendency towards cultural centreing since it is a process carried out by a full, complete, and well-defined self that targets the unknown and conceals the Other. Also, the discovery of the Other is not direct and innocent knowledge. It works through the mediation of the imaginary, through the images and representations that the culture creates about this Other. This supports the saying that there is no "discovery" in reality, since the self finds the Other as it (the self) wanted it to be, and if it finds it different, it (the discovering self) strives to transform it to the same image and status that it imagined before the discovery. Hence, the discovery of the Other could be a curse on the discovered Other. Most cases of discovering the Other that we know today are a blessing for the discovering self only but a curse on the discovered Other, who is subjected to destruction, extermination, displacement, exclusion, marginalization, contempt, and ridicule. Consequently, we know the value of Walter Benjamin's words: "There is no document of civilization which is not at the same time a document of barbarism"[125]; as if barbarism is a fellow of civilization, and the instinct of evil and destruction is a fellow of knowledge that, as Foucault postulates, feeds on wrong, injustice, cruelty, and "violence of prejudices" against the Other.

Notes

INTRODUCTION

1 Kadhem's original text uses the words *al-Sood/al-Sudan* (blacks), both of which are acceptable and commonly used in Arabic. Al-Sood/al-Sudan refers to people with very dark skin or with "classical" sub-Saharan, black African phenotype. The translator retained the word "blacks" throughout this work.
2 Salama Moussa, "Wells' Books and Novels," 121.
3 Ibid.
4 It is argued (especially in the United States) that blacks were not enslaved because they were inferior, but that they came to be regarded as inferior because they were enslaved. See Kendi, *Stamped from the Beginning*, 98.
5 The word "*zanj*" (singular, *zinji*) generally means "country of the blacks." It was used in medieval Arabic texts to refer to African blacks in general or blacks from southeast Africa, and more specifically to Bantu-speaking cannibals originally from the region of Zanzibar and Tanzania. During the Caliphate, it was mostly used to refer to slaves. However, for Muhammad al-Fayrouzabadi (d.1415), al-Zanj is "a nation of blacks." Arabic lexicographers in Europe, such as Hans Wehr and J.G. Hava, translate the Arabic word "zanj" as "negro." See Ali, *The 'Negro' in Arab-Muslim Consciousness*, 17.
6 Salama Moussa, *Al-Muqtataf*, 290.
7 Ibid.
8 Ibid., 291.
9 Salman, *Al-Muqtataf*, 787.
10 Ibn Taymiyyah, *Iqtida' as-Sirat al-Mustaqim*, 168.

11 "Bin" is used when the second name following is the father's name, such as Muhammad bin Abdullah (Muhammad, son of Abdullah). "Ibn" is used when the second name following is either the grandfather's name or the mother's name, such as Isa ibn Maryam (Isa/Jesus, son of Maryam/Mary). The translator retained both forms as used in Kadhem's original text.

12 Sirah (plural, Siyyar) is a genre in Arabic and Islamic literature. Depending on its contexts, it may refer to three meanings: life, journey, biography.

PART ONE

1 Castoriadis, *Interview by Hashem Salih*.
2 Bieger, Saldivar, and Voelz, *The Imaginary and Its Worlds: American Studies after the Transnational Turn*, xvii.
3 Freud, "Revision of Dream Theory," 47.
4 Lacan, "The Mirror Stage," 735.
5 Jung, "The Structure and Dynamics of the Psyche," 521.
6 Durand, *The Anthropological Structures of the Imaginary*, 37.
7 Alexander & Seidman, *Culture and Society*, 2.
8 Marx and Engels, *The German Ideology*, 47.
9 Bourdieu, *Language & Symbolic Power*, 245.
10 Althusser, "Ideology and Ideological State Apparatuses," 242.
11 Durand, *The Anthropological Structures of the Imaginary*, 41.
12 Caughey, *Imaginary Social Worlds*, 9.
13 Ibid.
14 Foucault, *The Order of Things*, 396.
15 Said, *Culture and Imperialism*, 106.
16 Ibid.
17 Todorov, "Coexistence of Cultures," 221.
18 Cashmore, *The Black Culture Industry*, 26.
19 Foucault, "Nietzsche, Genealogy, and History," 95.
20 Foucault, *Lectures on the Will to Know*, 218.
21 Said, *Orientalism*, 203–4.
22 Ibid., 92.

CHAPTER ONE

1 Al-Tunisi, *Tashhith al-thhan bi Sirat Bilad al-Arab wa al-Sudan*, 41–2.
2 Al-Askari, *Diwan al-Ma'ani*, 5001.
3 See Bhabha, *Nation and Narration*, 1.

4　Marshall, *Teaching the Postmodern*, 178.
5　White, "A Comment," 297.
6　Jameson, "On Interpretation: Literature as a Socially Symbolic Act," 261.
7　White, "A Comment," 297.
8　Ibid., 305.
9　Lerner, "History and Fiction," 334.
10　See Said, "Invention, Memory and Place."
11　See Whitelam, *The Invention of Ancient Israel*.
12　Bernal, *Black Athena*, vol. 1, *The Fabrication of Ancient Greece, 1785–1985*.
13　Medieval Muslim Arab sociologist, philosopher, and historian.
14　Al-Masudi, *Akhbar al-Zaman*, 63.
15　Haleem, *Kitaab al-Ansab*, 27.
16　All Bible citations are taken from the Bible Gateway, New International Version, www.biblegateway.com.
17　Haleem, *Kitaab al-Ansab*, 28–9.
18　*Qaisar* (Caesar) is the common name given by Arabs to the Byzantine emperor. Arabs have used it for a long time due to the historical relations between Arabs and the Romans, which flourished during the time of the Byzantine emperors. The reference to Caesar is mentioned in the poetry of the pre-Islamic poet Imru' al-Qays and the poetry that came after him. The word "Qaisar" is not mentioned in the Quran, but it is frequently mentioned in the Prophet's biography, Hadiths, interpretations of the Quran, and historical books. The word is used as an indefinite noun for the Byzantine emperors like Heraclius, along with other expressions such as "Caesar, the Great of the Romans" or "Caesar, the King of the Romans."
19　The story is mentioned in ancient history books, and in tafsir books, where it is believed that they are the ones to whom the following Quranic verse was revealed: "Cursed were the People of the Ditch. Fire supplied [abundantly] with fuel, When they sat by it [the Fire] ..." Surah Al-Burooj: 85.
20　Tabarsi, *Majma` al-Bayan fi Tafsir al-Qur'an*, 10:314. The strange thing in this narration is that Imam Ali speaks about an Abyssinian prophet, that is, a black prophet; however, according to the Arab belief, God did not send a black prophet, for all the prophets were from Shem's sons who lived in the moderate climes, according to Ibn Khaldun and others.
21　Lentricchia, *After the New Criticism*, 128.
22　Al-Masudi, *Muruj al-Dhahab wa Ma`adin al-Jawhar*, 2:182.
23　The word "al-Rum" was used in the Medieval Age to refer to Byzantine Christians. It is also used in the Quran (al-Rum/Ar-Rum, chapter 30).

24 Ibn Khaldun, *The Muqaddimah*, 172.
25 Al-Masudi, *Muruj al-Dhahab*, 2:182.
26 Ibid.
27 Ibid.
28 Ibid., 78.
29 Al-Masudi, *Muruj al-Dhahab wa Ma`adin al-Jawhar*, 2:186.
30 Shaarawy, *Surat al-Afriqi lada al-Muthaqaf al-Arabi*, 236.
31 Badawi, *Al-sood wal Hadharah al-Arabiyya*, 76.
32 Refers to a monotheistic religious movement that arose in pre-Islamic Arabia and was rooted in Prophet Abraham's patriarch.
33 Ibid.
34 Al-Masudi, *Muruj al-Dhahab wa Ma`adin al-Jawhar*, 1:190.
35 Ibid., 189.
36 Shaarawy, *Surat al-Afriqi lada al-Muthaqaf al-Arabi*, 236.
37 Gérard Genette's term for the perspective through which a narrative is presented.
38 Ibn Hisham, *Sirah Ibn Hisham*, 1:54.
39 See Badawi, *Al-sood wal Hadharah al-Arabiyya*, 85–6.
40 Ibn Saad, *al-Tabaqat al-Kubra*, 1:203–4.
41 Ibn Hisham, *Sirah Ibn Hisham*, 1:266.
42 Al-Ya'qubi, *Tarikh al-Ya'qubi*, 2:29.
43 Ibn Hanbal, *Musnad Ahmad*, 1:202.
44 Al-Sijistani, *Sunan Abu Dawood*, 3:212.
45 Ibn Hanbal, *Musnad Ahmad*, 4:198.
46 Al-Naysaburi, *Sahih Muslim*, Book 4, 527.
47 Al-Sijistani, *Sunan Abu Dawood*, 3:16.
48 Al-Haythami, *Majma' al-Zawa'id*, 4:235–36.
49 Al-Zirqani, *Mukhtaser al-Maqasid al-Hasana*, 185.
50 Jabar, *Wufud al-Qaba'l 'ala Rasool wa Intishar al-Islam fi Jazeerat al-Arab*, 62.
51 See Williams, *Marxism and Literature*, 123–7.
52 Al-Naysaburi, *Sahih Muslim*, Book 31, 6096.
53 Freud, "Five Lectures on Psychoanalysis," 2224.
54 All Quran citations are from the English translation by Saheeh International, https://quranenc.com/en/browse/english_saheeh, accessed 15 September 2022.
55 Al-Qurtubi, *Tafsir al-Qurtubi*, 4:322.
56 Al-Noori, *Mustadrak al-Wasa'l*, 11:94.
57 Tabarsi, *Majma' al-Bayan fi Tafsir al-Qur'an*, 9:225–26.

58 Othman, "Tijarat al-Muheet al-Hindi fi Asr al-Siyada al-Islamiyya," 41.
59 Davidson, *A Guide to African History*, 20.
60 Shaarawy, *Surat al-Afriqi lada al-Muthaqaf al-Arabi*, 240.
61 The word "Sudan" (blacks: plural) is derived from the Arabic word "aswad," which means black colour. The country name of Sudan is derived from the Arabic expression Bilad al-Sudan (land of the blacks).
62 Al-Manawi, *Faidh al-Qadir*, 3:532.
63 Al-Jahiz, *Risalat Fakhar al-Sudan 'ala Bidhan*, 1:197.
64 Al-Jazari, *Usd al-Ghabah fi marifat al-Sahabah*, 1:244.
65 Al-Jahiz, *Risalat Fakhar al-Sudan 'ala Bidhan*, 1:211–12.
66 Al-Azmeh, *Al-Arab wal Barabira*, 182.
67 Ibn Butlan, *Risala Nafi'a fi Shray al-Raqiq wa Taqleeb al-Abeed*, 1:386.
68 Ibid., 383.
69 Al-Turky, "Ilgha al-sifa al-qanunia lil Riq fi Saltanat Zanjibar al-Arabiyya 1897," 23.
70 Leitch, *Cultural Criticism, Literary Theory, Poststructuralism*, 171.
71 Geertz, *Islam Observed: Religious Development in Morocco and Indonesia*, 111.
72 Al-Ta'I, "Al-Itjah Nahwa al-Din," 12.
73 Afaya, *Al-gharb Mutakhayal*, 205.
74 See Todorov, *The Conquest of America*, 41.
75 Al-Ya'qubi, *Kitab al-Buldan*, 95.
76 Al-Masudi, *Muruj al-Dhahab wa Ma`adin al-Jawhar*, 2:115.
77 Al-Dimashqi, *Nukhbat al-Dahr, fi 'Aja'ib, i.e., al-Bar wa al-Bahr*, 318.
78 See Surah al-Furqan 25, verse 44; Surah al-A'raf 7, verse 179; Surah al-Ma'idah 5, verse 60.
79 Ibn Hanbal, *Musnad Ahmad*, 5:178.
80 Al-Kulayni, *Al-Kafi*, 1:105.
81 Majlesi, *Bihar al-Anwar*, 1:11.
82 Al-Baghdadi, *Tarikh Baghdad*, 2:221.
83 Ibn Hawqal, *Surat al-Ardh*, 19.
84 Al-Dimashqi, *Nukhbat al-Dahr, fi 'Aja'ib, i.e., al-Bar wa al-Bahr*, 358–9.
85 Ibid., 359.
86 Al-Rishhari, *al-Khair wal Barakah fil Kitab wal Sunnah*, 37.
87 Al-Maqdisi, *Ahsan al-Taqaseem fi Marifat al-Aqaleem*, 23.
88 Al-Shahrastani, *Al-Milal wa al-Nihal*, 1:37.
89 Abi Talib, *Peak of Eloquence (Nahjul-Balagha)*, 792.
90 Ibn Hanbal, *Musnad Ahmad*, 5:411.
91 Al-Bukhari, *Sahih al-Bukhari*, vol. 1.

92 Ibn Kathir, *Al-Sira al-Nabawiyya (The Life of the Prophet)*, 1:211.
93 See Shaarawy, *Surat al-Afriqi lada al-Muthaqaf al-Arabi*, 245; and Ahmed, *Al-Mar'a wal Jinusa fil Islam (women and sex in Islam)*, 70.
94 Shaarawy, *Surat al-Afriqi lada al-Muthaqaf al-Arabi*, 245.
95 Al-Masudi, *Muruj al-Dhahab wa Ma`adin al-Jawhar*, 3:70.
96 Shaarawy, *Surat al-Afriqi lada al-Muthaqaf al-Arabi*, 245.
97 Al-Tijani, *Tuhfat al-Aroos Wa Muta't al-Nofous*, 243.
98 Faqih (pl. Fuqaha) refers to a person who is an expert/jurisconsult in Fiqh (Islamic jurisprudence).
99 Al-Shafi, *Al-Umm*, 5:10.
100 Al-Qurtubi, *Tafsir al-Qurtubi*, 5:395.
101 Al-Suyuti, *Nuzhat al-'Umr fi al-Tafdeel bayna al-Beedh wa al-Sud wa al-Sumr*, 18.
102 Sabzevari, *Al-Jadid fi Tafseer al-Quran*, 2:118.
103 Al-Shirazi, *Taqrib al-Quran ila al-Athhan*, 4:20.
104 Al-Qurtubi, *Tafsir al-Qurtubi*, 19:148.
105 Al-Qurtubi, *Tafsir al-Qurtubi*, 13:316 and Al-Tusi, *al-Tibyan fi Tafseer al-Quran*, 9:477.
106 At-Tirmidhi, *Jami' at-Tirmidhi*, 5:42.
107 Ibn Manzur, *Lisan al-Arab*, s.v. "sakham."
108 Al-Kulayni, *Al-Kafi*, 6:533.
109 Ibn Sirin, *Muntakhabul Kalam Fi Tafsir al-Ahlam*, 110.
110 Bakr, *Salwat Al-Ahzan lil Ijtinab 'an Mujalasat al-Ahdath wal Niswan*, 39.
111 Al-Ghazzi, *Al-Kawakib al-Sa'irah Bia'yan al-Mi'ah al-'Ashirah*, 2:148.
112 Al-Tabari, *The History of al-Tabari*, 1:307.
113 Al-Jurjani, *Asrar al-Balaghah*, 341–2.
114 Durand, *The Anthropological Structures of the Imaginary*, 89.
115 Al-Qurtubi, *Tafsir al-Qurtubi*, 10:394.
116 Reilly, *The West and the World: A Topical History of Civilization*, 361.
117 Durand, *The Anthropological Structures of the Imaginary*, 91.
118 Leeming, *Creation Myths of the World: An Encyclopedia*, 1:165.
119 Ricœur, *From Text to Action*, 182.
120 In Arab/Muslim culture, dreams are of three kinds: good visions (Ru'yaa/prophetic: seeing "glad tidings from Allah"), bad dreams (hulum: seeing bad things from Satan) and self-talk (hadith annafs: reflection of inner thoughts and concerns).
121 Freud, "Five Lectures on Psychoanalysis," 2221.
122 Caughey, *Imaginary Social Worlds*, 83.
123 Ibid., 91.
124 Al-Bukhari, *Sahih Bukhari*, 9:114.

125 Ibn Sirin, *Muntakhab al-kalam fi tafsir al-ahlam*, 275.
126 Al-Jazari, *Usd al-Ghabah fi marifat al-Sahabah*, 5:448.
127 At-Tirmidhi, *Jami' at-Tirmidhi*, 5:167.
128 Al-Qazwini, *Sunan Ibn Majah*, 1:118.
129 Al-Kulayni, *Al-Kafi*, 6:592.
130 Ibid.
131 Al-Manawi, *Faidh al-Qadir*, 1:111.
132 Al-Jahiz, *Kitab al-Haywan*, 2:316.
133 Ibid., 207.
134 Al-Damiri, *Hayat al-Haywan al-Kubra*, 1:341.
135 As-Sijistani, *Sunan Abu Dawud*, 1:417.
136 At-Tirmidhi, *Jami' at-Tirmidhi*, 3:268.
137 Al-Jahiz, *Kitab al-Haywan*, 2:79.
138 Ibid., 314. See also Al-Damiri, *Hayat al-Haywan al-Kubra*, 2:103.

CHAPTER TWO

1 Hegel, *The Philosophy of History*, 93, 96.
2 Al-Dimashqi, *Nukhbat al-Dahr fi 'Aja'ib al-Bar wa al-Bahr*, 25.
3 See Al-Nadim, *Kitab al-Fihrist*, 33.
4 Al-Tahtawi, *Takhlees al- Ibreez fi Talkhees Pareez*, 12.
5 *Al-Franj* (the Franks) was widely used after the Crusades to refer to Western Christians as opposed to Eastern or Byzantine Christians.
6 Al-Suyuti, *Nuzhat al-'Umr fi al-Tafdeel bayna al-Beedh wa al-Sud wa al-Sumr*, 13.
7 Ibid., 14.
8 Shahrdar, *Al-Firdaws bi Ma'thoor al-Khitab*, 1:387.
9 Al-Qurtubi, *Tafsir al-Qurtubi*, 11:53.
10 Al-Askari, *Diwan al-Ma'ani*, 177.
11 Al-Tauhidi, *al-Imta' wal-Mu'anasa*, 1:71.
12 Al-Masudi, *Muruj al-Dhahab wa Ma`adin al-Jawhar*, 1:83.
13 Al-Jawziyya, *Naqd al-Manqool*, 1:88.
14 Al-Manawi, *Faidh al-Qadir*, 1:111.
15 Al-Mahali and Al-Suyuti, *Tafsir al-Jalalayn*, 1:785.
16 Al-Haythami, *Majma' al-Zawa'id*, 4:235.
17 *Tarab* refers to a state of ecstatic engagement, enchantment, or rapture promoted usually by music and singing.
18 Al-Masudi, *Muruj al-Dhahab wa Ma`adin al-Jawhar*, 1:81.
19 See Al-Qazwini, *Athaar al-Bilaad*, 22–3, and Al-Dimashqi, *Nukhbat al-Dahr, fi 'Aja'ib, i.e., al-Bar wa al-Bahr*, 359.

20. Al-Masudi, *Muruj al-Dhahab*, 2:103
21. Ibn Butlan, *Risala Nafi'a fi Shray al-Raqiq wa Taqleeb al-Abeed*, 1:398–9.
22. Al-Ya'qubi, *Tarikh al-Ya'qubi*, 1:15.
23. Al-Isfahani, *Kitab al-Aghani*, 3:273.
24. Al-Jahiz, *al-Bayan wal Tabyin*, 1:79.
25. Ibn Butlan, *Risala Nafi'a fi Shray al-Raqiq wa Taqleeb al-Abeed*, 404.
26. Al-Dimishqi, *Nukhbat al-Dahr*, 356.
27. Al-Nuwayri, *Nihayat al-Arab fi funun al-Adab*, 1:294.
28. Al-Tauhidi, *al-Imta' wal-Mu'anasa*, 1:215.
29. Al-Qazwini, *'Aja'ib al-Makhluqat wa Ghara'ib al-Mawjudat*, 31–2.
30. Ibn Khaldun, *The Muqaddimah*, 197.
31. Ibn Butlan, *Risala Nafi'a fi Shray al-Raqiq wa Taqleeb al-Abeed*, 409.
32. Khalaili, "al-Mutanabbi in His Role as a Eulogist and Satirist of Kafur."
33. It refers to narratives in hadiths that are assumed to be of foreign import: from Jewish, Christian, or Zoroastrian sources.
34. Al-Masudi, *Akhbar al-Zaman*, 83.
35. Ibid., 84.
36. Ibid.
37. Al-Masudi, *Muruj al-Dhahab wa Ma'adin al-Jawhar*, 1:38.
38. Al-Manawi, *Faidh al-Qadir*, 1:111.
39. Al-Masudi, *Akhbar al-Zaman*, 79.
40. Al-Masudi, *Muruj al-Dhahab wa Ma'adin al-Jawhar*, 1:38.
41. Ibn Khaldun, *The Muqaddimah*, 124.
42. Al-Katib, *Adab al-Mulook*, 115.
43. Muthhir, *Ta'athur al-Thaqafa al-Arabiyya bil Thaqafa al-Yunaniyya*, 47.
44. Isaac, *The Invention of Racism in Classical Antiquity*, 55–6.
45. Ibid., 72.
46. Al-Manawi, *Faidh al-Qadir*, 1:181.
47. Ibn Majid, *Kitab al-Fawa'id fi Usul 'Ilm al-Bahr wa 'l-Qawa'id*, 190.
48. Al-Masudi, *Muruj al-Dhahab wa Ma'adin al-Jawhar*, 1:86.
49. Al-Safa, *Rasa'il Ikhwan al-Safa wa Khilan al-Wafa*, 163.
50. Al-Dimashqi, *Nukhbat al-Dahr, fi 'Aja'ib, i.e., al-Bar wa al-Bahr*, 360.
51. See Al-Safa, *Rasa'il Ikhwan al-Safa*, 1:1171–9.
52. Al-Sirafi and Al-Tajir, "Akhbar al-Seen wal Hind," 1:970.
53. Ibn Battutah, *Tuhfat al-Nuzar fi Ghara'ib al-Amsar wa 'Aja'ib al-Asfar*, 263.
54. Al-Qazwini, *Athaar al-Bilaad*, 619.
55. Al-Hamadani, *Mukhtasar Kitab al-Buldan*, 9.
56. Minorsky, *Sharaf al-Zaman Tahir Marvazi on China, the Turks, and India*, 54.

57 Al-Idrisi, *Nuzhat al-Mushtaq fi ikhtiraq al-Afaq*, 110.
58 Ibn Butlan, *Risala Nafi'a fi Shray al-Raqiq wa Taqleeb al-Abeed*, 1:403.
59 Shahrdar, *Al-Firdaws bi Ma'thoor al-Khitab*, 1:387.
60 Al-Manawi, *Faidh al-Qadir*, 2:558.
61 Ibn Khaldun, *The Muqaddimah*, 125.
62 Al-Baghdadi, *Tarikh Baghdad*, 1:23.
63 Ibn Khaldun, *The Muqaddimah*, 124.
64 Al-Dimashqi, *Nukhbat al-Dahr, fi 'Aja'ib, i.e., al-Bar wa al-Bahr*, 362.
65 Al-Masudi, *Muruj al-Dhahab wa Ma`adin al-Jawhar*, 1:81.
66 Al-Qanwaji, *Abjad al-Uloom*, 1:168.
67 Ibid., 167.
68 Ibid., 168.
69 "Anti-Arab protest movement that had developed within intellectual and literary circles among the Mawali during the second and third Islamic centuries. The Shu'ubiyya phenomenon emerged as a reaction to Arab superiority and dominance in early Muslim society. Its spokesmen rejected the Arab right to hegemony within the *umma* and called instead for equality between non-Arab and Arab Muslims regardless of ethnic origins." Gershoni and Jankowski, *Egypt, Islam, and the Arabs*, 103.
70 Amin, *Dhuha al-Islam*, 1:386.
71 Ibn Ahmad, al-Dhahabi, *Siyyar A'lam al-Nubala*, 11:527.
72 Al-Anbari, *Nuzhat al-Alibba fi Tabaqat al-Udaba*, 149.
73 Al-Azmeh, *al-Arab wal Barabira*, 65.
74 Al-Taweel, *Abu Uthman al-Jahiz*, 8.
75 Al-Masudi, *Muruj al-Dhahab wa Ma`adin al-Jawhar*, 2:153.
76 See Al-Dinawari, *Ta'wil Mukhtalif al-Hadith*, 59.
77 Al-Jahiz, *Kitab al-Haywan*, 5:91.
78 Ibid., 466.
79 *Hulaq*, an archaic word, refers to a sexual disease that affects horses' and donkeys' genitals.
80 Ibid., 316.
81 *Fahl* (plural, *fuhul*, n. *fuhula*) linguistically means a male animal, but it generally refers to someone with virility, strength, courage, and honourable status. As for its critical meaning, it refers to a literary machismo in which a poetic prowess is interlinked with notions of masculinity. It is usually associated with a classification of poets theorized by Arab scholars such as philologist and grammarian Abd al-Malik ibn Quraib al-Asma'i (740–828 CE). A poet is *Fahl* (highest rank of poets) if he has: (1) a courageous and powerful ability to express poetry; (2) a unique creativity in versing poetry; (3) a mastery of the purposes (*aghrad*)

of poetry such as satire (*hija*) and panegyric (*madh*); (4) a noticeable impact on the poets of his time; and (5) an adherence to the previous fuhul poets and their poetic traditions. Imru' al-Qais (d. 544 CE) is considered as one of the outstanding examples of *Fuhul* poets.

82 Al-Jahiz, *al-Bayan wal Tabyin*, 1:164.
83 Ibid., 304.
84 Al-Jahiz, *Kitab al-Haywan*, 3:245.
85 Ibid., 2:314.
86 Ibid.
87 Al-Jahiz, *Manaqib al Turk*, 1:36.
88 Afaya, *Al-gharb al-mtkhyl: suar alakhàr fil fikr al-arabi al-islami al-wasiti*, 113.
89 Ibid.
90 Al-Jahiz, *Rasa'il al-Jahiz*, 1:196.
91 Ibid., 213, 219.
92 Ibid., 220.

PART TWO

1 Zanj revolution or rebellion, (869–883 CE), a black-slave revolt against the Abbasid caliphal empire.

CHAPTER THREE

1 Ibrahim, *Ashkal al-Ta'bir fil Adab al-Shabi*, 157.
2 Keller, "Otto Rank (1884–1939)."
3 Abdullah, *al-Sardiyya al-Arabiyya*, 164.
4 *Sirat Bani Hilal*, 27.
5 Al-Andalusi, *Tawq al-Hamamah*, 15.
6 It is defined as follows: "To accuse one's wife of committing adultery saying [to the judge] 'I have seen her committing adultery.' Or to deny his paternity what Allah has created in her womb." El-Jazaery, *The Approach of the Muslim*, 377.
7 Al-Qazwini, *Sunan Ibn Majah*, 3:145.
8 Barakat means blessings.
9 *Sirat Bani Hilal*, 27.
10 Ibid., 37.
11 *Sirat al-Amirah Dhat al-Himma wa Waladaha Abdul Wahab*, 1:592.
12 Ibid., 596.
13 Ibid., 631.

14 Ibid., 640.
15 Ibid., 782.
16 Ibid., 674.
17 See Al-Kulayni, *Al-Kafi*, 5:539, and Al-Mashhadi, *Kanz al-Daqa'iq wa Bahr al-ghra'ib*, 2:329.
18 Al-Sadiq was an eighth-century Shia Muslim scholar, jurist, and theologian. He was the founder of the Ja'fari school of Islamic jurisprudence.
19 *Sirat Antarah bin Shaddad*, 138.
20 Ibid., 147.
21 Ibid., 200.
22 Ibid., 346.
23 Ibid., 6:340.
24 Ibid., 5:277, 280, 290.
25 Ibid., 1:510.
26 Ibid., 4:25.
27 Ibid., 5:268.
28 Ibid., 316, 326, 322.
29 Al-Tijani, *Tuhfat al-Aroos Wa Muta't al-Nofous*, 229.
30 *Sirat Antarah bin Shaddad*, 1:108.
31 Ibid., 5:306.
32 *Sirat al-Malik Seif bin Dhi Yazan Faris al-Yemen*, 24.
33 Al-Masudi, *Akhbar al-Zaman*, 83.
34 Ibrahim, *Al-Sardiyya al-Arabiyya*, 90.
35 Encyclopedia.com, "The Arabian Nights: The Frame Tale."
36 *Alf Layla wa Layla*, 1:225.
37 Ibid.
38 Al-Kulayni, *Al-Kafi*, 5:460.
39 *Alf Layla wa Layla*, 2:238.
40 Al-Tifashi, *Nuzhat al-Albab*, 270-1.
41 There are several bestiality tales in *One Thousand and One Nights*, where women have sexual intercourse with, for instance, monkeys or bears to satisfy their excessive lust.

CHAPTER FOUR

1 Shaarawy, *Surat al-Afriqi lada al-Muthaqaf al-Arabi*, 250.
2 See "Al-Mawsu'a al-Shi'riya."
3 Abdullah, *al-Markaziyya al-Islamiyya*, 181.
4 Oven refers to a vagina.
5 Al-Isfahani, *Kitab al-Aghani*, 21:323.

6 Al-Suyuti, *Nuzhat al-'Umr fi al-Tafdeel bayna al-Beedh wa al-Sud wa al-Sumr*, 55–9.
7 Al-Tijani, *Tuhfat al-Aroos Wa Muta't al-Nofous*, 229.
8 Al-Suyuti, *Nuzhat al-'Umr fi al-Tafdeel bayna al-Beedh wa al-Sud wa al-Sumr*, 49.
9 Ibid., 50.
10 Al-Tijani, *Tuhfat al-Aroos Wa Muta't al-Nofous*, 230.
11 Al-Isfahani, *Kitab al-Aghani*, 1:323–4.
12 Ghada is a young beautiful delicate woman.
13 "Al-Mawsu'a al-Shi'riya."
14 Derived from "Tarab"; tarub refers to an exuberant person who is quickly and ecstatically engaged with music/singing/dancing. This is considered a distasteful feature and is often attributed to blacks.
15 "Al-Mawsu'a al-Shi'riya."
16 Al-Maqdisi, *Umraa al-Shi'r al-Arabi fil al-Asr al-Abbasi*, 287.
17 Al-Masudi, *al-Tanbih wa al-Ishraf*, 368.
18 Al-Tiqtaqa, *al-Fakhri fi al-Adab al-Sultaniyya wa al-Diwal al-Islamiyya*, 250–1.
19 Al-Masudi, *Muruj al-Dhahab wa Ma'adin al-Jawhar*, 5:186.
20 Foucault, *The Archeology of Knowledge and the Discourse on Language*, 216.
21 See Al-Ya'qubi, *Tarikh al-Ya'qubi*, 2:507; Al-Tabari, *Tarikh al-Tabari*, 7:566, 594, 597, 608; and Ibn Kathir, *Al-Bidayah wal Nihaya*, 11:23, 24, 34, 36, 37, 38.
22 *Diwan Ibn al-Rumi*, 135.
23 Ibid.
24 Ibid.
25 White, "A Comment," 294.
26 Lentricchia, *After the New Criticism*, 351.
27 Al-Qayrawani, *al-Umdah fi Mahasin al-Shi'r, wa Adabah wa Naqdah*, 1:121.
28 Diyab, *Khulasat al-Mutanabbi*, 213.
29 Sperl and Shackle, *Qasida Poetry in Islamic Asia and Africa*, 1:93.
30 Ibid., 95.
31 Ibid.
32 Ibid.
33 Diyab, *Khulasat al-Mutanabbi*, 2:626.
34 Al-Akbari, *Al-Tibyan fi Sharh al-Diwan*, 4:288, and Al-tha'alibi, *Yatimat al-Dahr fi Mahasin Ahl al-Asr*, 1:190.
35 Sperl and Shackle, *Qasida Poetry in Islamic Asia and Africa*, 95.

36 Diminutive form used to express smallness.
37 Hussein, *Ma'a al-Mutanabbi*, 330.
38 Al-Wahidii, *Sharah Diwan al-Mutanabbi*, 2:629.
39 "'Father of Whiteness' (i.e., bounty) is ironically applied to the black miser Kafur" (Sperl and Shackle, *Qasida Poetry in Islamic Asia and Africa*, 422).
40 Sperl and Shackle, *Qasida Poetry in Islamic Asia and Africa*, 103–4.
41 Khalaili, "al-Mutanabbi in his Role as a Eulogist and Satirist of Kafur," 168.
42 Ibid., 169.
43 Ibid., 315.
44 Ibid., 180.
45 Sperl and Shackle, *Qasida Poetry in Islamic Asia and Africa*, 103.
46 Khalaili, "al-Mutanabbi in his Role as a Eulogist and Satirist of Kafur," 185.
47 Al-Ghathami, *al-Naqd al-Thaqafi: Qira'a fil Ansaq al-Thaqafiyya*, 168–9.
48 Khalaili, "al-Mutanabbi in his Role as a Eulogist and Satirist of Kafur," 59.
49 Abbas, *Tarikh al-Naqd al-Adabi 'inda al-Arab*, 281–2.
50 Khalaili, "al-Mutanabbi in his Role as a Eulogist and Satirist of Kafur," 163.
51 Al-Wahidii, *Sharah Diwan al-Mutanabbi*, 2:666.
52 Khalaili, "al-Mutanabbi in his Role as a Eulogist and Satirist of Kafur," 174.
53 Al-Rumi, *Qalb Kafuriyyat al-Mutanabi min al-Madih ila al-Hija*, 176–7.
54 Hussein, *Ma'a al-Mutanabbi*, 303.
55 Foucault, *The History of Sexuality*, 1:95.
56 Leitch, *Cultural Criticism, Literary Theory, Poststructuralism*, 92.
57 al-Furusiyya (Arabian knighthood dates back to pre-Islamic era) generally refers to knightly/equestrian martial exercise, and includes noble qualities such as chivalry, bravery, generosity, altruism, forgiveness, faithfulness, and love, and the ability to compose/recite powerful poetry.
58 "White character" here refers to the "white Arab character," which generally includes virtuous behaviours, manners, qualities, values, and deeds.
59 Al-Isfahani, *Kitab Al-Aghani*, 8:250.
60 *Diwan Antarah*, 22.
61 Ibid., 25.
62 Ibid., 201.
63 Ibid., 211.
64 Ibid., 126.

65 Ibid., 103.
66 Ibid., 22.
67 Ibid., 59.
68 Al-Jumahi, *Tabaqat al-Shu'ra*, 72.
69 Thuhni, *Sirat Antarah*, 77.
70 Ibid., 86.
71 Al-Isfahani, *Kitab Al-Aghani*, 1:339.
72 Ibid., 325.
73 Ibid., 337.
74 Ibid., 315.
75 Ibid.
76 Ibid., 316.
77 Ibid., 323–4.
78 Ibid., 325.
79 Ibid., 337.
80 Ibid., 338.
81 Ibid., 339.
82 Ibid., 313.
83 *Nasib* refers to amatory poetry. In the pre-Islamic era, nasib was a prelude to qasidah (e.g., al-Mu'allaqat/Odes), where the poet starts his poem reminiscing about people (his beloved), things, and times lost and absent.
84 Ibid., 332.
85 Ibid., 329.
86 Ibid., 312.
87 Ibid., 349.
88 *Diwan Abu Dulamah*, 79.
89 Ibid., 109–10.
90 Ibid., 48–9.
91 Ibid., 112.
92 Ibid., 94.
93 Al-Isfahani, *Kitab Al-Aghani*, 10:300.
94 Ibid., 281.
95 Al-Jahiz, *Al-Taj fi Akhlaq al-Muluk*, 63.
96 Badawi, *Al-sood wal Hadharah al-Arabiyya*, 198.
97 *Diwan Suhaim Abd Bani al-Hashas*, 66.
98 Referring to all fingers of her hands and feet, i.e., her whole body embraced him.
99 Al-Jumahi, *Tabaqat al-Shu'ra*, 89.
100 Al-Jahiz, *Fakhr al-Sudan*, 1:198.
101 Ibid., 182.

102 Al-Julanda family ruled Oman from the sixth century CE until their overthrow in the Umayyad era.
103 Harith ibn Abi Shamir al-Gassani was the Ghassanid Arab Christian governor of Sham.
104 The poet claims that those people refused to believe in and accept Muhammad's prophethood and his invitation to Islam.
105 Hawthah bin Ali al-Hanafi, a poet and orator of Banu Hanifa, before and during Islam.
106 Accepted and believed in Muhammad's prophethood and mission.
107 "it" refers to Mecca (Arabs' honour).
108 The country that does not pay tax to its kings.
109 Water spring in Bahrain.
110 Banu Kulaib (tribe of Kulaib) were accused of having intercourse with lambs and ewes.
111 Al-Jahiz, *Fakhr al-Sudan*, 1:183–5.
112 Maternal uncle relationship.
113 *Kulaib* is an Arab tribe, but also a diminutive form of the word "Kalb" (a dog).
114 Al-Farazdaq's noble forefathers.
115 Name of Jarir's mother.
116 Khufaf bin Nudbah from Sulaym's tribe.
117 Al-Jahiz, *Fakhr al-Sudan*, 1:190–1.
118 Ghumdan Palace in Yemen was destroyed by Abrahah al-Habashi.
119 Refers to The Battle of al-Harra (63 AH).
120 Refers to Abraha's attack (using elephants) on Mecca around 552 AD.
121 Dhu al-Qarnayn (He of the Two Horns).
122 From Ham's offspring.
123 Hammarah refers to a hybrid mare, but it also has other meanings such as muleteers or (slow) horses that run like donkeys.
124 Ibid., 199.
125 Steinberg, *Walter Benjamin and the Demands of History*, 209.

Bibliography

Abbas, Ihsan. *Tarikh al-Naqd al-Adabi 'inda al-Arab*. Beirut: Dar al-Thaqafa, 1971.
Abi Talib, Ali b. *Peak of Eloquence (Nahjul-Balagha)*. New York: Tahrike Tarsile Qur'an Inc., 2009.
Afaya, Muhammad Nur al-Din. *Al-Gharb al-Mutakhayal: Suwar al-Akhar fil fikr al-Arabi al-islami al-wasit*. Beirut/Casablanca: The Arab Cultural Center, 2000.
Ahmed, Layla. *Al-Mar'a wal Jinusa fil Islam*. Cairo: al-Majlis al-'Ala lil Thaqafa, 1999.
Al-Akbari, Abu Al-Baqa. *Al-Tibyan fi Sharh al-Diwan*. Vol.4. Cairo: Dar al-Kitaab al-Islami, n.d.
Alexander, Jeffrey, and Steven Seidman. *Culture and Society: Contemporary Debates*. Cambridge: Cambridge University Press, 1991.
Alf Layla wa Layla. Vol. 1. Beirut: Maktabat al-Hayat, 2000.
Ali, Abdullah bin Hamid. *The 'Negro' in Arab-Muslim Consciousness*. E-book: Claritas Books, 2018.
Althusser, Louis. "Ideology and Ideological State Apparatuses." In *Critical Theory since 1965*. Tallahassee: Florida State University Press, 1986.
Amin, Ahmed. *Dhuha al-Islam*. Vol. 1. Beirut: Dar al-Kitab al-Arabi, n.d.
Al-Anbari, Abu al-Barakat. *Nuzhat al-Alibba fi Tabaqat al-Udaba*. Jordan: Manar Library, 1985.
Al-Andalusi, Ibn Hazm. *Tawq al-Hamamah*. Damascus: Dar al-Mada lil Thaqafa wal Nashr, 2002.
Al-Askari, Abu Hilal. *Diwan al-Ma'ani*. Beirut: Dar al-Kutub al-Ilmiya, 1994.
As-Sijistani, Abu Dawud Sulayman ibn al-Ash'ath. *Sunan Abu Dawud*. Vol.1. Translated by Yaser Qadhi. Riyadh: Darussalam, 2008.

At-Tirmidhi, Hafiz Abu Eisa. *Jamiʿat-Tirmidhi*. Vol. 3. Translated by Abu Khaliyl. Riyadh: Darussalam, 2007.
– *Jamiʿat-Tirmidhi*. Vol. 5. Translated by Abu Khaliyl. Riyadh: Darussalam, 2007.
Al-Azmeh, Aziz. *Al-Arab wal Barabira: Al-Muslimoon wal Hadharat al-Okhra*. London/Cyprus: Riyadh al-Rais lil Kutub wal Nashir, 1991.
Badawi, Abduh. *Al-sood wal Hadharah al-Arabiyya*. Cairo: General Egyptian Book Organization, 1976.
Al-Baghdadi, al-Khatib. *Tarikh Baghdad*. Vol. 1. Beirut: Dar al-Kotob Al-Ilmiyah, n.d.
– *Tarikh Baghdad*. Vol. 2. Beirut: Dar al-Kotob Al-Ilmiyah, n.d.
Bernal, Martin. *Black Athena: The Afro-Asiatic Roots of Classical Civilization*. Vol. 1, *The Fabrication of Ancient Greece, 1785–1985*. Rutland: Rutland Local History and Record Society, 1987.
Bhabha, Homi K. *Nation and Narration*. London: Routledge, 1990.
Bieger, Laura, Ramon Saldivar, and Johannes Voelz, eds. *The Imaginary and Its Worlds: American Studies after the Transnational Turn*. Hanover: Dartmouth College Press, 2013.
Bourdieu, Pierre. *Language & Symbolic Power*. Translated by Gino Raymond and Matthew Adamson. Cambridge: Polity Press, 1991.
Al-Bukhari, Muhammad. *Sahih Bukhari*. Vol. 1. Translated by M. Muhsin Khan. Riyadh: Darussalam, 1997.
– *Sahih Bukhari*. Vol. 9. Translated by M. Muhsin Khan. Riyadh: Darussalam, 1997.
Cashmore, Ellis. *The Black Culture Industry*. United Kingdom: Taylor & Francis, 2006.
Castoriadis, Cornelius. Interview by Hashem Salih. *Al-Karmel*, no. 40–1 (1991).
Caughey, John L. *Imaginary Social Worlds: A Cultural Approach*. United Kingdom: University of Nebraska Press, 1984.
Al-Damiri, Kamal al-Din Muhammad ibn Musa. *Hayat al-Haywan al-Kubra*. Vol. 1. Cairo: Mostafa Bab Halabi & Sons Press, 1978.
Davidson, Basil. *A Guide to African History*. New York: Zenith Books, 1971.
Al-Dimashqi, Shams al-Din. *Nukhbat al-Dahr, fi ʿAja'ib al-Bar wa al-Bahr*. Beirut: Dar Ihya al-Turath al-Arabi, 1988.
Al-Dinawari, ibn Qutayba. *Ta'wil Mukhtalif al-Hadith*. Beirut: Dar al-Jil, 1973.
Diwan Abu Dulamah. Beirut: Dar al-Jil, 1994.
Diwan Antarah, edited by Majid Tarad. Beirut: Dar al-Kitab al-Arabi, 1994.

Diwan Ibn al-Rumi. Beirut: Dar al-Hilal, 1991.
Diwan Suhaim Abd Bani al-Hashas. Cairo: al-Dar al-Qawmiyya lil Tibaʿa wal Nashir, 1950.
Diyab, Abdul Majid. *Khulasat al-Mutanabbi*. Vol. 2. Kuwait: Dar Souad al-Sabah, 1992.
Durand, Gilbert. *The Anthropological Structures of the Imaginary*. Translated by Margaret Sankey & Judith Hatten. Brisbane: Boombana Publications, 1999.
– *Introduction à la mythodologie: Mythes et sociétés*. Paris: Albin Michel, 1996.
El-Jazaery, Abu Bakr. *The Approach of the Muslim*. Translated by Ayman Muhammad. Beirut: Dar al-Kotob al-Ilmiyah, 2016.
Enderwitz, S. "Al-Shuʿubiyya." In *Encyclopedia of Islam, Second Edition*. Edited by P. Bearman, Th. Bianquis, C.E. Bosworth, E. van Donzel, and W.P. Heinrichs. Accessed 10 August 2022. http://dx.doi.org/10.1163/1573-3912_islam_SIM_6997.
Foucault, Michel. *The Archeology of Knowledge and the Discourse on Language*. Translated by A.M. Sheridan Smith. New York: Pantheon Books, 1972.
– *The History of Sexuality*. Vol. 1. New York: Pantheon Books, 1978.
– *Lectures on the Will to Know*. Translated by Graham Burchell. New York: Palgrave Macmillan, 2013.
– "Nietzsche, Genealogy, and History." In *Language, Counter-Memory, Practice: Selected Essays and Interviews*. Ithaca, NY: Cornell University Press, 1980.
– *The Order of Things: An Archaeology of Human Sciences*. Taylor and Francis e-Library, 2005.
Freud, Sigmund. "Five Lectures on Psychoanalysis." Translated by J. Strachey et al. In *The Standard Edition of the Complete Psychological Works of Sigmund Freud, Volume XXII*. London: Hogarth Press, n.d.
– "Revision of Dream Theory." In *Essential Papers on Dreams*. Edited by Melvin Lansky. United Kingdom: NYU Press, 1992.
Geertz, Clifford. *Islam Observed: Religious Development in Morocco and Indonesia*. Chicago and London: University of Chicago Press, 1971.
Gershoni, Israel, and James P. Jankowski. *Egypt, Islam, and the Arabs: The Search for Egyptian Nationhood, 1900–1930*. Oxford: Oxford University Press, 1986.
Al-Ghathami, Abdullah. *Al-Naqd al-Thaqafi: Qiraʾa fil Ansaq al-Thaqafiyya*. Beirut: al-Dar al Baidha, al-Markaz al-Thaqafi al-Arabi, 2000.

Al-Ghazzi, Najm al-Din Muhammad. *Al-Kawakib al-Sa'irah Bia'yan al-Mi'ah al-'Ashirah*. Vol. 2. Jounieh: Lebanese Missionaries Publisher, 1949.
Al-Hamadani, Ahmad ibn Muhammad ibn al-Faqih. *Mukhtasar Kitab al-Buldan*. Beirut: Dar Ihya' al-Turath al-Arabi, 1988.
Al-Haythami, Nur al-Din. *Majma' al-Zawa'id*. Vol. 4. Cairo: Dar al-Rayan lil Turath, 1987.
Hegel, Georg Wilhelm Friedrich. *The Philosophy of History*. New York: The Colonial Press, 1899.
Hussein, Taha. *Ma'a al-Mutanabbi*. Cairo: Dar al-Ma'arif, n.d.
Ibn Abd Al-Haleem, Salih. *Kitaab al-Ansab*. Madrid: Consejo Superior de Investigaciones Científicas, 1996.
Ibn Ahmad, Muhammad. *Al-Dhahabi, Siyyar A'lam al-Nubala*. Vol. 11. Beirut: al-Risala Institute, 1993.
Ibn Battutah, Abu Abdullah Muhammad. *Tuhfat al-Nuzar fi Ghara'ib al-Amsar wa 'Aja'ib al-Asfar*. Beirut: Dar Ihya' al-Uloom, 1987.
Ibn Butlan, al-Mukhtar bin al-Hasan. *Risala Nafi'a fi Shray al-Raqiq wa Taqleeb al-Abeed*. Vol. 1. Beirut: Dar Al Jil, 1991.
Ibn Hanbal, Ahmad. *Musnad Ahmad*. Vol. 1. Giza: Mu'asasat Qurtoba, n.d.
– *Musnad Ahmad*. Vol. 4. Giza: Mu'asasat Qurtoba, n.d.
– *Musnad Ahmad*. Vol. 5. Giza: Mu'asasat Qurtoba, n.d.
Ibn Hawqal, Muhammad Abdul-Qasi. *Surat al-Ardh*. Beirut: Maktabat al-Hayat, 1979.
Ibn Hisham, Abd al-Malik. *Sirah Ibn Hisham*. Vol. 1. Cairo: Dar al-Hadith, 1996.
Ibn Kathir, Imad al-Din Ismail ibn Umar. *Al-Bidayah wal Nihaya*. Vol. 11. Beirut: Dar Ihya al-Turath, 1993.
– *Al-Sira al-Nabawiyya (The Life of the Prophet)*. Vol. 1. Translated by Trevor Le Gassick. UK: Garnet Publishing Limited, 1998.
Ibn Khaldun, Abd Ar-Rahman bin Muhammed. *The Muqaddimah*. Translated by Franz Rosenthal. London: Routledge & Kegan Paul, 1978.
Ibn Majid, Ahmed. *Kitab al-Fawa'id fi Usul 'Ilm al-Bahr wa 'l-Qawa'id*. UAE: Markaz al-Dirasat wal Watha'iq fil Diwan al-Amiri Biras al-Khaima, 1989.
Ibn Manzur, Muhammad ibn Mukarram ibn Ali. *Lisan al-Arab*. Cairo: Dar El Maaref, n.d.
Ibn Saad, Muhammad. *Al-Tabaqat al-Kubra*. Vol. 1. Beirut: Dar Sadir, n.d.
Ibn Sirin, Muhammad. *Muntakhab al-Kalam fi tafsir al-Ahlam*. Beirut: Dar al-Fikr al-Arabi, 1999.

Ibn Taymiyyah, Taqi al-Din Ahmad. *Iqtida as-Sirat al-Mustaqim.*
Cairo: al-Sunna Al-Muhammadiyah Library, 1950.
Ibrahim, Abdullah. *Al-Markaziyya al-Islamiyya: Surat al-Akher fi
al-Mukhyal al-Islami khilal al-Quroon al-Wista.* Beirut: al-Dar
al-Baydha, 2001.
- *Al-Sardiyya al-Arabiyya.* Beirut: al-Marqaz al-Thaqafi al-Arabi, 1992.
Ibrahim, Nabila. *Ashkal al-Ta'bir fil Adab al-Shabi.* Cairo: Dar Gharib,
1981.
Al-Idrisi, Mohammad. *Nuzhat al-Mushtaq fi ikhtiraq al-Afaq.* Cairo: El
Thaqafya El Diniah, n.d.
Al-Isfahani, Abu al-Faraj. *Kitab al-Aghani.* Vol. 1. Beirut: Dar al-Kutub
al-ilmiya, 1992.
- *Kitab al-Aghani.* Vol. 3. Beirut: Dar al-Kutub al-ilmiya, 1992.
- *Kitab al-Aghani.* Vol. 21. Beirut: Dar al-Kutub al-ilmiya, 1992.
Isaac, Benjamin. *The Invention of Racism in Classical Antiquity.*
Princeton: Princeton University Press, 2004.
Jabar, Hassan. *Wufud al-Qaba'l 'ala Rasool wa Intishar al-Islam fi
Jazeerat al-Arab.* Kuwait: Ministry of Information, 1987.
Al-Jahiz, Abu Uthman Amr bin Bahr. *Al-Bayan wal Tabyin.* Vol. 1.
Beirut: Dar Maktabat al-Hilal, 1992.
- *Al-Taj fi Akhlaq al-Muluk.* Beirut: al-Sharika al-Lubnaniyya lil Kitab, n.d.
- *Kitab al-Haywan.* Vol. 2. Beirut: al-Majma' al-Ilmi al-Arabi
al-Islami, 1969.
- *Kitab al-Haywan.* Vol. 3. Beirut: al-Majma' al-Ilmi al-Arabi
al-Islami, 1969.
- *Kitab al-Haywan.* Vol. 5. Beirut: al-Majma' al-Ilmi al-Arabi
al-Islami, 1969.
- *Manaqib al-Turk.* Vol. 1. Beirut: Dar al-Hadatha, 1988.
- *Rasa'il al-Jahiz.* Vol.1, *Fakhr al-Sudan.* Beirut: Dar al-Hadatha, 1988.
- *Risalat Fakhar al-Sudan 'ala Bidhan.* Vol. 1. Cairo: Maktabat
al-Khanji, n.d.
Jameson, Fredric. "On Interpretation: Literature as a Socially Symbolic
Act." In *Twentieth-Century Literary Theory A Reader*, edited by
K.M. Newton. London: Macmillan, 1989.
Al-Jawziyya, Ibn Qayyim. *Naqd al-Manqool.* Vol. 1. Beirut: Dar
al-Qadri, 1990.
Al-Jazari, Ali 'Izz al-Din Ibn al-Athir. *Usd al-Ghabah fi marifat
al-Sahabah.* Vol. 1. Beirut: Dar Ihya al-Turath al-Arabi, 1970.
- *Usd al-Ghabah fi marifat al-Sahabah.* Vol. 5. Beirut: Dar Ihya al-Turath
al-Arabi, 1970.

Al-Jumahi, Muhammad Ibn Sallam. *Tabaqat al-Shuʻra*. Beirut: Dar Ihya al-Uloom, 1998.
Jung, Carl. "The Structure and Dynamics of the Psyche." Vol. 8. In *The Collected Works of C.G. Jung*, edited and translated by Gerhard Adler and R.F.C. Hull. Princeton: Princeton University Press, 1969.
Al-Jurjani, Abd al-Qahir. *Asrar al-Balaghah*. Beirut: Dar Al-Kotob Al-Ilmiyah, 1988.
Al-Katib, Ali bin Razin. *Adab al-Mulook*. Beirut: Dar al-Taliʻa, 2001.
Keller, Carrie. "Otto Rank (1884–1939)." In *The Embryo Project Encyclopedia*, 2019. Accessed 30 May 2022. https://embryo.asu.edu/pages/otto-rank-1884-1939.
Kendi, Ibram X. *Stamped from the Beginning: The Definitive History of Racist Ideas in America*. New York: Nation Books, 2016.
Al-Khaffaf, Abu Bakr. *Salwat Al-Ahzan lil Ijtinab ʻan Mujalasat al-Ahdath wal Niswan*. Al-Maktaba al-Shamela (online), 2022.
Khalaili, Kamal. "Al-Mutanabbi in His Role as a Eulogist and Satirist of Kafur: A Study, Edited Text and Annotated English Translation of the Kafuriyyat." PhD diss., University of Manchester, 1978. ProQuest (27733487).
Al-Kulayni, Muhammad ibn Yaʻqub. *Al-Kafi*. Vol. 1. Translated by Muhammad Sarwar. N.p: Islamic Seminary Incorporated, 2015.
– *Al-Kafi*. Vol. 5. Translated by Muhammad Sarwar. N.p: Islamic Seminary Incorporated, 2015.
– *Al-Kafi*. Vol. 6. Translated by Muhammad Sarwar. N.p: Islamic Seminary Incorporated, 2013.
Lacan, Jacques. "The Mirror Stage." In *Critical Theory Since 1965*, edited by Hazard Adam and Leroy Searle. Tallahassee: University Presses of Florida, 1992.
Leeming, David Adams. *Creation Myths of the World: An Encyclopedia*. Vol. 1. Part I–II. Santa Barbara, CA: ABC-CLIO, 2010.
Leitch, Vincent. *Cultural Criticism, Literary Theory, Poststructuralism*. New York: Columbia University Press, 1992.
Lentricchia, Frank. *After the New Criticism*. Chicago: University of Chicago Press, 1980.
Lerner, Laurence. "History and Fiction." In *Literature in The Modern World*. New York: Oxford University Press, 1990.
Al-Mahali, Jalal al-Din and Jalal al-Din al-Suyuti. *Tafsir al-Jalalayn*. Vol. 1. Cairo: Dar al-Hadith, n.d.

Majlesi, Muhammad Baqir. *Bihar al-Anwar*. Vol. 1. Tahran: al-Matba al-Islamiyya, 1966.

Al-Manawi, Abdul Ra'uf. *Faidh al-Qadir*. 3 vols. Egypt: al-Maktaba al-Tijariyah al-Kubra, 1937.

Al-Maqdisi, Anis. *Umraa al-Shi'r al-Arabi fil al-Asr al-Abbasi*. Beirut: Dar El Ilm Lilmalayin, 1989.

Al-Maqdisi, Shams al-Din. *Ahsan al-Taqaseem fi Marifat al-Aqaleem*. Beirut: Dar Ihya al-Turath al-Arabi, 1987.

Marshall, Brenda. *Teaching the Postmodern: Fiction & Theory*. New York/London: Routledge, 1992.

Marx, Karl, and Frederick Engels. *The German Ideology*. Edited by Christopher John Arthur. New York: International Publishers, 1970.

Al-Mashhadi, Mohammed al-Qummi. *Kanz al-Daqa'iq wa Bahr al-ghra'ib*. Vol. 2. Tehran: Ministry of Culture and Islamic Guidance, Printing & Publication Organization, 1947.

Al-Masudi, Abu al-Hasan. *Akhbar al-Zaman*. Cairo: Abdel Hamid Ahmed Hanafi Press, 1938.

– *Al-Tanbih wa al-Ishraf*. Leiden: Brill Publishers, 1893.

– *Muruj al-Dhahab wa Ma`adin al-Jawhar*. Vol. 1. Translated by Tarif Khalid. Jerusalem: Khalidi Library, 2020.

– *Muruj al-Dhahab wa Ma`adin al-Jawhar*. Vol. 2. Translated by Tarif Khalidi. Jerusalem: Khalidi Library, 2020.

– *Muruj al-Dhahab wa Ma`adin al-Jawhar*. Vol. 3. Translated by Tarif Khalidi. Jerusalem: Khalidi Library, 2020.

– *Muruj al-Dhahab wa Ma`adin al-Jawhar*. Vol. 5. Translated by Tarif Khalidi. Jerusalem: Khalidi Library, 2020.

"Al-Mawsu'a al-Shi'riya." Abudhabiculture.ae. Accessed 25 August 2022. https://abudhabiculture.ae/ar/learn/national-library-programmes/poetry-encyclopedia.

Minorsky, Vladimir F. *Sharaf Al-Zaman Tahir Marvazi on China, the Turks, and India*. London: The Royal Asiatic Society, 1942.

Moussa, Salama. *Al-Muqtataf*, no. 3 (1910).

– "Wells' Books and Novels." *Al-Muqtataf*, no. 2 (1910).

Muthhir, Ismail. *Ta'athur al-Thaqafa al-Arabiyya bil Thaqafa al-Yunaniyya*. Cairo: Hindawi Org., 2017.

Al-Nadim, Abu al-Faraj Muhammad ibn Shaq. *Kitab al-Fihrist*. Beirut: Dar al-Ma'rifa, 1997.

Al-Naysaburi, Muslim ibn al-Hajjaj. *Sahih Muslim, Book 4*. Translated by Abd-al-Hamid Siddiqui. Online: 2009.

- *Sahih Muslim, Book 31*. Translated by Abd-al-Hamid Siddiqui. Online: 2009.
Al-Noori, al-Muhadith. *Mustadrak al-Wasa'l*. Vol. 11. Qum: Mu'sasat aal al-Beit li Ihya' al-Turath, 1988.
Al-Nuwayri, Shihab al-Din Ahmad bin 'Abd al-Wahab. *Nihayat al-Arab fi funun al-Adab*. Vol. 1. Cairo: Wazarat al-Thaqafa wal Ershad al-Qawmi, n.d.
Othman, Showqi. "Tijarat al-Muheet al-Hindi fi Asr al-Siyada al-Islamiyya." In *A'lam al-Marifah Series*, no. 151. Kuwait: National Council for Culture, Arts and Literature, 1990.
Al-Qanwaji, Sadiq bin Hassan. *Abjad al-Uloom*. Vol. 1. Beirut: Dar al-Kutub al-Ilmiya, 1978.
Al-Qayrawani, Ibn Rashiq. *Al-Umdah fi Mahasin al-Shi'r, wa Adabah wa Naqdah*. Vol. 1. Beirut: Dar Sadir, 1993.
Al-Qazwini, Muhammad bin Yazeed Ibn Majah. *Sunan Ibn Majah*. Vol. 1. Translated by Nasiruddin al-Khattab. Riyadh: Darussalam, 2007.
- *Sunan Ibn Majah*. Vol. 3. Translated by Nasiruddin al-Khattab. Riyadh: Darussalam, 2007.
Al-Qazwini, Zakariya. *'Aja'ib al-Makhluqat wa Ghara'ib al-Mawjudat*. Beirut: Dar Ihya al-Turath al-Arabi, 1989.
- *Athaar al-Bilaad*. Beirut: Dar Beirut lil Tiba'a, 1984.
Al-Qurtubi, Abdullah Muhammad. *Tafsir al-Qurtubi*. 19 vols. Cairo: Dar al-Shaab, 1954.
Reilly, Kevin. *The West and the World: A Topical History of Civilization*. New York: Harper & Row, 1980.
Ricœur, Paul. *From Text to Action: Essays in Hermeneutics*. Vol. II. Translated by Kathleen Blamey and John B. Thompson. Evanston: Northwestern University Press, 1991.
Al-Rishhari, Muhammad. *al-Khair wal Barakah fil Kitab wal Sunnah*. Qum: Dar al-Hadith, 2007.
Al-Rumi, Husam Zadah. *Qalb Kafuriyyat al-Mutanabi min al-Madih ila al-Hija*. Beirut: Dar Sader, 1993.
Sabzevari, Mohammad Bagher. *Al-Jadid fi Tafseer al-Quran*. Vol. 2. Beirut: Dar al-Taarif lil Matbooat, 1983.
Al-Safa, Ikhwan. *Rasa'il Ikhwan al-Safa wa Khilan al-Wafa*. Beirut: Dar Sadir, n.d.
Said, Edward. *Culture and Imperialism*. New York: Vintage Books, 1993.
- "Invention, Memory and Place." *Critical Inquiry* 26, no. 2 (2000).
- *Orientalism*. New York: Vintage, 1979.
Salman, Dalwar. *Al-Muqtataf*, no. 2 (1910).

Shaarawy, Helmy. *Surat al-Afriqi lada al-Muthaqaf al-Arabi*. Beirut: Center for Arab Unity Studies, 1999.
Al-Shafi, Abu Abdillah Muhammad ibn Idris. *Al-Umm*. Vol. 5. Beirut: Dar Al-Marifah, 1973.
Al-Shahrastani, Muhammad. *Al-Milal wa al-Nihal*. Vol. 1. Beirut: Dar Saab, 1986.
Shahrdar, Abo Shuja' Sheeraway. *Al-Firdaws bi Ma'thoor al-Khitab*. Vol. 1. Beirut: Dar al-Kutub al-Illmiya, 1986.
Al-Shirazi, Mohammad. *Taqrib al-Quran ila al-Athhan*. Vol. 4. Beirut: Mu'sasat al-Wafa, 1980.
Al-Sijistani, Abu Dawud. *Sunan Abu Dawood*. Vol. 3. Beirut: Dar Al Fikr, n.d.
Al-Sirafi, Abu Zaid and Suleiman al-Tajir. "Akhbar al-Seen wal Hind." *Al-Mawsim* 1, no. 7 (1990).
Sirat al-Amirah Dhat al-Himma wa Waladaha Abdul Wahab. Vol. 1. Beirut: al-Maktaba al-Thaqafiyya, 1980.
Sirat al-Malik Seif bin Dhi Yazan Faris al-Yemen. Vol. 1. Beirut: al-Maktaba al-Thaqafiya, n.d.
Sirat Antarah bin Shaddad. Vol. 5. Beirut: al-Maktabah al-Sha'biyah, n.d.
Sirat Bani Hilal. Beirut: Dar al-Kutub al-Shabiyah, 1981.
Sperl, Stefan, and C. Shackle. *Qasida Poetry in Islamic Asia and Africa*. Vol. 1. New York: E.J. Brill, 1996.
Steinberg, Michael P., ed. *Walter Benjamin and the Demands of History*. Ithaca: Cornell University Press, 1996.
Al-Suyuti, Jalaluddin. *Nuzhat al-'Umr fi al-Tafdeel bayna al-Beedh wa al-Sud wa al-Sumr*. Cairo: Maktabat al-Turath al-Islami, n.d.
Al-Tabari, Muhammad ibn Jarir. *The History of al-Tabari*. Vol. 1, *General Introduction and from the Creation to the Flood*. Translated by Franz Rosenthal. Albany: State University of New York Press, 1989.
– *Tarikh al-Tabari (Tarikh al-Rusul wal Muluk)*. Vol 7. Beirut: Dar al-Kutub al-Ilmiya, 1986.
Tabarsi, Shaykh. *Majma' al-Bayan fi Tafsir al-Qur'an*. Vol. 9. Beirut: al-'Alami Institute, 1995.
Al-Tahtawi, Rifa'a. *Takhlees al- Ibreez fi Talkhees Pareez*. Beirut: Dar Ibn Zaidon, n.d.
Al-Ta'i, Nizar. "Al-Itjah Nahwa al-Din." *The Annals of the Arts and Social Sciences*, no. 12 (1992).
Al-Tauhidi, Abu Hayyan. *Al-Imta' wal-Mu'anasa*. Vol. 1. Beirut: al-Maktaba al-Asriya, n.d.

Al-Taweel, Ahmed. *Abu Uthman al-Jahiz*. Tunisia: Institute of Abdul Kareem bin Abdallah, 1992.

Al-tha'alibi, Abu Mansour. *Yatimat al-Dahr fi Mahasin Ahl al-Asr*. Vol. 1. Beirut: Dar al-Kutub al-Illmiya, 1979.

Thuhni, Mahmoud. *Sirat Antarah*. Cairo: Dar al-Ma'arif, 1984.

Al-Tifashi, Ahmad. *Nuzhat al-Albab*. London: Riyadh al-Rais, 1992.

Al-Tijani, Muhammad bin Ahmed bin Muhammad. *Tuhfat Al-Aroos Wa Muta't al-Nofous*. London: Dar Riyadh Al-Rais, 1992.

Al-Tiqtaqa, Muhammad bin Ali bin Tabataba. *Al-Fakhri fi al-Adab al-Sultaniyya wa al-Diwal al-Islamiyya*. Beirut: Dar Sadir, n.d.

Todorov, Tzvetan. "Coexistence of Cultures." Translated in *Fusuul Journal*, no. 2 (1993).

– *The Conquest of America: The Question of the Other*. New York: Harper Perennial, 1982.

Al-Tunisi, Muhammad bin Umar. *Tashhith al-thhan bi Sirat Bilad al-Arab wa al-Sudan*. Edited by Khalil Asaker and Mustafa Massad. Cairo: Al-Dar al-Misriyah for Composition and Translation, 1965.

Al-Turky, Binyan Soud. "Ilgha al-sifa al-qanuniyya lil Riq fi Saltanat Zanjibar al-Arabiyya 1897." *The Annals of the Arts and Social Sciences*, no. 13 (1993).

Al-Tusi, Muhammad b. Hasan. *Al-Tibyan fi Tafseer al-Quran*. Vol. 9. Qum: Maktab al-Ilam al-Islami, 1988.

Al-Wahidii, Abu al-Hassan. *Sharah Diwan al-Mutanabbi*. Vol. 2. Edited by F. Dieterici. Berlin: N.p., l861.

White, Hayden. "New Historicism: A Comment." In *The New Historicism*, edited by Aram Vesser. New York: Routledge, 1989.

Whitelam, Keith. *The Invention of Ancient Israel: The Silencing of Palestinian History*. London: Taylor & Francis, 1996.

Williams, Raymond. *Marxism and Literature*. Oxford: Oxford University Press, 1977.

Al-Ya'qubi, Ahmed bin Abi Yaqub. *Kitab al-Buldan*. Beirut: Dar Ihya al-Turath al-Arabi, 1988.

– *Tarikh al-Ya'qubi*. Vol. 1. Beirut: Dar Sadir, 1995.

– *Tarikh al-Ya'qubi*. Vol. 2. Beirut: Dar Sadir, 1995.

Al-Zirqani, Muhammed. *Mukhtaser al-Maqasid al-Hasana*. Riyadh: Arab Bureau of Education for the Gulf States, 1981.

Index

Aba Bakra bin Kalda
   al-Thaqafi, 46
al-Abbas Bin al-Ahnaf, 117
Abbas bin Merdas, 153
Abd al-Aziz bin Marwan, 139,
   140, 142
Abd al-Malik ibn Quraib
   al-Asma'i, 165n81
Abd al-Muttalib bin Hashim
   ibn Abd Manaf, 35, 36
Abd al-Wahhab al-Mo'dab, 6
Abd al-Wahhab bin al-Amira of
   al-Himma, Prince, 98, 99, 103,
   104–5, 106
Abdul Allah bin Ja'far, 142
Abdullah bin Abi Rabia, 39
Abdullah bin Khazim al-Salmi, 153
Abdullah bin Masoud, 40
Abdul Malik bin Marwan, Prince,
   140, 142
Abi al-Shis, 117
Abraha al-Ashram Abu Yaksum:
   campaign against the Kaaba, 28,
   31, 34; construction of al-Qalis
   cathedral, 39; death of, 32;
   march to Mecca, 34
absolute Other, 68, 69, 70

absolute slavery, 68–9
Abu al-Abbas al-Nashi'
   al-Akbar, 71
Abu al-Abbas Muhammad bin
   Khalaf bin al-Marzuban, 71
Abu al-'Ala al-Ma'arri, 116–17
Abu al-Hasan Ali bin al-Abbas
   (a.k.a. Ibn al-Rumi): background
   of, 121, 123; imagination of,
   125; influence of, 120; poetry of,
   95, 120, 123–4, 125; portrayal
   of revenge as a holy war, 124;
   representation of black women,
   117, 118
Abu Ali al-Basir, 117
Abu al-Misk Kafur, vizier of Egypt,
   119, 125–6
Abu Burda, 41, 42
Abu Dulamah, 119; assimilation
   into society, 145; background of,
   133; blackness and ugliness
   of, 143, 144; caliphs and, 145;
   concealment of blackness, 134;
   drinking of, 144; humour and
   witticism of, 144, 145;
   imprisonment of, 144; poetry
   of, 143; satire of, 144

Abu Hayyan al-Andalusi, 117
Abu Hayyan al-Tawhidi, 72, 75
Abu Nawas, 116
Abu Ruhm, 41
Abyssinia: characteristics of people of, 84; Christianity in, 32; conflict between Arabs and, 29, 30, 37; historiography, 40–1; imaginary of, 43; invasion of Yemen, 28, 30–1, 34; Muslim migration to, 28, 38–9, 41–2, 43; religion of, 34–5
Adler, Alfred, 16
Adnanite Arabs, 154
adultery, 114, 166n6
Afaya, Muhammad Nur al-Din, 12
Afro-Iraqis, vii
Ahmed bin Majid, 82
Alf Layla wa Layla (*One Thousand and One Nights*): authorship of, 111; bestiality tales in, 167n41; genre, 95, 97; "Ghanim bin Ayyub" tale, 114; origin of, 111; plotlines, 112–13; representation of blacks in, 14, 111–12, 113–14; sexual desire in, 111–12, 113, 114–15; slaves in, 113–14
Ali bin Abi Talib, 31, 44, 53, 54, 121
Ali Bin al-Jahm, 117
Ali bin Muhammad, 121, 123
Althusser, Louis, 18, 116
al-Waleed bin Abdul Malik, 142
Amr bin al-'as, 39, 40
al-Anbari, Abu al-Barakat: *Nuzhat al-Alibba fi Tabaqat al-Udaba*, 88
al-Andalusi, Ibn Hazm, 100
Antarah bin Shaddad: background of, 14, 133, 136; blackness of, 107, 134, 135–6, 137, 153; identity crisis, 108; insults of, 136; metaphors used by, 62; personal Other of, 107–8; poetry of, 95, 119; popularity of, 134–5; studies of poems of, 138–9; in Sudan, 109; tribal Other of, 107; whiteness of character of, 136–7
anthropological dialectic, 19
Anthropological Structures of the Imaginary (Durand), 19–20
anti-Arab protest movement, 165n69
Arab Africanism (*al-Istifraq al-Arabi*), vii, 23, 27, 72
Arab culture: Biblical myth of, 77; dusk in, 63; Greek knowledge and, 81; interest in other cultures, 22–3; mechanism of, 8–9; Other in, 8–9, 12
Arab imaginary, 38–9, 119–20
Arab Renaissance (*al-Nahda al-Arabiyya*), 3–4, 11
Arab representations of blacks. *See* Arab Africanism
Arabs: Abyssinians and, 34–5, 36, 37, 38–9; backwardness of, 11; call for unity of, 38; collective memory of, 28; conquests of, 45; difference between blacks and, 46–7, 69–70, 154; identity formation, 7–8, 30; kinship between Persians and, 35; nationalism of, 36; poetry of, viii, 126; rationality and materialism of, 11; religious difference between Romans and, 33; representations of others, 71
Arabs of Jazeera, 151

Index

al-Arab wa al-Barabira
  (Arabs and the barbarians)
  (al-Azma), 12
The Archeology of Knowledge
  (Foucault), 122
Ariat bin Ashama, 31
Aristotle, 74, 81
Arkoun, Mohamed, 11
al-Ashtar, Malik, 54
al-Askari, Abu Hilal, 26
Asma bint Umais, 41–2, 43
"assabiyyah", 36
'Attab bin Usayd, 44
Ayman bin Khuraim, 140–1
al-Azma, Aziz, 12

Babel, Tower of, 77–8
Babylon, 85
Bachelard, Gaston, 16
Badawi, Abduh, 146
al-Badawi, Sayyid Ahmed, 25, 26
Baghdad School, 81
Bani Asad bin Khuzaimah, 145
Bani Dhamrah bin Bakr, 140
Banu al-Hubab, 153
Banu Hilal, ruler of Mecca, 99
Banu Kulaib (tribe of Kulaib), 151, 171n110
al-Baqir, Abu Ja'far Muhammad, 31, 61
Barakat (Abu Zaid al-Hilali), Prince, 98, 99, 100, 101–2, 104, 105
Bashar bin Burd, 117, 118, 130
Basra: destruction of, 122, 123, 124
al-Bayhaqi, 72
Bayt al-Hikma (the House of Wisdom), 81
Benjamin, Walter, 155

Bernal, Martin, 28
Bhabha, Homi, 27
Bilal (the Prophet's muezzin), 9, 40, 44, 46, 93
birth trauma, 98
blackness: in animal world, 66–7; Arab representation of, 60–1, 62, 63, 64, 77; Biblical interpretation of origin of, 77–80, 87, 93; Christian symbolism of, 63; denial of, 134; in dreams, symbolism of, 65–6, 67; hell and, 63; in Judaism, 63; metaphors of, 59–60; negative connotations of, 62–4, 66–7; seven climes theory of, 81–7; sin and, 61–2, 63; slavery and, 66, 77–80
black poets: confrontation with the host culture, 146; counter-representation of, 95, 132, 133; cultural identity of, 134; defence strategy against mockery, 150; desire to assimilate, 135; historical and cultural resistance of, 145–6, 148–9; humor of, 145; re-emploting of Arab culture by, 149, 150–1, 152–3; satire of poetry of, 150; social status of, 133
blacks: animality of, 73–4, 76, 84; Arabic term for, 157n1; Arab imaginary of, 3, 7, 13–14, 49–50, 51, 52, 72–3, 75, 109; criminalization of, 110; enslavement of, 48, 76, 98, 114–15, 147, 157n4; identity of, 134; inability to self-representation, 70–1, 132; lack of religion, 53; literary

representations of, 95; medieval descriptions of, 74–6; mental state of, 53; non-fictional representations of, 14; Otherness of, 7, 8, 9–10, 14, 67, 70, 98; poetic representation of, 14, 116–55; in popular discourse, 97; praise of qualities of, 91–2; relations between Arabs and, 46–7, 69–70, 154; sexuality of, 74, 75; stereotypes about, 7, 14, 47; as subject of mockery, 116; submissive, 134; tendency to "*tarab*," 73, 74–6; virtues of, 92–3
Bourdieu, Pierre, 11, 116
Brantlinger, Patrick, 10
bricolage, 32
al-Buhturi, 120, 121, 122

Caesar (King of the Romans), 31, 33, 34, 149, 151, 159n18
Canopus star, 76
Cashmore, Ellis, 76
Cassirer, Ernst, 16
Castoriadis, Cornelius, 15
children: three stages of development, 16
Chinese people, 87
Christian calendar, 34–5
Christians, 34–5, 56
civilized nations, 87, 91, 155
collective cultural imaginary, 19
Collingwood, R.G., 27
colour difference ("al-Jibla"), 31, 33
Columbus, Christopher, 50
concord: narrative of, 38, 41, 46
conflict: narrative of, 41, 43
contrapuntal reading, 14

counter-representation, 95, 132, 133
cultural identity, 28
cultural imaginary, 14, 19, 97
cultural system, 49

al-Dhahabi, 88
Dhul-Qarnayn, 83
Dhu Nawas (Damianus), 31
Dhu Tha'laban, 31
dialectic of concealment and revelation, 137, *138*
Di'bil al-Khuza'i, 116
al-Dimashqi, Shams al-Din, 51, 52, 53, 69, 72, 75, 81, 128
Diwan Antarah bin Shaddad (Antarah's anthology), 133, 138
dominant narrative, 41
dreams, 64–5, 162n120
Durand, Gilbert, 11, 64; *Anthropological Structures of the Imaginary*, 19–20

Earth: theory of division of, 82–3
Elephant, Battle of, 34, 151, 153, 154
Eliade, Mircea, 16
exclusion: narratives of, 45

Fahul poets, 165–6n81
fakhr (self-exaltation poetry), 142
Fakhr al-Sudan 'ala al-Beedhan (The pride of blacks over whites) (al-Jahiz), 46, 88, 91–2
Faraj al-Hajam, 93
al-Farazdaq, 117–18, 130, 141
al-Fath bin Khaqan, 92
Fish, Stanley, 28
Foucault, Michel, 20, 22; *The Archeology of Knowledge*, 122

Frankfurt School, 18
Freud, Sigmund, 16
al-Furusiyya (Arabian knighthood), 134, 135, 136, 169n57

Galen, 74, 81
Gama, Vasco da, 45
Geertz, Clifford, 11, 49, 51
Ghana, 45
al-Gharb wal Mutakhayal (The West and the imaginary) (Afaya), 12
al-Ghathami, Abdullah, 12
al-Ghazali, Muhammad, 47

Hafs bin Ziyad bin Amr al-Ataki, 152–3
Hakim bin Ayyash al-Kalbi, 149, 153
Ham (Biblical character), 30, 79, 80, 110, 111
al-Hamadani, Ahmad ibn Muhammad ibn al-Faqih, 84
Hamites, 29–30, 31
Hammarah, 153, 154, 171n123
Harasa bin Shaddad, 153
al-Harith bin Abi Shamir, 151
al-Harith bin Hisham, 44
al-Harith bin Zalim (character), 99, 102, 104
Harith ibn Abi Shamir al-Gassani, 149, 171n103
Harra, Battle of, 154
Hassan Bin Thabit, 72
Hawtha bin Ali al-Hanafi, 151, 171n105
al-Hayqutan, 93, 95, 119, 133; on Arab prophethood, 151; defence against mockery, 149–50; reputation of, 148; satire of, 151; vilification of Arab civilization by, 151; on wisdom of blacks, 151
Hegel, Georg Wilhelm Friedrich, 68
Herodotus, 81
Hidayat al-Mureed fi Taqleeb al-Abeed (Guiding the follower in inspecting slaves) (al-Ghazali), 47
Hippocrates, 74
Hisham bin Abdul Malik, 142
history: definition of, 26; fabrication of, 29; ideology and, 28; imaginary dimensions of, 27; language and, 28; as narrative, 26–8
Hunayn bin Ishaq, 81
Hussein, Taha, 127, 132

Ibn Abbas, 40, 59, 72
Ibn al-Khayat, 117
Ibn al-Muqaffa, 72, 73
Ibn al-Muʻtaz, 117, 122
Ibn al-Nadim, 72
Ibn al-Rumi. *See* Abu al-Hasan Ali bin al-Abbas (a.k.a. Ibn al-Rumi)
Ibn al-Shajari, 127
Ibn al-Wardi, 117
Ibn Battuta, Abu Abdullah Muhammad, 72, 83
Ibn Butlan, al-Mukhtar bin al-Hasan, 47, 75, 76
Ibn Habib, 44
Ibn Hawqal, Muhammad Abdul-Qasi, 52, 53, 72
Ibn Husam, Abd al-Malik, 130, 131
Ibn Jinni, 130, 131
Ibn Jubayr, 72
Ibn Kathir, Imad al-Din Ismail ibn Umar, 56

Ibn Khafajah, 117
Ibn Khaldun, Abd Ar-Rahman bin Muhammed, 29, 33, 36, 72, 74, 75, 76, 77, 80, 81, 86
Ibn Manzur, Muhammad ibn Mukarram ibn Ali, 47
Ibn Misjah, 75
Ibn Nadeem, 74, 122
Ibn Rastah, 72
Ibn Saad, Muhammad, 39
Ibn Sirin, Muhammad, 61
Ibn Sukkara, 117
Ibn Tauus, 73
Ibrahim, Abdullah, 13
Ibrahim bin Hani, 75
Ibrahim bin Hisham, 142
al-Ibshihi, 72
idealism, 17
ideology, 18
imaginary: collective cultural dimensions of, 19; cultural representation of, 13; external social dimension of, 15, 16; popular culture and, 11–12; psychological dimension of, 15, 16, 19; studies of, 10–12, 16–19; tension in, 38–9
imaginary kinship, 29, 36
Imru' al-Qais, 62, 166n81
Indian people, 86, 87
individual psychological imaginary, 19
The Invention of Racism in Classical Antiquity (Isaac), 81
Isaac, Benjman: *The Invention of Racism in Classical Antiquity*, 81
Ishaq bin Hunayn, 81
Islam: first human being in, 51, 52, 54; human equality in, 57; Other in, 49; principles of, 54; slavery in, 49, 58; spread of, 45; systemic nature of, 49; universality of, 55; view on religion, 49–50
Israel: fabrication of history of, 29

al-Jabri, Muhammad Abed, 11–12
Ja'far bin Abi Talib, 40, 41
al-Jahiliya (the ignorance age), 52, 56
al-Jahiz, Abu Uthman Amr bin Bahr: on black animals, 67; black origin of, 88–9; books of, 88, 90, 91–2; on civilized nations, 91; collective memory of, 88–9; grandfather of, 88; on Islam, 89; on Luqman the Wise, 91; reputation of, 88; on stupidity, 76; view of blacks, 46, 72, 90–1, 92–3
Japheth (Biblical figure), 78, 79, 110
Jarir ibn Atiyah, 149, 151–2
Jewish-Christian hostility, 31–2
Jews: Arab's perception of, 56–7
al-Julanda people, 149, 151, 171n102
Julaybib, 93
al-Jumahi, Muhammad Ibn Sallam, 137
Jung, Carl, 16, 17

Kadhem, Nader, vii–viii
Kafur al-Ikhshidi (Ikhshidid ruler), 95
al-Kafuriyyat (Poems on Kafur) (al-Mutanabbi): Arab Imaginary and, 125, 128; image of eunuch, 129; panegyric poem, 127–8; portrayal of Kafur, 125, 126–7,

128, 129; representation of blacks, 126, 128, 129, 130; representation of slavery, 126; satire in, 127, 128–9; type of poetry in, 126
Karam al-Bustani, 138
al-Katib, Ali bin Razin, 81
al-Khadra, 99, 100, 103, 106
Khalil Sharaf al-Din, 138
al-Khatafoon (the kidnappers), 48
al-Khatib al-Baghdadi, 88
al-Khatib al-Tabrizi, 138
Khorasan people, 85
Khosrau Anushirwan, king of Persia, 33, 34, 151
Khufaf bin Nudbah, 119, 135, 153
Khuza'ah, 140
Kitaab al-Ansab (The genealogy book) (al-Haleem), 29
Kitab Akhbar Sahib al-Zanj (The book of the news of al-Zanj revolt leader), 122
Kitab al-Haywan (Book of animals) (al-Jahiz), 90
Kitab Rasa'ilihi (The book of his letters), 122
knowledge, 22

Lacan, Jacques, 16
Leach, Vincent, 49
Levi-Strauss, Claude, 32, 77
Luqman al-Hakim (Luqman the Sage), 40, 46, 91, 93, 144, 149, 151

Ma'bid bin Wahab, 75
Makhoul al-Faqih, 93
Mali, 45
Malinowski, Bronisław, 51

Manaqib al-Habshan (Virtues of Abyssinians), 40
Manaqib al-Najashi (Virtues of the Negus), 40
Manaqib al-Turk (Virtues of the Turks) (al-Jahiz), 88, 92
al-Maqdisi, Anis, 53, 72
al-Mar'a wa al-Lugha (The woman and language) (al-Ghathami), 12
al-Markaziyya al-Gharbiyya (The Western centricity) (Ibrahim), 13
marriage, 58–9, 63–4
Marxism, 17–18
Masruq bin Abraha, 32
al-Masudi, Abu al-Hasan: on al-Jahiz, 89; on division of the Earth, 82; on Noah's story, 29, 79; view of blacks, 50–1, 72, 74, 75, 76, 128; on war between Arabs and Abyssinia, 34–6
materialism, 11, 17
Matta bin Yunus, 81
Mecca, 151, 153, 154
menstruation: Islamic prohibition of intercourse during, 106, 107
minority literature, 132
al-Miqdad bin al-Aswad, 93
Moussa, Salama, 4–5
Muhammad, Prophet, 31, 36, 39, 41–2, 43, 45
Muhammad al-Hafni al-Qana'i, 41
Muhammad bin al-Hassan bin Sahl, 121
Mihja', 93
al-Mukhtara: destruction of, 122, 123
al-Muqawqis, 151
Al-Muqtataf (magazine), 45
Musa bin Dawood al-Hashimi, 143

Index

Muslims: conflict between Jews and, 55, 56; identity of, 6
al-Muʿtadhid, Calif, 121
al-Mutakhayal wa al-Tawasil (The imaginary and communication) (Afaya), 12
al-Mutanabbi: *al-Kafuriyyat* (Poems on Kafur), 119, 120, 125–30; depiction of blacks, 14, 95; greatness of poetry of, 130; satirical poems of, 128–9; on slaves, 76; view of ownership, 130
al-Muwaffaq, 123
mythical thinking, 32

al-Naqd al-Thaqafi: Qira'a fil Ansaq al-Thaqafiyya (Cultural criticism: A reading of cultural patterns) (al-Ghathami), 12
narrative identity, 7
nasib (amatory poetry), 142, 170n83
Nasir al-Din al-Tusi, 47
Negus, king of Abyssinia, 39–40, 43, 45, 151
neo-Marxist scholars, 18
Nimrod (Biblical figure), 78
Noah (Biblical figure), 78, 79, 80, 110–11
Nubia, 28
Nukhbat al-Dahr fi ʿAja'ib al-Bar wa al-Bahr (The elite of time in the wonders of land and sea) (al-Dimashqi), 69
al-Nuʿman bin Jayfar bin al-Julandi, 153
Nussaib bin Rabah: background of, 139; competition with al-Farazdaq, 118; connections to caliphs and princes, 134, 142; poetic excellence of, 119, 133, 142, 143; praise of white in poetry of, 139–43; satire of, 142; shame of blackness, 139, 141; whiteness of character and deeds, 141
al-Nuwayri, Shihab al-Din Ahmad bin ʿAbd al-Wahab, 72, 75

Omar bin Abdul Aziz, 142
Orientalism, 22, 23
Other/Otherness: Arab representation of, 6–8, 20, 21, 116, 154; concept of, 9; discovery of, 154–5; exclusion of, 116; historical, 108; in Islamic imaginary, 13, 53–7; narrative, 108; practice of learning about, 9; relationships between self and, 12; types of, 53–4; violence of prejudices against, 155. *See also* absolute Other

People of the Ditch, 31
Piaget, Jean, 16
Plato, 81
plotting (emplotment), 27
poetic violence, 116
polytheists, 56, 58
popular folk narratives, 97, 98–9
power relations, 119
proto-racism, 81
Ptolemy, 74, 77, 82
punishment: power of, 20

al-Qafa, 100, 103
Qahtanite Arabs, 154

al-Qahtaniyya wal Adnaniyya
  (Qahtanites and Adnanites)
  (al-Jahiz), 88
al-Qalis church, 39
al-Qalqashandi, 21, 72, 118
al-Qayrawani, Ibn Rashiq, 117, 126
al-Qazwini, Zakaria, 72, 75,
  76, 128
Quraishi Arabs, 37, 151
Quran: metaphors of blackness in,
  59, 60; on unity of humanity,
  56, 57
al-Qurtubi, Abdullah
  Muhammad, 60

racism, vii, viii, ix, 4–5, 6, 81
al-Radd 'ala al-Nasara (Refutation
  of the Christians) (al-Jahiz),
  88, 92
Rafi' Sha'n al-Habshan (Raising
  the status of the Abyssinians)
  (al-Suyuti), 40
Rank, Otto, 98
rationalism, 11
regimes of reason/unreason, 49
religion: as cultural system, 49–50;
  human civilization and, 50,
  51, 53
representation: definition of, 7, 19;
  dimensions of, 21; in discourses
  of Others, 21; of foreign
  cultures, 22; as mechanism of
  domination, 20; studies of, 11.
  See also counter-representation
Ricoeur, Paul, 7, 11, 27
*Risala Nafi'a fi Shray al-Raqiq
  wa Taqleeb al-Abeed* (A useful
  treatise on buying and inspecting
  slaves), 47
Rizq, Prince, 99, 100

al-Sabi, 117
al-Sadiq, Ja'far bin Muhammad,
  104, 106, 167n18
Saeed bin Jubayr, 93
Sahib al-Zanj, 122, 123
Said, Edward, 11, 14, 22, 28
Saif bin Dhi Yazan: background of,
  32–3; on colour difference, 31;
  fabricated kinship of, 34; king of
  Persia and, 33–4, 36; on unity
  of Arabs and other nations, 33
Salim bin Mansour, 9
Salman, Dalawer, 5
Sana'a cathedral, 39
savagery, 51
self, 12, 16
seven climes theory: classification
  of peoples in, 84–5, 86–7;
  on colours of people, 83–4;
  explanation of blackness and
  whiteness, 82–3, 85; geographical
  distribution of regions in, 85–6;
  origin of, 77
Sharia, 58
al-Sharif al-Radi, 117
Shem (Biblical figure), 78, 79, 110
Shemites, 29–30, 31
Shu'ubiyya phenomenon, 165n69
singing: art of, 75
Al-Sira al-Nabawiyya (*The Life
  of the Prophet*) (Ibn Kathir), 56
al-Sirafi, Abu Zayd, 72
al-Sirafi, Amr, 84
Sirah genre, 158n12
Sirat al-Amirah Dhat al-Himma
  (Life of Princess of high resolve),
  14, 95; audience of, 106–7;
  on causes of outbreak of war,
  103–4; criterion for virtuousness
  in, 105; Islamic of values of

tolerance in, 105–6; plot, 102; reference to menstruation, 106, 107; representation of blackness, 103, 104–5, 106
Sirat Antarah bin Shaddad (*Life of Antarah bin Shaddad*), 14, 95, 107, 108, 109
Sirat bani Hilal (Chronicle of the al-Hilalis), 14, 95; birth trauma, 100–2; plot, 99–100; representation of blackness, 103, 106
Sirat Seif bin Dhi Yazan (Biography of Seif bin Dhi Yazan), 14, 95, 110–11
slavery: barbarism and, 48; blackness and, 66, 77–80; dimensions of, 48; Islamic conception of, 48–9, 58; marriage in, 58; Muslim jurisprudence on, 66; sources of, 58
slave trade, 45, 47–8
social imaginary ("al-Mikhyaal al- Ijtima'i "), 12
speech: as tool of representation, 118
Sudan, 45–6
Suhaim Abd Bani al-Hashas: blackness of, 146; confrontation with the host culture, 95, 146, 147–8; death of, 146; new image of blacks, 119; poetry of, 145, 147; rebellious voice of, 14, 133
al-Sulayk bin Salaka, 119, 153
Suleiman bin Abdul-Malik, 118, 142
Sunaih bin Rabah, 93, 119, 133, 148, 152
al-Suraha wal Hujana (Purebred and half-breed) (al-Jahiz), 88, 92

al-Suyuti, Jalal al-Din, 40–1, 71
Swahilis, 45

al-Tabarani, 45
al-Tabari, Muhammad ibn Jarir, 72, 121, 122
Tafdheel al-Kilab 'ala Katheer mimen Labasa al-Thiyab (Superiority of dogs over many who wear clothes [humans]) (al-Suuty), 71
al-Tahtawi, Rifa'a , 4, 70
al-Tajer, Sulayman, 72
Tamtheelat al-Akher (*Representations of the Other*) (Kadhem), vii–viii, 3
Ta'neeth al-Qasida wal Qari' al-Mukhtalif (Feminization of the poem and the different reader) (al-Ghathami), 12
Tarikh al-Rusul wa al-Muluk (Annals of the prophets and kings), 123
Tarrad, Majid, 138
tarub, 118, 168n14
al-Tha'alibi , Abu Mansour, 127
al-Thaqafa al-Arabiyya wal al-Marja'yat al-Musta'ara (Arab culture and the borrowed references) (Ibrahim), 13
Thaqafat al-Waham (The culture of illusion) (al-Ghathami), 12
al-Tiraz al-Manqush fi Mahasan al-Habush (The coloured brocade on the virtues of the Abyssinians) (al-Suyuti), 41
al-Tunisi, Muhammad bin Umar, 25–6
al-Tusi, Muhammad b. Hasan, 60

Index

'Ukaim al-Habashi, 93, 95, 119, 133, 148, 153–4
Umarah bin al-Waleed, 39
Umar bin al-Khattab, 41–2, 43, 61, 147
Um Habiba, 40

Wahrez (Sasanian general), 38
Wahshi ibn Harb (a.k.a. Abu Dusmah), 9, 46
Wells, H.G.: *The Future in America*, 4
White, Hayden, 11, 26, 27
whiteness: interpretations of, 65
Whitlam, Keith, 28
Williams, Raymond, 41
writing: as tool of representation, 118–19

Yahya bin Adi, 81
Yahya bin Masawaih, 81

Yamut bin al-Muzarra, 88
al-Ya'qubi, Ahmed bin Abi Ya'qub, 39, 50, 51, 79, 121, 122
Yaqut al-Hamawi, 37, 88
Yazid bin Abdul Malik, 142
Year of the Elephant (Aam al-Fil), 31
Yemen: Abyssinian invasion of, 30–1, 34, 153, 154; Persian liberation of, 34, 38; rulers of, 32

Zafar: story of, 37
Zaghawa: people of, 84
zanj (zinji), 5, 50, 68, 73, 116–17, 157n5. *See also* blacks
Zanj Revolution, 119, 120–2, 123, 132, 166n1
al-Zubair, 58